*38 year-old Robert Sands is taking a hands-on approach in his research on JC football.*
John Zant, *Santa Barbara News-Press*, November 17, 1995

*"I felt I'd become and integral part of the team," Sands said, "even though the guys don't know my first name. They call me Doc. They love to hit me."*
John Zant, *Santa Barbara News-Press*, Nov. 17, 1995

*One player is the same age as Chuck Melendez (Head Coach)–Dr. Robert Sands.*
Dave Loveton, *Santa Barbara New-Press*, September 9, 1994

*Another possible target of not only footballs but certainly media attention will be 37-year-old anthropology professor/back-up wide receiver Dr. Robert Sands. In his first ever attempt at organized football, the longtime runner and former SBCC track man made the squad and earned the respect of thousands of sofa jocks and couch potatoes. Just once this season, I'd like to see him beat some 20-year-old kid for a long touchdown. Makes all us grown-ups feel proud.*
Jim Buckley, *Santa Barbara Independent*, September 15, 1994

*Middle-Age Crazy-Anthropologist Discovers Pain and Fun of Football at SBCC*
*Santa Barbara News-Press* Headline, November 17, 1995

# GUTCHECK!

## Also by Robert R. Sands

*Instant Acceleration: Living in the Fast Lane* (1995)

*Sport and Culture: At Play in the Fields of Anthropology* (1999)

*Anthropology, Sport and Culture* (1999)

# GUTCHECK!

## AN ANTHROPOLOGIST'S WILD RIDE INTO THE HEART OF COLLEGE FOOTBALL

### ROBERT R. SANDS

**Rincon Hill Books**
**Carpinteria, California**

Rincon Hill Books
Carpinteria, CA 93014

The Library of Congress Cataloging-in-Publication Data:

Sands, Robert R
        GutCheck!: An Anthropologist's Wild Ride into the Heart of
        College Football/Rincon Hill Books—1st ed.


p. cm.
        ISBN 0-9672973-0-3
Sands, Robert R.—anthropologist. 2. College Football—Junior college football—United States—California. 3. Anthropology—Sport and culture studies—Case study. I. Title.
        GV 958.S26 1999     Library of Congress Catalog Number: 99-93335

Grateful acknowledgment is made for permission to reprint the following composition:
*The Dance* by Tony Arata
© 1989 Morganactive Songs, Inc. and Pookie Bear Music
All rights outside US and Canada administered by WB Music Corp.
All rights Reserved                    Used by permission
Warner Bros. Publication U.S. INC., Miami, FL 33014

# *Foreword*

---

met Robert Sands five years ago on the Santa Barbara City College football field. It was almost Christmas, the 1994 football season had been over for a month, but Sands and a friend were tirelessly running routes. I asked if they minded if I threw to them. It had been a while since I had thrown a football and it took me a couple of throws to loosen up. I was curious what they were doing and Rob informed me they were practicing for City College's next season. Small talk followed and in the course of the conversation, he found out that I played quarterback at the University of Illinois where he received his Ph.D. from and I found out he was a 38 year-old sophomore wide receiver for City College. I was just as impressed with his achievements as he was with my collegiate and professional experience with New England and New York. After I had run his legs off with post patterns, we talked about race and sport; although it was more like he asked questions and I gave him my opinions. A year and a half later, his agent tracked me down and wondered if I would read parts of a manuscript Rob was working on. Now half a decade later, Rob's manuscript has become a reality.

Sands invested two years of his life playing, teaching and being a student and probably took at least that much off his life, so he could understand the culture of junior college football.

Many books have been written on college football and about college football players. Most of these are about the high profile programs, coaches and players. Too many people see what is wrong with big time college football, the grade scandals, athletes taking payments, booster clubs, win at all costs attitude, and think that all college football is like that. Robert Sands takes us to a college football program that is free of all that, where the players are there just to play and most of the coaches have real jobs on the side. Football is football, no matter if 100,000 fans are screaming their approval in Ann Arbor, Michigan, or 2000 are watching two junior colleges battle 100 yards from the Pacific Ocean. Sands' teammates loved the game no less, some probably even more, than scholarship players; they played just as hard and hurt just as much; celebrated each win and despaired every loss just as much as a Heisman Trophy winner would.

As I read, the years rolled back and I found myself remembering the two years I played junior college football in California, before going to the University of Illinois. The story line then was just the same as Sands experienced 15 years later; the more things change, the more they stay the same. In talking to Robert Sands and reading about what he experienced, I am reminded of a scene in *Field of Dreams*, where Shoeless Joe Jackson is telling Ray Kinsella about his love of the game. At the end of that discussion, he says, "I would've played for nothing." Sands and his teammates and those they played against did play for nothing, but what they took out was priceless. In many ways, players I know would envy them.

Besides, it's a good story.

Tony Eason

# *Acknowledgments*

---

This book is the genesis of two full years of living football while I tried to lead a normal life as a college professor. Many times I found myself drawn into the swirling cauldron that was college sport and if not for the help and friendship of a few, I would have had a much more difficult time balancing my life. As acknowledgments usually go, this book would not have been possible without the help of the following individuals.

First off, I would like to publicly thank Head Coach Chuck Melendez, coaches Steve Dudley, Joe DiPaulo, T.K. Walter, Mark Johnson, Don Hopwood, Colin Flynn and the rest of the Vaquero coaching staff for seeing me first as a player and then as an eccentric busybody. As a player, I found myself going through a gamut of emotions daily concerning my feelings toward those coaches, especially Chuck and Steve. Now that four years has passed by, those feelings have become mediated with time and I write these words knowing, above all else, they are my friends. My experiences could have easily focused around being tacitly accepted, much like a mascot or, worse yet, like an interloper. They allowed me to grow as a player and this opened up the world of football to my eyes, ears and heart. I thank them for answering all my questions even when they didn't want to, which I imagine was often.

I would also like to publicly thank the 1994 and 1995 Vaquero football squads for their enthusiasm and interest in my fieldwork and willingness to be a part of it, as well: Eric Mahanke, Ryan Capretta, David Weismiller, Stuart Boyer, Stephan Kratzer, Troy Tremblay, Benjy Trembly and the rest of the receivers. Also, I would like to thank Jarrett Thiessen, Mike Hayes, Tony Coffey, and Chris Hill for their help; they were on the defense, but in the end we were all one team. Special thanks go to Pat Aguilera and Casey Ray for letting me hang around them when I wasn't on the field and keeping me posted on things I didn't know, which were many.

There were those who weren't players and listened to my ranting and ravings about being wrapped up in an experience that turns you into an entirely different person. Lorena Stehmeier was a good friend during this period in my life and it seems that thanks are not enough. She listened well. My two brothers, Eric and Stephen, also listened while their middle-aged brother constantly talked football whenever I had their ears. I think that they were just a little bit envious, but they would never admit to it. My mother, Betty Volm, was against this project from the start; in fact I tried to hide my involvement from her but, as mothers usually do, she found out. During my first season, I wrote letters to her every Sunday about my experiences, but never mailed them. It was enough to know that she would be there if needed. My son, Parker, living in Illinois, never understood my fascination with football, but our numerous phone calls during the season reset my life compass so that the important things in life did not take a back seat. I would like to extend gratitude to Lisa Rath for her efforts to help reorganize the mish-mash that were first drafts, and Tracey Lennon for putting on the final touches. My thanks also to Ron Mason, graphics designer, for his artistic genius. My agent, Linda Petersen, *Zola Peters Agency*, spent tireless hours searching for a publisher, going well beyond what is expected of an agent. For this I can only give thanks, but again thanks is not enough.

And last, but never least, I would like to thank my wife Linda who, when the project was all but dead, helped resurrect it with her confidence. She wasn't a part of my life when I played, but not a day goes by that I don't wish she had been there; I only know the experience would have been that much more enjoyable.

# *Preface*

---

**A**s an anthropologist, I started out to study and write about the culture of college football from the inside, not just as a description of the game but, far more interesting, the stories of the players themselves and how each of these personalities were woven into the fabric of sport. I also wanted to incorporate, as much as possible, my own experiences in the equation; the oftentimes conflicting, or at least contrasting, roles of prof and jock. The structured violence and mind-numbing obedience to an autocratic authority inherent in football preyed upon the liberal, humane and creative side of my profession. But as the seasons wore on, I found burning inside of me a being that sought out the violence, adrenaline and mind-numbing regimentation of football. As an anthropologist, I have grown accustomed to keeping separate the mind and soul, but for two years of living a Walter Mitty fantasy I found that the boundaries between each blurred. For a month, at the end of my second season, these boundaries disappeared altogether. I lived to play and my reality and future were dictated by whims of coaches who were the same age as myself. The simplicity of my life, for those two seasons, was invigorating and liberating. I was never more alive, never more in tune with my body than during that period of time. And once it was over, I experienced a free-fall that plunged me deep into a natural state of competition withdrawal. That same simplicity that had stoked my fires smoldered and flickered in the deprived atmosphere where no more did adrenaline course through my veins, electrifying my soul.

Junior college football is full of diversity, but behavior is constrained by a number of cultural factors. In other words, the personalities that populated those two years that I played were from a diverse spectrum: players and coaches, Ukrainians, Blacks, Whites, Hispanics, Native Americans, Australian, Danish, surfers, gang bangers, leaders and followers, Democrats and Republicans, criminals and ex-cons, fathers, teenagers, middle-agers, intellectuals and those who could give two shits about a college education, drug users, drug abusers, drug sellers and abstainers, those religious and those who didn't know what the inside of a church looked like, those fundamental and those liberal, hunters and pacifists, those fast, those slow, on and off the field, those large, extra large and those freeze-dried. Some of these distinctions could be found inhabiting the same player and the same coach and the blending of all these different types and backgrounds into a functioning team was one of the most exciting, frustrating and satisfying experiences I have ever had the fortune to be a part of.

At the same time to play football, more than any other sport, demands all this diversity to be channeled, minimized, and even exorcised by coaches and players alike for the success of the team. Football is seen by some as dehumanizing and autocratic, stripping the very things that make a player what he is and forcing him to fit a specific mold and follow only certain prescribed behaviors. Individuality takes away from blind obedience; creativity is only good when it is driven by instinctual athleticism on the field. To be a James Dean in football is contrary to the needed chiefs and Indians mentality.

In these two years, experiments blew up as many times as they succeeded. These rebellious players' ability was never in question but, unfortunately, football is just as mental as it is physical. And for reasons, some known and some unfathomable, the same players didn't buy into the necessary formula for team success: discipline, sacrifice, wanting and being able to play in pain, hard work, and subjugation of personal goals for team triumphs.

There were players who were able to chase personal goals, as well as fuel team success. They weren't automated to completely ignore the need to build up receptions and touchdowns. It was important to them and the others to showcase their talents. Their performance was the only way to meet the criteria for grabbing a scholarship to move on to two more years of organized football. But they never forgot the ultimate reason we were risking our bodies, and that was to win.

On defense, it was easier to find players who filled the role of team player. Defensive coaches Joe and Carmen preyed on the desire to play as a motivating factor and performance became the only deciding factor whether a player contributed. For a defense to be successful, a sense of team unity is paramount. Everybody needs to not only do their job right, but also be willing to go the extra mile to back up teammates.

And then there were those players who epitomized the role of "Rudy," only wanting to be a part of the team and its successes. I remember in the 1994 Chaffey game when, in the 4th quarter, just how bad we were going to be blown out was the only question left unanswered, one player, who saw very little action that season, came up to the receivers coach, almost frothing at the mouth and screamed at him, "Put me in, let me get out there and hit those guys! You don't have to throw to me, I just want to hit them!"

The nature of college football produced the need for not only physical types of players, defensive linemen as opposed to receivers, but for a certain type of mentality that lay at the heart and soul of the game. That is why the best coaches are ex-players. They understand all too well the traditions that have gone into the culture of the game. Football is not static; innovation and creativity become the lifeblood of success. Decades ago, outside of a few coaches that saw the game as more than one dimensional in developing strategy, the game was methodical and a symbolic struggle for possession and territory. This shouldn't be surprising, as the world was seen in a similar light—a struggle by the strongest nations for territory and resources. World wars and police actions involved long, drawn out contests of will as much as overcoming entrenched ideology.

Mike Oriard, Oregon State University American literature professor and ex-NFL player, sees the initial promotion of football as a "manly sport." Football was piggybacked with a macho far-reaching foreign policy, the beginning of a social obsession of the male physique, and the elevation of power hungry corporate raiders and tycoons like Rockefeller and DuPont into the ideal of the American warrior.

To an extent, the Korean War and the Viet Nam conflict added to this way of thought. Technology lulled generals into a false sense of security and acquisition of territory was subsumed by body counts. War became high tech and fought at Mach 1. Society began to move at the same speed and, in time, sport accelerated at the same rate. It wasn't long before sports like basketball, baseball, hockey and football felt the acceleration of change. Now, just three short decades later, what was football in many ways has no resemblance to the run and shoot, high-powered passing game you find from high school to the professional ranks. Junior college football, at least in southern California, like minor league baseball, is a culture wrapped around student-athletes not elevated to the high powered programs so visible on Saturday afternoons. Players with skills are forced to hone their abilities in backwater programs while attempting to improve academic skills to bring them a chance to play with the best.

More times than not, they fail. They fail at school, they fail at keeping focused and using the experience to make them better players and better people and, for an unfortunate few, they fail at life. Receivers coach Steve Dudley still wavers on the edge of finding a career, 17 years after strapping on his cleats for the last time. Football gave him opportunities, football continues to help support him, but football also consumed him to a point where nothing else mattered.

And finally, junior college football mimics the experience of the junior college education. Santa Barbara City College offers community-based programs such as vocational, certificated, and professional as well as a program for the continuing student. In a way, City College is like a microcosm of society; it takes all kinds. Vaquero football was that way, too. Ex-cons playing with Ph.D.s.

One of my students asked me, not too long ago, what I learned from playing junior college football. "I mean if you are an anthropologist, what did your playing tell you about our culture, our society, about the life of an American?" was the question.

I didn't have time to lay out an answer for her then, but I told her I would get back to her. She left for school in the Bay area with no forwarding address and I have no way to tell her, but perhaps she will read this sometime in the future. Football is like a cultural black box or, maybe better yet, like the old sausage grinder my mother used, where you jammed in a hunk of meat into a metal grinder and you cranked the handle and kept pushing the meat in and on the other side, the meat came out prepared for cooking.

In a crude way, we were the meat and the coaches' expectations of what a player should be "made" of was the giant hand that pushed. And the game, complete with the history, traditions, acceptable and unacceptable behavior and the required education that allowed you to participate, was the grinder. The coaches and the players' addiction to the game greased the handle, making it much easier to ram through the meat.

In the end, what came out was a football player. Every season, the handle cranked and, every season, the identity of football player spit out the other side of the grinder. The experience of football was more than just wearing pads and cleats and butting heads for 60 minutes. Players were a diverse lot, different shapes and sizes, backgrounds and beliefs, but once that whole mess was shoved through the grinder, out popped 80 sweating, grunting, violent, adrenaline-crazed machines programmed to beat up and destroy 80 other crazed machines.

Football is a culture of controlled mayhem. Injury, even death, lurks just around the corner of the next play or quarter or game. It is called a war and a battle. Author Sally Jenkins boils football down to "bullying the opposition into retreat via a mob action, with only a handful of rules restraining the conduct of those on the field. What few rules do exist are to be circumvented or exploited, or simply changed when things get too boring or nonviolent." Jenkins quotes Missouri football coach Larry Smith as saying, "It's about war. I don't know if it's in men's genes or what. But you're out there to hurt the other guy. I mean, to absolutely physically destroy him. We promote it, we encourage it, hell we teach it."

After these two seasons, I have come to appreciate the game of football as a choreographed dance of precision patterns and defense danced by the surprisingly nimble feet of overgrown men-children. When I was on the field, I found football to also be a game of chess with the physical contact and the thrill of victory and agony of defeat thrown in. However, football doesn't occur in the quiet, cerebral arena of a room with a view or fireplace. Nor does it take place at the slow, measured pace of glaciers melting.

Football plays out in microseconds with the added complexity of moving your body. To move a pawn, capture a rook or harass a king before abducting the queen requires a touch of a finger. To move a 250 pound tackle when you are a 160 pound wideout, or cut a blitzing backer at the knees demands at least the mental imagery of chasing a bishop through the diagonal and living the chase and feeling the fear and adrenaline, placing yourself *In Harm's Way* like John Wayne did in Otto Preminger's sprawling, never-ending, bigger than life epic film of the same title.

In chess, you are far removed from the human senses involved in combat; strategy is painless and threatening only to one's ego. In football, you pay for your mistakes in pain and feel the coach's ire. John McKay, the first coach of the Tampa Bay Buccaneers, once said, when asked about the execution of his team following a particularly poor performance, "I think it is a good idea." In a game that celebrates violence, failure to perform at your best expects–no demands–punishment. In football, you applaud minor triumphs, a well-placed block, a catch, and a misdirection, sometimes with pain, but also with a triumph of combining intellect with brawn. To risk defeat in a room warmed by a flickering fire or even in an auditorium filled with many chess enthusiasts is adrenalizing, yet removed from the experiential sense that many of us crave in American sport and American society overall. But to expose both you and your body to your opponent is the ultimate risk. Death is extremely rare, yet bodily injury is imminent at each passing moment.

Dan Jenkins, famous *Sports Illustrated* and author of *Semi-Tough*, once wrote "Football (is) more than chess with human beings. It is the supreme test of bravery in sports, as close as man could come to war without death."

At its simplest level, in practice, before the lowly judges of your teammates and coaches, it is a ritual of attempted perfection. Most of us demand perfection at some point in our life–not to fulfill obligation or appeal to others, but to satisfy our nagging internal drive for order. It is only when the ritual is played out before others, in an arena of competition, that one comes to appreciate the game and its risks, the ubiquitous ballet, and internal consistency. Perfection is superseded by an appeal to the Homeric deeds of its contestants. Then the players become gladiators in a struggle that may include honor, courage, and sacrifice, but always includes the element, victory at all costs.

*GutCheck!* is about the culture of junior college football, not from a view of an observer, stuck on the other side of reality, but from the inside, wrapped in the cocoon of experience. This is a book that utilizes the canons of anthropological research, but the message is expressed in the sardonic and mirthful voice of George Plimpton with a jolt of electricity supplied by the *King of Gonzo*, Hunter S. Thompson. The culture of football demands both voices; it is not for the idealists, nor for the passive or faint of heart. *GutCheck!* is more about the players and coaches than about the Xs and Os. It is more about the pressures of marginal athletes and students trying to succeed at both football and academics, than about the glitz and glitter of big time college football.

The following pages are snapshots of a culture of football; at times not a pretty picture, but then one should not assume that football is played out in a vacuum without the foibles of human personalities added in. Football as a sport is far different than football as a culture. Traditionally, in anthropology a culture was a collection of people who shared many common elements of life such as religion, art, morals, law, leisure, etc. In fact, this 1871 definition of E.B. Tylor, one of the first American anthropologists, is still used in introductory anthropology texts today.

To some anthropologists, like William Haviland, culture operates as a set of mental rules or standards shared by society that produces acceptable behavior. Others also see culture, beyond behavioral manifestation, as the material expression of a lifestyle. To me, today, culture has taken on a more selective definition. It is a concept that applies more to the mental construction of how people access, process, and store information that is gleaned from the environment around them. It is not so much the traditional commonalities that tie people together in a culture, it is more the nature of people thinking alike and interacting together during a social situation over a period of time that forms a culture. During this period of time that the group of individuals are together, how they think and how they think of themselves become the defining attributes of the "culture."

The upshot of all this is that "culture" no longer refers only to an ethnicity or nationality, like Mexican-American or even the American culture; it can also refer to smaller groups of people who share only parts of their lives together, like athletes. During that shared time, the feeling of togetherness and common identity is very strong.

The 1994 and 1995 the Santa Barbara City College football squad was a culture tied together by the long afternoons of practice, the highly charged, emotional games, and the long bus rides before and after away games. For those extended and intensive periods of time spent together, we became our own little self-contained culture, complete with similar ways of thinking and responding to the environment of college football and all that goes into that environment. Interaction between players and players and coaches in this culture were raw, earthy, profane, and biting. We swept the bowels of human dignity and, just as often, soared with sacrifice and courage. In short, Vaquero football was, as Dan Jenkins wrote, "life its ownself."

In my journey, I became just another player and experienced the same raw emotions. At times, I found myself wondering how as a college professor, I could become just as raw and profane as my 20-year younger teammates. How I could scream for the other team's blood, or mentally picture an opponent face down on the turf, my helmet gouged into his back, or shout at a defensive back to "fuck off" ten different ways after getting tangled up in a pattern. At other times, I wondered how I could have gone so long without becoming part of, at least for a short time, this experience called college football.

In between these extremes, I did what all the other players did; persevered and survived. In the end, I was no stronger or less mobile than when I started (after a couple months of rest and rehabilitation following the 1995 season) although I am a much better player but, for sure, I am much wiser about what makes young men into college football players.

Robert R. Sands
Ventura, CA

# Section One
## Pregame
### Bakersfield versus Santa Barbara

*Leaving the field after the first fall scrimmage. It is a long season, but try telling us that, with the excitement yet to come.*

*For those who rest and wait...good things will come.*
*Starting wideout, Benjy Trembly.*

# Introduction

## In the Beginning

I t was 1964. Football had already slowly and surely grabbed the fancy of America. The fledgling American Football League would soon escalate interest, money and television viewing with such names as George Blanda, Lance Alworth, Len Dawson, and Jack Kemp. The established National Football League stars like Bart Starr, Don Meredith, Paul Horning, and Alex Karras were already legends. In 1964, the NFL was tradition, work ethic and starting the meteoric rise in the number of black players in the league. Alex Karras and Paul Horning became headlines, suspended for that season because of gambling. George Plimpton was a Harvard-trained journalist trying to tap into the Walter Mitty psyche of the American sports fan. He was searching for a way into the magical, ritualized world of storybook heroes on the Sunday gridiron. He had warmed up this idea in an earlier book entitled *Out of My League* where he pitched in a post season all-star game in Yankee Stadium.

"It described what happened to someone with the temerity to climb the field-box railings to try the sport oneself, just to see how one got along and what happened," he wrote. "The notion behind the book was to play out the fantasies, the daydreams that so many people have seeing themselves on the center court at Wimbledon, or sinking long putts in the U.S. Open, or ripping through the Green Bay secondary."

The brooding, iconoclastic, male centric dean of macho, Ernest Hemingway, deemed it an interesting experiment and described Plimpton's brief professional baseball career as "the dark side of the moon of Walter Mitty." Friends questioned George's sanity. "Why do you want to embarrass yourself like that? It's terrible. Either you're the most frustrated athlete there ever was, or you're nuts."

Frustrated or nuts. What a choice.

George responded in defense of his method of madness, "the idea is also to get a firsthand knowledge of the professional athlete. By being one of them, in a sense being a teammate," he said. From the American pastime to the ultimate expression of masculinity, George shopped his idea of experiencing football to selected pro teams and finally caught on with the Detroit Lions for a month of pre-season training. This culminated in a four down exhibition at quarterback in the team's pre-season intra squad scrimmage. Along the way he bonded with the common man's heroes and opened a door into the fraternity.

His story was a revelation into the sporting world and a journal of his journeyman's attempt at performing with the best. What provided muscle to his experience was that Plimpton was not a good athlete. He had dabbled in high school soccer, but he indeed was just like the couch potato next door. "My credentials as a football player may not have been of the first order," Plimpton would rationalize, "but I kept assuring myself that the purpose of my participation in professional football was not to represent the skilled performer, but the average weekend athlete."

His journey was so successful that his exploits became the best selling book, *Paper Lion*, and a movie by the same name. With the mass appeal of his message, Plimpton became synonymous with experiential sports journalism furthering his "investigative" work by reporting on boxing, basketball and ice hockey. Plimpton raised the ante on getting the real sport story across to the American public. Now I was going to continue it, 30 years later-for two seasons, 24 months of living, breathing and dreaming football, four years older than Plimpton when he performed for one series of downs on a hot July Detroit evening.

*Whitworth begins to vomit on the grass, which stinks in the heat and has been torn to bits by cleats and the crash of helmets and the endless screams of the fans. No one pays attention except for Trapper, the Permian trainer, who starts shouting at him from the sidelines, "Gut check, baby! Gut check!" Yes, it is a gut check, test of how much Kevin Whitworth wants to play this game.*

H. G. Bissenger
*Friday Night Lights*

# Chapter 1

---

## Vaqueros on the air and Home Locker Room
### LaPlaya Stadium, Santa Barbara City College
### Bakersfield/Santa Barbara City College Football Game
### (November 18, 1995)

**Radio Station KIST 1340**

*Santa Barbara City College football is on the air! Here is the voice of the Vaqueros, John Martony.*

*Pleasant afternoon to everybody. John Martony live and the SBCC Vaqueros are on the air. Santa Barbara 4 and 0 at home this year. For the first time since 1991, looking for a piece of the Northern Conference Championship in the Western states Conference. The fifth ranked Bakersfield Renegades are in town. Bakersfield coming into town, most impressive, 4 and 1 in the Northern Conference, with an overall record of 8 and 1. They were a preseason rank of #2 behind City College of San Francisco, dropped to 12 following an early season loss to LA Valley, 33-30 and the Renegades have not been headed off since, averaging 48 points per game, over 50 points per game the last 6 weeks. So this team is a powerful offensive machine and has it in high gear.*

*Santa Barbara City College coming off three emotional wins last week, a come from behind fourth quarter game against*

*Glendale, Santa Barbara down 30-26 entering the fourth quarter, but the fans would not let them leave LaPlaya a beaten team, a TD to Arthur Williams gave the Vaqueros a three point margin and Mike Hayes on a fourth down play, sealed it with a 44 yard touchdown interception, the final Santa Barbara 40, Glendale 30. That victory makes today's all the more important, Santa Barbara alive for a bowl bid and also a share of the Western States Conference Division.*

### Home Locker Room

"This is the biggest challenge of your life. This is a big time gut check! This is the most important game in your lives," said Chuck Melendez, the florid-faced, olive-skinned 6-foot, 280-pound head football coach of Santa Barbara City College as he challenged 55 football players, of which I was one, that crowded into the team locker room. A huge circulating fan sat in the corner and swirled the sweet stench of sweat, the wet turf, week-old socks and jocks, unwashed gloves and the last minute emptying of protesting stomachs around the room.

This was the real scent of football.

Industrial-strength Glade couldn't battle these fumes.

They thrived in this environment where so many bodies undressed, dressed in unwashed practice-gear some guys proud of the fact that gear went weeks without seeing a washer–undressed again three hours later swimming in perspiration and then stashed away gear in closed, confined lockers only to be revisited in less than 24 hours.

The smell assailed a visitor the first thing when he stepped in the team room. Even beyond that, it attacked you and caused some rethinking about whether it was truly safe to enter without a gas mask, like an image of Dustin Hoffman chasing a viral monkey in *Outbreak*. For the last 14 weeks, six days a week, the scent became an integral part of just who you were and what you were doing–a cultural scent of identity. You didn't have to love it. You just had to breathe it in and make it part of the experience.

The coach's black mustache and hair offset the white of his teeth as he offered a quick smile to the assembled throng of highly strung grotesquely-padded players sitting on two long rows of benches that stretched the length of the locker room. Many of them missed the smile as they stared at the floor and watched almost

2

disinterestedly as their cleats beat a staccato rhythm on the stained red carpet. Others held red helmets in laps and fingered the scratches and cuts carved into the plastic, compliments of past battles and skirmishes. I alternated between the floor and my helmet, occasionally looking up at the coach, catching his eye and tracking the words as they left his mouth. "These guys don't respect you and that pisses me off. You have to go out and show these sons of bitches that you can play with them. You have to run, block, tackle and catch the football, and it starts in here and here!" The coach pointed at his head and then his heart.

I looked at my Reebok cleats and then glanced down and caught a little bit of the huge #25 emblazoned on my red jersey, the one-time Oakland Raiders' great Fred Bilitnikoff's jersey number, one of my boyhood idols. He had long, shaggy blonde hair, with hands like flypaper and ran very precise routes. The other idol was #19, Lance Alworth with the San Diego Chargers. Bambi. His strides were as graceful as a gazelle and he could jump like a, well, like a deer. I wanted his number, but the school had retired it as a memorial to a player who died.

What Chuck really wanted to say was, "Okay guys, time to grab your balls and find out what they are made of. Time to quit fucking around and run, not walk, after your miserably brief teenage destiny." But he didn't. The coach wanted a class program, so he was attempting to clean up his act. More often than not, he slipped and laid some choice "fuck" or "God Damn" on us that made us feel comfortable and at home. Football players demand a sense of blunt and no-nonsense honesty that in a classroom would generate an atmosphere of hostility. In the primal setting of brute strength and intense competition, the words ran not like a sewer, but in some warped way, like the water jets of a hot tub, soothing the strung-out nerves and that made us comfortable in our existence as assassins and human projectiles.

He did say, "You got to keep your heads. We are not going to start any fights. Walk away from trouble and come back on the next play and get back at them, cleanly, between the lines and within the rules. Win with class."

The problem with college football seasons is that there are only ten or eleven games and each one assumes monumental proportions. Since the beginning of this 1995 season, every game was the storming of the beach at Iwo Jima or the Battle of the Bulge, a must win, gotta have it situation. Like an apocalypse, the approaching game loomed before us during the week of practice. The coaches kept saying, "this game (fill in the blank) is our season, our bowl game. It is the game of your life." It's a wonder many of us didn't become screaming idiots from the pressure applied like vise grips.

The players aren't the only ones honed to a razor's edge. Coaches, with eyes bugged out, stalk the sidelines in a state of near frenzy. I was used to the wild swing of emotions of coaches and players that paraded up and down the sidelines and was inextricably woven into the fabric of the action on the field. I remembered the 1995 Santa Monica game. We had the vaunted Corsairs down 31-16 with six minutes to go. Santa Barbara had never beaten Santa Monica in the history of Vaquero football. During the fourth quarter, we pissed away the lead and allowed them to score twice. The last score came with no time left on the clock and then we gave up the two-point conversion that gave us a tie.

Joe DiPaolo, the defensive coordinator, took off his sunglasses and with a primal "Fuck" at the top of his lungs, heaved them 40 yards down field and stomped off the turf. Joe was still almost incoherent with a simmering rage an hour later in the parking lot, unable to talk without peppering his words with venom. The team showered and dressed in silence, without the usual bitching about playing time, or lack of it, from those who didn't play. We didn't see any of the coaches until Monday afternoon.

Win with class. I looked around the room. We sat crowded like sardines, red jersied shoulder pads rubbing into each as players fidgeted. Others stood behind, helmets dangling at their sides. Eighteen-year-old faces with stubble of youthful beards and closely cropped hair, not unlike fresh recruits in the army, somehow followed the coach's message. As they had heard it before, from any number of coaches, this season, last season and the countless years of youth and high school football. As my gaze drifted, I thought that to most, I could be a father or an uncle. For the lucky ones, I could have been the father who played catch with them, attended their games, and taught them about life. For many, I could have been the father that deserted them or the father or uncle that abused and beat them. Or worse yet, I could have been the father that cared less if they lived or died. But I wasn't. I was a teammate and, to a few, their professor.

Santa Barbara City College Vaqueros were a collection of individuals trying to be a team. We were unpredictable, loaded with talent, and as the heart and soul of the defense, monsterback Jarrett Thiessen remarked on many occasions, "We suck because some of us are just too fucking good." Too good because many played beyond their abilities, trying too hard to be the big guy. Too good because too few realized that raw talent without restraint was self-destructive. Too good, because too many were in love with their one-handed catches and huge numbers that showed up in newspapers and stat sheets. Like last season, the painful reality was we lacked the simple equation that made champions: teamwork + controlled ability + sacrifice = winners.

We had a Fun 'n Gun offense that could score at will, a quarterback with a shotgun for an arm and by the last game, four receivers who had 40 or more catches. We were a machine that tallied first downs like a lucky Vegas slot and amassed real estate like Century 21. We also had a schizophrenic personality where players disappeared and went "south" when adversity came to visit, but we had players who thrived on that same adversity and came through in the clutch. Too bad the numbers were split almost evenly.

Still, after the tumultuous season, on this final Saturday of the regular season, destiny lay in our hands. A coveted bowl bid dangled in front of us, like a mechanical rabbit that lay just beyond the furious charge of the racing greyhounds. That bowl bid would only come on the heels of a consistently brilliant performance by all the receivers this afternoon. This effort had lived sporadically through the season.

Looking around, I saw the jet black hair of the Mexican-American players, brown and blond hair of the Anglo players, some surfers, the shaved heads and 'fros of the brothers, the ash-colored stubble of D.J. Molina, the huge 275-pound Chumash offensive lineman and the shaved bullet head of Rick Millers, the Australian defensive end. If one looked down the two rows of benches, they were the "colors" of the team, but these weren't the true colors we experienced each day of this long 14-week season. There really were no true colors, no visible lingering images of shades or hues. In many ways, athletes are the most colorblind of all people, because when you get right down to it, the only color that matters is the "color" of performance and effort. Whether you get the job done on the field in practice, and in the game, whether you bring it till you collapse on the turf from exhaustion on the 50-yard line are the most important hues that color a team portrait.

Chuck's voice cut through the background din of the fan once more. "I am going to be proud of you, win or lose today. Just give 100%. When you leave the field, leave your heart and soul out there, too." This was a new line. Chuck was bending to the reality of playing our opponent, Bakersfield College, ranked fifth in the state and huge favorite. All week long during practice it was win, win, win; bowl game, bowl game, bowl game. Beating Bakersfield would almost assure us of a post-season game, first in five years of Vaquero football and the first for the second-year coach. Now it was down to avoid embarrassment. I wondered if anybody else caught the shift in perception.

I felt the stinging of sweat from my long hair as a couple of drops rolled down my forehead and washed the scratches and abrasions that lay in the path on the way to my neck and into my jersey. I had lived with pain constantly for the last 24 months like my fellow gladiators, and the stinging of sweat into the wounds was a balm and tonic for my mind, "I hurt, therefore I am." We were all hot, baking in our uniforms after going through the 45 minutes of pre-game warm-up drills in the near-perfect Santa Barbara Fall day where temperatures comfortably sat in the 70s.

The coach put his hands on his hips, his eyes and teeth flashing against the brown skin, and squared his squat body off, as if to challenge us to prove our manhood on the field. "I am not going to lie to you. Bakersfield is huge. They tackle, block and run the ball better than we have seen all year." Indeed, an assessment of Bakersfield program by a local journalist was that it could beat the crap out of many Division One programs. "I am not bullshitting you when I say, to beat these guys, you have to play the game of your career. How bad do you want it? Do you guys want this game that bad?" he yelled.

A collective "yes sir" roared out of the mouths of babes, resonating a determination of Davids and aftershocks seemed to rumble through the room. Now, not so strange to me, I heard a similar yell of affirmation escape from my lips, as well. No longer resided in me a rational, thinking academic. Instead, the moment shoved the educator aside and replaced him with a middle-aged crazed automaton and a David facing the Bakersfield Goliath.

"You guys win today, it's a bowl game."

I knew it wasn't far from the surface. Bowl-mania.

"You guys lose, your season is over. I want you guys to go to a bowl game, especially you sophomores."

A bowl game. What we had been playing for since the beginning of the year, and as well, an undefeated season and a division championship. We lost the undefeated season the second game of the season, deep in the California desert against Antelope Valley and probably the Division championship (within the Western States Conference) when we bowed to arch rival "The 'Cock" (Hancock College) in the sixth game of the season. Ranked as high as 15th in Southern California in the middle of the season, a big deal to us at the time, we were now staring down the barrel at a probable 5-4-1 season with a loss to Bakersfield.

Following Chuck's initial 5-5 season, we were improving, albeit slowly. This year, Chuck's nemesis was not so much our opponent, but our own team and the strain of balancing out-of-control egos dogged him every game this season. "Nobody thinks we can win," the coach said with feeling. "But I think differently, the coaches think differently, and you have to think differently. Now go out and prove them wrong!" He paused and looked at the coaches, scattered around the room. "You guys got anything to say?"

Each one shook his head. Words had become unnecessary. They were obstacles now to the final moment of preparation. Even veteran Carmen DiPaolo, the sagacious secondary coach, who had been coaching football for 25 years, had nothing else to say. Carmen usually cut through the bullshit with observations that were bare and stark. Following a Friday practice last season before a game, he had chopped down the problems of playing to, "You guys want to win tomorrow, you have to go out and fucking play like we have taught you and you will win. You don't play like we taught you, you fucking lose. That is all there is to it. It is not the coaches who play, it's you."

"Okay, let's get a prayer, a break and then, captains, out onto the field. All sophomores are captains," Chuck yelled as players got to their feet and began massing in the center of the room.

Like water swirling toward a drain, players were drawn to the growing huddle, kneeling with heads bowed and hands reaching out for others. All but a couple of players hung back and seemed disinterested, offering only a half-hearted stab of hands toward the pile of humanity. In all of football, this moment is the most puzzling to me. It is an intersection of such unlikely bedfellows as religion and the brutish and no-holds-barred activity of trying to flatten your opponent into the fresh smelling turf. As the French sociologist Emile Durkheim believed, the world, and all its experience, can be divided into two spheres, the profane and the sacred. Now for a minute, before charging out onto the field and for the three-and-a-half hours of the game, we were entering the sacred; far different than the mundane and ordinary "profane."

Begging for guidance and benevolence, we knelt before each player's God–that, to many, was even more powerful than a head coach–and entered the sacred. At this very moment, upstairs in the women's locker room, Bakersfield was doing the same damn thing.

Beggars can't be choosers.

As Chris Hill, the black safety from Florida, steeped in the Southern Baptist tradition of fire and brimstone, began his hypnotic and lyrically rich chant to "Dear God," I stood in the back, hands resting lightly on the two players kneeling in front of me. As players and coaches alike bowed their heads in the last moment of reflection, Chris took us on a metaphysical search for the elusive edge. I listened, with eyes wide open, my only concession to the juxtaposition that confronted my intellect, and part of me was drawn into the web of Chris' soliloquy. I wondered which team would Chris' God grant the edge to today and, if both teams begged enough, didn't that balance out the god effect and lead us back to square one, dependent on our heart and soul and determination? Just in case, I hoped that Chris pleaded his case more eloquently than the Bakersfield designated prayer.

Dueling prayers.

Evidently, Chris felt the same way because his words rose on the wings of his chant and danced out of his mouth. Sacrilegious as it may have been, I muttered an appreciative and impressed "damn" to myself as Chris rammed home the final words of offering. A moment of silence followed, just a tick of the clock hanging on the wall above the doorway and then the room erupted with screams of emotional triumph.

"Let's kill them!"

"Fuck Bakersfield!"

"You got to want it!"

"Fuck Bakersfield!"

Bodies leaped from the huddle and arms reached for the ceiling as we crushed into a standing pile of heavily padded warriors. As bodies jumped and jostled, somewhere in the bowels of that human pile, Rick Owens, a sophomore defensive end, screamed out "Vaqueros on three, Vaqueros on three. One two, three!" In unison, all of us responded in kind. "Vaqueros!"

And we were done. Ready to face the challenge of our young and not so young lives. I turned and, with the other 18 sophomores, slipped out the team locker room door. I was a 38-year-old captain of the Santa Barbara City College Football team and anthropologist, headed to flip the coin and decide the fate of the beginning of our last game of the 1995 season and, for many of us, the last game of our lives.

# Chapter 2

---

## A Nineties Masculinity
### Bakersfield/Santa Barbara Pregame
### (continued)

**KIST**

*Welcome back, crowd still filing in on this pleasant Saturday afternoon. Santa Barbara City College looking for a share of the Northern Division title for the first time since 1991.*

*Today Bakersfield is in town at LaPlaya Stadium. Let's chronicle Santa Barbara City College to date. J.T. Stone having a phenomenal year leading the conference in individual total offense and passing, 3108 yards, net passing and running with 20 touchdowns and he has passed for 2696 yards and 17 TDs. Having just a terrific season, the freshmen from Dos Pueblos, and he is only getting better every week, the technique, the footwork and his decision making has improved from week one immeasurably.*

Out the locker room door, we flinched at the bright sun and then all eighteen of us went down the concrete winding stairs that led onto the parking lot where the ticket office was. A big crowd of parents and kids pushed us through the 10-foot high gate that led to the stadium floor. Slowing slightly to give the rest of the sophomores time to catch up, the pack crossed the nine-lane synthetic tartan track and reached the turf, a group of helmeted players ready to do battle and challenge the odds. We marched across the field to the sidelines opposite the huge, old 10,000 seat concrete grandstand. Already there was a large group of red clad Bakersfield fans settling on the worn and weathered seats. The Vaquero contingent was slow in arriving, fashionably late and in half the numbers of the Bakersfield supporters. No surprise to us. Usually, at our home games, the visiting team had more fans than we did.

One of the officials met us at the 50-yard-line and told us only four could walk all the way to midfield to meet the Bakersfield captains. The rest would have to stop at the near hash. Mike Hayes, a starting cornerback, lone halfback Twuan Hill, Jarrett Thiessen, the monsterback, and I lined up with the rest falling in behind us. We grabbed hands and waited for the official to lead us out. A minute passed before the Bakersfield contingent was ready to go. Silent, we stood there lost in our own thoughts, hands resting in each other's grasp. Conscious of what this particular display of male bonding would be thought of outside this stadium, at a different time and place, the anthropologist in me rudely intervened and pushed aside the player. I remembered a particular passage from a book I had just recently read.

Mariah Burton Nelson, the author of *The Stronger Women Get, The More Men Love Football*, wrote of bonding in male athletes by describing the cover photo of H.G. Bissenger's *Friday Nights Lights*. Three high school football captains striding through the stadium tunnel on their way to the pre-game ceremony were described as an irony, a social-sexual paradox in an otherwise hyper-masculine activity. "Were these same young men," said Nelson, "to hold hands in a different setting on a city street...without their football uniforms, they would be thought of as gay. They might be taunted by other men, football players perhaps. Yet in this picture their hand holding projects a solemn, unified sort of group power that conveys both threat and affections. It illustrates the fact that male power is based on male bonding. Together they feel powerful. Together, they act powerful."

Standing there, my hands wrapped in two different hands, I felt some of that unified power. A feeling of togetherness was

11

generated to approach a monumental task and gather strength. I didn't feel a power that held dominion over women. My thoughts were not of us males dominating women by our linking of rough and callused hands. I could feel the texture of Jarrett's skin that lay in mine and its roughness reminded me of the feeling of security I felt when my father's giant paw, giant to a six year old, used to settle around my hand. It wasn't threatening; it was comforting in it maleness.

However, Nelson continued, "together, they fall in love with power, with masculinity. They also fall in love with each other." I wasn't ready for some psychosexual analysis of hand holding and attempted to push the thought from my mind. I didn't need to look at Twuan on one side of me and Jarrett and Mike on the other side to know that I was not in love with either of them or any others on the team. In some real way, Nelson's male bashing is a condemnation of male athletes. She was saying that only in hyper-masculine sports like football could a man physically show another male how he feels without fear of negative labeling.

"While sport offers a man a place to worship traditional manhood, paradoxically it also offers a man a place to loosen the rigid masculine role without losing status," wrote Nelson. Mary Boutilier and Lucinda SanGiovanni added those men "can embrace each other unself-consciously, holding and hugging, touching and kissing without threat of ridicule and suspicion. They can express fear, hesitancy, pain and doubt and be nurtured by other men. They can be irrational, cooperative, sentimental, and superstitious in the accepting presence of male camaraderie. In sum, in the absence of women, they can allow themselves to express what sexist ideology insists must be suppressed if they are to lay valid claim to being 'real men.'"

Pat Griffin, a lesbian athlete and author, in her book, *Strong Women, Deep Closets* took a similar tack, "It is not a coincidence that expressions of male-to-male physical affection and love are acceptable in few other contexts. In athletics, men can admire other men's bodies and their physical accomplishments openly without arousing suspicions about their heterosexuality." More simplistically, said Nelson, "Much of sport...is an elaborate stage set to enable men to feel."

A folklorist, Allen Dundes, contributed a thought-provoking

piece for a volume I edited on anthropology, sport and culture based on his belief that football was a ritual that allowed for the expression of male homosexuality combat rites. Not unique to American culture, Dundes found these rites fairly common in other cultures. Echoing other feminist writers, Dundes suggested that beyond serving as a male initiation right, football promotes the continuation of a male preserve that manifests both the physical and cultural values of masculinity. In the speech and behavior from penetration of one's end zone to the postural stances of lineman and the center, football, he suggested, is full of homosexual connotations. Yet Dundes didn't stop there; he saw football as "a ritual combat between groups of males attempting to assert their masculinity by penetrating the end zones of their rivals. The ritual aspect of football provides a socially sanctioned framework for body contact and is a form of homosexual behavior." Although these male initiation rites are a doorway to manhood in many cultures, college and professional athletes, especially football players, extend and retard this period of adolescence for many years.

Nelson and many other feminist writers accuse sport of creating a safe, artificially constructed haven where a man can show and express real emotion and attachment to other males without being labeled a "fag" by his friends. I know that the turf is a rectangular harbor where feelings of males find asylum and I wonder, what is wrong with that? Human ritual and football can be considered an activity that supersedes normal or profane reality. Ritual is the result of thousands of years of human evolution to accommodate behavior that is necessary for the function of culture. It finds a home above and beyond normal reality. Famous sports attorney and once philosopher of sport, Howard Slusher, suggested that religion and associated rituals play less and less an important role in human's existence. Sport is one of those rites humans now turn to to impose order on a chaotically changing world. Why should males, or for that matter females, today be exempt from that same evolutionary need? Why not let order come out of chaos through a ritual that stretches back in our evolution?

Many feminists stick male athletes with a label of latent homosexuals. In a twist of logic, lesbian and female athletes are now discovering the strength, power and bonding that participating in sports can bring to the athlete. Wrote Griffin, "Women in athletics develop strong relationships with other women as teammates, friends, and lovers; they challenge, comfort, and support each other.... The truth is that women do develop passionate feelings for other women in the sport context, and for some women these feelings are sexual. Now women find out sport is a venue, removed from real life, and yet part of real life, that offers them a sanctuary to express affection and camaraderie."

The academic liberal inside me acquiesced to their logic, but the player in me tried to escape it. I could rationalize telling myself that it isn't the game that I have come to cherish that creates the homophobic masculine-only locker room feelings. It's the players and the coaches and the men who sit back in their easy chairs and in smokey bars that create the need to ritualize male affection. The game, the camaraderie, the surge of adrenaline, the goal of team victory all are connected together in some ritual zeitgeist that propel the players forward and brings out the worst in those who play and watch.

In the minute before marching toward midfield, 18 young men and one old guy held hands in full view of 2000 fans. And this wasn't the first time we held hands. We held hands in practice and games in the offensive huddle. We held hands during team prayers. We hugged players with a happy embrace after a good play and mauled them when they scored a touchdown, made an interception, or recovered a fumble. We consoled players after mistakes by draping an arm over a shoulder and telling them to shake it off. We grabbed facemasks or shoulders to make them focus after loosing their cool during a play or on the sidelines after coming off the field. And after the game, some would walk toward the locker room with arms hanging loosely over shoulders reveling in that emotional high of a victory or the bittersweet feeling of a loss.

Very vividly, I can recall the end of the San Francisco-Minnesota *Monday Night Football* Game on December 18, 1995. Two old warriors, quarterbacks Steve Young and Warren Moon, met in the middle of the field at the end of the close game. One white, one black. Young is a devout Mormon and Moon had just recently spoken out and begged forgiveness for his alleged spousal abuse. Uniforms covered with Candlestick/3ComPark moist turf, sweat glazing their faces, steam rolling off their helmetless heads in the late evening Bay fog, they met and embraced and then pulled away, but kept their arms resting on each other's shoulders. The *Monday Night Football* camera remained on this image for what seemed like hours, but was probably only a minute. The viewer could not hear what they were talking about but, whatever the game, the season or just renewing a friendship, the affection and respect each had for the other was there for 20 million viewers to see.

Defined during this context of spent souls and bodies as exhaustion takes its toll, there are feelings of deep respect and maybe love that transcend the profane and pass between players. With society constructing such loaded and dangerous labels and rigidly defining acceptable behavior, is it any wonder that none of us 18 hand holding sophomores would ever admit that this display was nurturing or even slightly affectionate. It has to remain unlabeled and undefined, underscoring the brutal, violent and lightning quick context of what Nelson calls the "manly sports." In those seconds of charged combat, I didn't wonder if grabbing a fellow player is socially acceptable. I grabbed a player because I felt. I bowed to the elation of the moment and it felt good. My mind didn't categorize and compartmentalize my actions. In that instance, those brief seconds of time swallowed up social boundaries and my heart was allowed to run rampant. Is football solely an elaborate stage constructed so that these moments of passion can be allowed to surface? According to Nelson, I went through months of training so that I could stand here holding hands with two other guys and not feel uncomfortable. Nelson and others dwelled at length on the physicalness of male sport, but conveniently, or maybe without knowing, overlooked that sport is a celebration of achievement where one or a group triumph and the passion is not the end result of participation. It is something that sweetens the already enjoyable experience.

I stood on the sideline knowing that in the ensuing march to midfield, it would be wrong not to hold hands. It was the final piece to complete the experience, not the experience itself. Whether the experience is called love or something else, I couldn't deal with it now. I had other things to think about. I banished Nelson from my thoughts. In the future, the anthropologist in me would have to deal with her claims.

I had been one of the four captains at two previous games and I enjoyed the feeling of pomp and circumstance attached to the display of unity and representation. Finally, the far-side official waved that the Renegades were ready and the four of us stepped out on the field. We began the symbolic journey honoring the age-old context of the agonal contest found in the ancient Olympics and in the mythical battlefields of the Greek Gods. Honor and courage were the foundation of all athletic contests and the structure of the contest was the combat of equals. Behind us, 14 others followed in our footsteps, stopping at the near hash mark, leaving the four of us to finish the journey.

We stopped ten yards short of midfield with hands still clasped, matching the movement from the opposite sideline of the handholding Bakersfield quintet of captains. An official stood to either side of us and one stood behind. We dropped hands. The head linesman introduced the other officials and then asked a Bakersfield captain to call the coin in the air to determine possession and field direction. I watched the Bakersfield captains, some large lineman and some secondary or receivers, and made out their grim expressions underneath the facemasks. So this was the great juggernaut that had beaten teams by an average of 40 points, the Nebraska of California junior colleges. Their uniforms were white with red piping on their shoulders, white helmets with a simple circled red B and black cleats, the white of the good guys, the white of angels, of purity and virtue.

"We are going to flip this coin to decide possession," said the official and he showed both sides of the coin to each team. "Bakersfield, call when the coin is in the air." The coin went up and seemed to hover at its zenith. "Heads," said the middle Bakersfield captain urging the coin to correct its revolutions and land on the favorable side. The coin lazily fell to the turf and 13 heads craned toward the glint of pseudo steel that lay perched on the only two blades of grass that remained on the worn down, mostly bare 50-yard line. "Heads it is," said the lineman. "What goaline do you wish to defend, Santa Barbara?" asked the official. "We want to defend the east," said Jarrett, before I could get it out.

We wanted the westward ocean breeze that usually blew in the late afternoon at our backs the last quarter so if by some miracle we were within striking distance, J.T.'s bombs would have help.

The flip side of this decision was that, by four in the afternoon the sun was low on the horizon and, without any helpful cloud cover to cut the glare, would bore solar lasers into Vaquero receiver's eyes. This would create an additional problem, along with holding onto the ball after getting whacked by the league-leading defense. Balancing out the good with the bad, it was wind over sun.

The head linesman then directed us to change positions on the field, our backs to the east goal and Bakersfield to face us. "Okay, gentlemen, Bakersfield has elected to kickoff," and he switched and stood to the side of the Renegades, pantomiming a catching motion. Switching positions, he stood with his back to us and continued, "Santa Barbara has chosen to defend the east goal." He then moved to the middle and said, "Have a good clean game and good luck to both of you. Now shake hands." An order from on high. Both sides stepped toward the middle of the field, hands outstretched, reaching to make some kind of connection.

"Good luck."

"Have a good game."

"Play well."

These words greased the clasps of flesh as we shook hands all around, some hands being shook more than once. I tried to make eye contact with the soon-to-be enemy. A couple of them returned my gaze for longer than a couple of seconds, but the huge numbers on our respective uniforms would be forgotten even before we reached the sidelines. We turned and made our way back the way we came. The rest of the Vaquero captains that had waited while the four of us represented them joined like a growing wave and we headed for the sideline.

The rest of the team broke from the gate and sprinted to the near side goal and formed a huge moving mass of players. The latecomers leaped on top of the group like kids diving off of huge speakers at a rock concert. Once this year, I got caught in the middle of that and feared for my life as my body was crushed under several tons of males and football gear. For the rest of the season, I stayed on the periphery, away from flying human missiles. I was glad that today I was already out on the field. From where I stood, it looked like the huge huddle was even more bent on reducing those in the middle to quadriplegics. The huddle finally broke and the players streamed across the field. Bakersfield was already on their sideline, waiting patiently for the anticipated slaughter to begin.

J.T and starting wide receiver/back-up quarterback Benjy drilled warm-up passes to receivers. The balls spiraled back and forth in a crisp and comforting way. There was little talking. Every now and then, leather hit the grass signaling the tension that was felt. Other players mingled up and down the sideline stopping to slam into somebody or beat a player's shoulder pads with their forearms.

Chuck and defensive coordinator Joe DiPaolo plugged themselves into the headsets. Chuck connected to his friend that helped spot for Chuck sitting high above the field in the press box and Joe to his father, Carmen, sharing the same space. The scratchy voice of the PA announcer floated down from above, asking us to listen to Whitney Houston sing, "our National Anthem." What seemed like hours later, it was the extended extra slow version, Whitney was mercifully over and we turned our attention to the field and raised helmets in anticipation of the kick-off.

It was time. It was time for the biggest game in our lives and, as an anthropologist, I had more than a first row seat. I was there as a player and as a describer of culture. More often than not, each role got lost in the other. But that was one of the pitfalls of doing anthropology fieldwork; trying to figure out where science ended and real life began.

**KIST**
*If you are not doing anything, come out to the ballpark this afternoon. Tickets are still available. If not, stay in the backyard or your easy chair and keep it right here on KIST. The Renegades and Vaqueros ready to do battle. When we come back we will preview both teams, give you the pregame stats and stories and set up the final regular season game from LaPlaya stadium that Vaquero fans hope is only the regular season finale. They would like to get a bowl game. Santa Barbara one of 18 teams still negotiating bowl rights with the state of California.*

*Bakersfield, boy they are tough. The fifth ranked team in the state, coach Dallas Grider has this squad continuing the excellence tradition that Bakersfield football knows.*

*Last year Bakersfield went 10-1, finished third ranked in the state, number 7 in the nation. Won the Potato Bowl, defeated Long Beach City College, 31-9. They were a preseason rank #2 this year, after City College of San Francisco lost their opening game to Laney College of Oakland, Bakersfield jumped up to #1 in the State. But the loss to LA Valley moved them down a few notches, but they are right back up into the top five.*

*Coming into La Playa stadium today and Bakersfield has a most impressive offense. 431 points this season, as I mentioned, and they average 48 points per game. Santa Barbara, a big win as we have talked about 40-30 last week and it has been an uphill climb since the 34-18 loss to Hancock back in the first week of Division play. But since then, Santa Barbara has hung tough and battled back and has won three straight to set up the showdown today.*

# Chapter 3

## Santa Barbara: Football in Paradise

A past Santa Barbara College football brochure read, "Students are privileged to live in beautiful Santa Barbara, 'where the mountains meet the sea' declared by many world travelers to be one of the most beautiful cities in all the world.... One-half of the streets end at one of the world's most beautiful beaches; the others end in the foothills of the Santa Ynez Mountains. With the mountains and the sea, with a climate unsurpassed, and with flowers blooming every day of the year, nature has made Santa Barbara a most enjoyable place to live."

Standing at Chumash Point, the small memorial to the Chumash Indians, high on a cliff face 100 feet above Cabrillo Boulevard and Santa Barbara City College's LaPlaya Stadium, one can see the mountains meeting the ocean. One can also almost imagine seeing the Chumash big block canoes gracefully paddling out into the Santa Barbara Channel for the 21-mile trip to Santa Cruz Island, one of the several islands that naturally form the boundaries of the Channel. The last island westward in the chain, San Miguel, signals the end of the channel and the lazy meandering California coastline takes a hard right at Point Conception and continues racing north toward the awesome, breathtaking beauty of the jagged cliffs and crashing surf of Monterey and Santa Cruz.

A little off to the right, and directly below Chumash Point, sits LaPlaya Stadium. The venerable 10,000 seat concrete grandstand climbs 72 bleacher steps up and, at its highest, is the same level as Chumash Point. Night or day, the bleachers are constantly in use by the community recreational enthusiasts doing "stadiums," running up and down the steps. Over 60 years old, the stadium shows it's age. With crumbling cement steps in some areas and paint peeling from the press box, the antiquated structure harbors memories of football games when helmets were leather and one could easily see the pain, triumph, and ecstasy etched on the players' faces.

LaPlaya was constructed in the 1930s by the Civilian Conservation Corps during Roosevelt's Great Plan for putting America back to work and, without a doubt, contained one of the most picturesque views in all of college football. Dramatically rising off the beach, gray wooden bleacher seats, many with carved initials of those who sat on them in the past, seemingly climb toward the heavens or least the coastal mountain range just a short five miles away. The concrete edifice runs the entire length of the field with the end zones and ocean side of the field empty of seating. An old scoreboard, complete with a few missing light bulbs, stands behind the West End zone and a very fast, state-of-the-art track encircles the field. The track is perhaps the best, or one of the best, in Southern California and was a result of a rare surplus of funds from the 1984 Los Angeles Summer Games.

The turf was the worst we played on all year and it was our home field. The man in charge of the field, John, tried his hardest, but he was always fighting a losing cause. In places, the turf was below sea level and water seeped up from below, creating muddy areas that needed sand for the games. Sinkholes dotted the field and the shape of the crown, the highpoint of the field, resembled a chewed watermelon slab. It was way too easy to twist and sprain an ankle on sections of the field.

But it was home, and it was ours.

It is not too difficult, standing at Chumash Point, to transport oneself back in time over 450 years ago when there were no

Anglos, no Spanish, no Mexicans, just the Chumash. On October 10, 1542, the intrepid Spanish explorer, Juan Rodriguez Cabrillo, was trying to locate a northern passage back to Europe. A little off on his geography, his two little ships dropped anchor off what is now Ventura, California. This is the point where the coast heads northward from Los Angeles and makes a hard left turn and heads west into the Pacific for 60 miles. Cabrillo took possession of the country for his Royal benefactors. For the 10-15,000 Chumash Indians that inhabited over 40 large villages up and down the central California coastline, and the added villages that occupied the vast wilderness of the Inland Empire, it signaled a tragedy soon to play out. Four days later, Cabrillo continued his explorations westward and made landfall at what is now Carpinteria, just 11.5 miles by Highway 101 to Santa Barbara City College, less by following the coastline. Cabrillo found a laid back, content and happy people living on the beach and the islands were only a day's paddle away. These true Californians did not want, for the coastal life produced plenty: seals, whales, shellfish and other resource-rich marine life. Hundreds of smaller villages dotted the coastline clustered around the mouths of little streams and creek deltas that emptied out into the Channel.

The 2000-foot Coastal Mountains just three miles away acted to keep the climate almost ideal year round. The inland Chumash inhabited what is now Los Padres National Forest and faced soaring temperatures in the summer, topping out at over 100 degrees and close to zero in the dead of winter. Most Chumash lived on the narrow strip of coastline between the mountains and the surf.

Numerous canoes bringing fresh fish to barter met Cabrillo, and many Chumash boarded the two ships in welcome. A diarist from Cabrillo's party wrote, "a magnificent valley, densely populated with level land and many groves." Cabrillo spent the rest of the fall exploring the Channel Islands and coast. He did not live to see the spring. He suffered a freak fall that injured his arm and died in early winter. He is supposedly buried on San Miguel Island, but the whereabouts of his grave remains a mystery.

A follow-up expedition wasn't mounted for another 60 years. In 1602, Sebastian Viscaino retraced Cabrillo's sail steps up the coast and named points of interest and villages after the patron saint of the day. He entered the Channel on December 4 and promptly named it after the patron saint, Barbara. The islands became Santa Cruz, Santa Rosa and San Miguel and modern-day Ventura became San Buenaventura. Viscaino was faced with the usual December Channel weather of fog and rain, and landfall was infrequent and brief. He continued his journey westward passing and naming Point Conception. He journeyed farther north and discovered a peaceful natural harbor at Monterey Bay.

One of the first maps of the Channel coastline drawn by a member of the expedition shows three of the four islands. The present day, still lush, Montecito and Carpinteria Valleys, home of many Hollywood stars and security gates and high hedges, were identified as the Coastal del Arborledo (wooded coast). Dos Pueblos, 10 miles further west of Santa Barbara, was labeled as Pueblo Grande. Today this stretch of coast is not only one of the most scenic in Southern California, it is probably one of the most affluent.

The Chumash were granted a respite from foreign meddling for 167 years after Viscaino's visit. The Spanish found little to interest them about the central coast; the peoples were too peaceful and, worse yet, had no gold. To plug up the drain on pocketbooks of royal and private enterprise, the California coast, north of Mexico, was judged too costly to offer dividends and left alone.

The saber-rattling Russians began a series of advances southward from Alaska and the Spanish grew concerned for their claims on the Pacific. In 1769, a small land force was sent north, from the just-built San Diego Mission, to build an outpost and establish a military deterrent to the Russian advance at Monterey Bay. Juan de Portola led the intrepid band northward and on August 16 they camped at the edge of Carpinteria Valley near Rincon Creek. A village of 38 houses lay further to the west at what is now Carpinteria. The soldiers happened on the construction of one of many canoes and the village was named Carpenter after the builders. The expedition continued through present day Santa Barbara and Goleta, both locations bustling communities. At soon to be named Santa Barbara, the party was inundated with gifts of fresh fish and finally they told the Indians, no more, for it would spoil. Said one Lieutenant Flages, "The gentleness and good disposition of the Indians gives good reason for entertaining a

23

moral certainty of their reduction, provided they be preached the word of God." A priest wrote, "we journeyed along the Santa Barbara Channel and rejoiced to find there so many pagans upon whom the light of our Holy Father was about to dawn." In a miscarriage of social justice and one of life's cruelest ironies, the friendliness of the "natives" was to prove to be their downfall. Less than 70 years later, a healthy, carefree 15,000 Chumash had dwindled to a scant 234 men, women and children.

Missions were soon established in five locations; the largest of the five was built in Santa Barbara. Two years prior to the construction of the mission at Santa Barbara, a presidio, or military base, was constructed just south of the eventual mission and slightly lower on the slope leading to the beach. Both stand today; the Presidio recently has been archaeologically reconstructed, and the Mission, with a little facelift, looks out on a panoramic view of the islands and the Channel from its perch nestled up against the Riviera.

In the name of God, the missions quickly became the center for an indentured Indian labor. Besides being rounded up and virtually imprisoned within the missions' walls, the Indians suffered through epidemics of white man's diseases; syphilis and pleuropneumonia and a rapidly decreasing birth rate. They were made to worship against their traditions and myths. In 1833, the Mexican government secularized the missions and the vast holdings were squandered in a few short years. Wrote Campbell Grant, "In the space of a single lifetime, a great Indian nation, one of the largest and most culturally advanced in California, had ceased to exist."

On a clear day, from Chumash Point, mainly during the late fall and early spring, one can see the ridges and canyons of Santa Cruz and San Miguel Islands, the flat top of Anacapa and all the way down the coastline to Ventura. If you don't look too closely, you can also feel the centuries roll back to the 1500s and let your eyes focus on the mountains as they meet the Pacific in the distance. It is not too hard to imagine Cabrillo's tiny ships, lordly to the Chumash canoes, slowly making their way up the Channel, passing the many villages that stretched from Malibu Canyon to Point Concepcion.

I have stood at Chumash Point after practice and watched the sun set and the entire Channel turn from light orange to pink to blood red in the cooling evening. In the final two weeks of the season, when the clock was set back an hour, practice finished under the lights. The last 20 minutes of scrimmage we either looked into the sinking orb or watched the reflection of the dying light on the clouds and mountainsides and the rolling surf.

The cultural heritage in Santa Barbara and elsewhere is Mexican and Spanish. This legacy percolates down through the social classes and the masses. It is found on the street signs and fiestas, the phone books, the names of towns along the coasts, and the vistas in Santa Barbara and highlands behind. It is owed to the conquistadors or Mexican soldiers sent by the government to maintain the territorial rights to a land swiped from the Chumash.

The Santa Barbara City College mascot is a Vaquero, a Spanish cowboy that rode the huge sprawling rancherias in the 1800s. The silhouette of a cowboy on a rearing horse graces the walls of the training and weight room and is featured on tee shirts. The message portrayed is a tough, independent, resourceful and skilled cowboy.

The true legacy of the coastline is the rich image of pristine and fertile valleys inhabited by the Chumash hunters and gatherers in harmony with their universe. The Chumash tamed the forests, enjoyed the immaculate beaches and mined the abundant marine life, not by altering it to their needs, but by letting the land and ocean speak to them about what was possible. What those first explorers must have felt as they sailed along these plentiful resource-rich islands to the west and just beyond the surf, a veritable gold mine of teeming wildlife and fertile soil to the east. A sense of paradise found.

Santa Barbara City College sits on what was a bustling mesa of Chumash habitation. At the time of contact, the village of Syuhton sat on the beach, nestled up against the delta of Mission Creek that empties into the Channel. State Street now slams into Cabrillo at this location and the wharf juts obscenely out into the harbor. Even before contact time, prior to Syuhton, there was a memory of a village sitting "on top" of the Mesa in the same exact location as East campus. "When they started building East Campus back in the 1960s," said Dennis Ringer, anthropology instructor at City College, "the whole area was full of artifacts and signs of habitation." The name of this village was Mispu, or cradle of the hand. Right behind Chumash Point, where Mispu was located, our practice field sat in a clearing with a view that parallels none. I would lay back after practice and the rich sweet smell of Eucalyptus would combine with the salt air of the Pacific and settle around my sweat-covered nose and I would know this was the closest to playing in paradise.

It always seemed to me that since we toiled, sweated and practiced our balls off on the site of an Indian village and played our games on a field just 60 years ago that was awash with surf, identity with a culture that raped the countryside and exterminated the original inhabitants was more than an irony. For two years, I played a sport that incorporated elements of Chumash life: cooperation, speed, guile, the velocity and accuracy of throwing, even the raw strength and power of the animal world they exploited. I played this sport on the same grass where trod the light feet of Chumash warriors hundreds of years before. And for two years, I wore the symbol of those who destroyed that life.

Santa Barbara was a soap opera, still is a lifestyle, and features million dollar Montecito and Riviera mansions tucked into mountainsides. Interwoven in the fabric of everyday life are the affluence of European visitors, the close ties with the glitz and glitter of Hollywood and LA that lie two hours south on a good day, with only a moderate amount of traffic, and the extremes of the social classes, rich and famous, white and Hispanic. In between the high and low resides a financially-stressed middle class, struggling to own homes and bring up children. You must pay to live in paradise.

There is another social stratum of Santa Barbara, that of traditional Mexican families, who have been here for generations and purchased houses on the Mesa and other residential neighborhoods way back when $25,000 bought you a house on Shoreline Drive, just a two-minute walk from City College. Now, you are lucky to buy one for under $750,000. Many of these families are third and fourth generation Mexicans who are now entrenched in the real Santa Barbara, like Head Coach Chuck Melendez.

Just on the other side of Cabrillo Boulevard, in front of LaPlaya Stadium, is the bike path that spans the three miles of city beach in the heart of tourist Santa Barbara. A spit from the stadium is the fountain of dolphins that is the center of the year round vacation atmosphere and sits in a roundabout at the busiest light in Santa Barbara. West of the campus, Cabrillo changes into Shoreline Drive and rises up to meet another section of the Mesa, paralleling for the first mile Leadbetter Beach where any time during the day surfers can be seen wave-riding. On the backside of campus, the mountains loom and the city majestically unfolds beneath you only to climb up to meet the foothills on the other side of the tiny valley. Line of sight from campus across the city is the Riviera; a neighborhood built on the first series of foothills. The mission is quite visible from campus and sits right below the Riviera. At the foot of City College, on the backside, sits a mile square barrio, filled with tiny houses jammed full of Hispanic families. Many residences contain two or three families. Some of them are illegal aliens. Downtown splits residential Santa Barbara into the East and West Side, both predominantly Hispanic.

On the periphery, but very much a defining element of Santa Barbara, are Montecito, Summerland and Carpinteria. Just a mile or two from Santa Barbara, the rich and famous live in hedged fortresses in the still-wooded valleys that jut up against the mountains just a mile or two from Santa Barbara. Kenny Loggins, Rob Lowe, Cathy Ireland, Michael Douglas are just a few that call Montecito home. Former supermodel Cheryl Tiegs does the LaPlaya steps once a week and the Clintons spent the week after winning the 1992 election on Padaro Lane in Summerland. Michael and Arianna Huffington tried to squeeze in the White House while residing in Montecito. Kevin Costner has a Carpinteria address.

Take a ride through Montecito in the late afternoon and the bus stops will be jammed with Mexicans leaving their jobs as domestics, gardeners, and nannies to stream home to a house, filled with humanity, the size of garage or tool shed on their employer's acreage. This is the Santa Barbara of extreme contrast. And in the middle of all, like Mt. Olympus, sits Santa Barbara City College, offering redemption, salvation and a modern-day educational spiritualism.

The college has the highest transfer rate of all junior colleges to the University of California system and the largest number of

Ph.D.'s per student population, as well. Walking across campus is a trip through multicultural diversity featuring the sun-bleached blonde hair, the dark tresses and olive complexion of the Hispanic, and the serene countenance of the many Asian students. Few blacks can be found on campus, as Santa Barbara is too far north of LA County and way too expensive to call home. City College students, many who have to work one or even two part-time jobs to live in Santa Barbara, take much longer to transfer to a four-year program and a large number make the cross-town trek to UCSB where they spend even more time finishing.

City College is situated in what my mother described as the envy of all geographical locations: on a beach, smack dab in the middle of a resort town. Indeed, everybody is laid back in an ideal climate where, outside of two weeks of rain in the wet season, why wear clothes. Wait. Doesn't this sound like the Chumash?

# Section Two
## The Game
## Bakersfield versus Santa Barbara
## 1st Quarter

*LaPlaya Stadium*
*A crumbling edifice, testament to the New Deal, with*
*weathered and splintered seats.*
*But it was home.*

*The view from our practice field, down the coast*
*and back in time*
*We shared it with the memories of Chumash centuries old*

# *Chapter 4*

## The Team

**KIST**

*Bakersfield coming out from the tunnel here at LaPlaya Stadium and City College will be following, I am sure. So the battle for first place in the Northern division, Bakersfield 4-0 is guaranteed a share of the title, Santa Barbara and Hancock trying to grab a piece of their own. On a gorgeous afternoon here at LaPlaya Stadium facing the Pacific Ocean, flag flying a slight breeze, the temperatures which had dropped into the mid 50s in Santa Barbara are now climbing. The sun is back out and should be a very pleasant afternoon. Crowd filing in, the red and white on both sides, Bakersfield bringing a large contingent, media crews to the game. A festive atmosphere.*

*Santa Barbara City College has won the toss. They will receive. Bakersfield will be going left to right on your radio dial. Getting ready to tee it up on the 35-yard line, Brian Walker. He will be doing the punting duties for Bakersfield. The Renegades fans hope they don't see Brian on the field very much. Santa Barbara fans hope he kicks all day long. But he will get it up on the 35-yard line. Back deep for SBCC, Mike Hayes, standing at his 4 yard line with hands on hips, Torlando Bolden, the Santa Barbara High School Don product, also flanking Hayes. Renegades' white uniform, red trim. Santa Barbara in their home red with black pants*

31

*and red helmets, 4-0 at home this year.*
*And this game from LaPlaya stadium is underway.*

Along with everybody else, I watched from the sidelines anticipating the kickoff. Our helmets were thrust toward the heavens as Mike and Torlando waited for the kick from Bakersfield. Mike and Torlando were as different as night and day, white and black, short and tall, defense and offense, father and fancy-free. Torlando received the kick.

**KIST**
*Walker's kick is taken by Bolden at the 7-yard line.*

Up and down the sideline, players were screaming at the top of their lungs as 22 heavily-padded teammates collided all over the field of play. Torlando stuttered-stepped, moving more laterally than vertically and in a rare occurrence only made a few yards before being stopped by a swarm of Bakersfield tacklers.

**KIST**
*Torlando nimbly dances up past the 20 before he is crushed by four Renegades at the 23-yard line. Renegades at the 23-yard line. Torlando a cautious run right there. Taking baby steps and looking for a hole. Bakersfield wouldn't let him do it. Santa Barbara City College will take over at the 23-yard line against the seventh state ranked Bakersfield defense. Santa Barbara coming in the #5 offense in the WSC. Bakersfield with the number 2 offense in the WSC, Santa Barbara's defense ranked eighth in the conference.*

Mike offered a hand and helped Torlando get back on his feet. He effortlessly got up and then, shifting gears, ambled off the field. When Torlando stepped onto the game's sacred arena, he was the closest thing to a god we had. He wasn't like an omnipotent deity of the Great Religions, but was more the humancentric personality of the Greek Gods; jealous, vain, arrogant, brash and, for the benefit of the mortals that created them in their own image, insecure. He was immortal to us because his exploits lived in our minds long after his feet and hips had danced to another touchdown. By age 19, "Touchdown" Torlando Bolden was already a convicted felon when he stepped onto the practice field for 1995 spring ball. One night, that summer before, as Torlando readied for his freshman year at San Jose State, he decked a 5'3" Mexican-American one block off of State Street. Torlando knocked him cold after an exchange of racial taunts, and his victim spent several days in the hospital with cerebral bleeding. Torlando was arrested and stood trial for aggravated assault. He was convicted of a misdemeanor and received a lifetime full of probation and community service.

Touchdown was also perhaps the most electrifying back to come out of Santa Barbara High School since Randall Cunningham followed his brother Sam "Bam" Cunningham into the NFL. Torlando's football feats were prodigious, turning short pass patterns and kickoff returns into touchdowns at will. He was not very big, maybe 6 feet and 170 pounds, but was one of those rare athletes who could out sprint a horse and make it look so easy. Torlando was made for the pass-happy AirChuck offense. With three other receivers, set him out wide, suck up the man on man and hit him short underneath or streak him deep down the sideline. Either way, just get him the ball and stand back and marvel.

As exceptional on the field as Torlando was, off the field he was an enigma, aloof and ice cold one day, outgoing and funny the next. Torlando carried with him the baggage of a broken family environment and a temper that, when ignited, was like a brush fire on a dry late summer day in the browned-out mountains behind Santa Barbara. His father was in prison, so was a cousin. His mother and a doting grandmother brought him up. He loafed through high school. Classes were just a passing thought, hidden far down the ladder of priority, below his on-the-field accomplishments. Coming out of high school, Torlando was a non-qualifier scoring well below 750 on his SAT scores. San Jose State wanted him bad enough to get him there and line him up with enough financial aid to pay for five others, if need be. If he could survive his freshman year, Torlando was guaranteed a scholarship the second year. The end of the first week of football practice at San Jose did not feature Torlando Bolden. He had already left and returned back home after spending three days in campus dorms. The rumor was that he ended up in fights and that the football team, to him, was a joke. Some said it was because he missed his grandmother and the security of friends.

Chuck talked Torlando into going to City College for the 1995 school year and tried to get him into a weightlifting and the spring football class. For some reason or other, known only to the enigmatic Torlando, he decided not to enroll, but did show occasionally during the football class. While twirling a ball in his large hands, he watched from the sideline. Everybody had their favorite Torlando play: a 98-yard kickoff return, a long bomb, a short dig that turned into a mad sprint to the goal line with Torlando easily outdistancing the defenders. Most of the City College players were from local high schools and had played with or against Torlando. He was treated with a certain amount of deference that befit his recognized, legitimized position as king of, at least, our turf.

He could be the life of the locker room. His humor was biting and always on target, but you could never get past, or maybe it was Torlando would never let you pass, his surface layer or comfort zone. He would sit on the bench in front of his locker as he went through his own ritual of getting his pads stuffed into his pants and lazily watch the swirl of players getting ready for practice or a game. Every now and then he would single out a player around him and fire off a salvo of biting commentary concerning a sister or a girlfriend of the player, how she was a loose or too easy, how she should be in the army, she's had enough march through, anyway. The player would squirm, but underneath would feel honored he was chosen by the King. In those situations, Torlando's disinterested look would disappear and his broad forehead would wrinkle and his face would light up with a toothy grin and let loose a laugh that echoed off the lockers in the team room and drifted into the hallways. You never knew from one day to the next when his mercurial disposition was on vacation. Torlando could disappear during the game faster than water in Death Valley. He would be sitting on the trainer's table on the sidelines; ice on his knee by the beginning of the fourth quarter, and was done for the day. When Torlando did show up to play, he was a human highlight film.

Torlando didn't understand why his talents couldn't take him the same places others' talents had. Look at Napoleon Kaufman, from Lompoc, just 40 minutes away; now with the Oakland Raiders and Sam and Randall Cunningham. Torlando knew he wasn't into books and had trouble learning or paying attention enough to learn.

But he didn't want people to think he was stupid. School just wasn't interesting enough for him. It wasn't like dunking a ball or grabbing a bomb and scoring a TD. Besides, you had to show up when the classes started and then had to sit there. Torlando hated schedules. Things got going when Torlando arrived.

He didn't worry about things working without him. In fact, things didn't work until he was a part of the game. Nobody had the hops he did or the moves on the field. Big schools wanted him. They were ready to deal for his services, and things he could do were worth something. It was a pain in the ass that the road to the pros took him through something he wasn't or had never been good at. City College wanted him to go through a slow learners program and get him tutors for all of his subjects. He wasn't going to go through a program for dummies. School was never easy for him; it just didn't seem to be worth the effort.

Torlando didn't start for us anymore. The best player on the team came off the bench. That honor of starting went to others with lesser talents. Torlando didn't start because his practice habits were nonexistent. All fall, Torlando did not finish one practice. Rarely did he make it past the team scrimmage in practice before taking himself out and visiting the trainers on the sidelines. Still, Torlando led the team in every offensive category except carries and yards rushing, and that was because he only saw the ball from the air.

Mike, one of the starting cornerbacks, jogged ahead of Torlando, cutting toward the defensive side of the sideline. Mike had more than a couple of interceptions to his credit. He returned one for a score the week before to seal a victory against Glendale and was a fearless kick-off and punt returner. He accepted the pats on the back from his teammates, a far different reception than Torlando received. Mike was the glue to the defense.

Standing a shade over a blade of grass, Mike Hayes was an overachiever and loved football. He loved the feeling of snaring a pass intended for a receiver and then juking and faking his way back up the field. He loved the excitement of returning punts, him versus a swarm of defenders. He also loved the concussion of a collision, knocking the ball loose, and flattening the receiver. He lived for the moment at the end of a game where he could barely drag himself off the field after leaving his heart, soul, and body on the turf.

Mike also loved his two-year-old daughter and her mother, just as much as football. That, in part, was the reason for Mike's success. He had to grow up fast in high school. Fatherhood waits for no one. Mike was used to having people depend on him. While other players were greeting waiting girlfriends or parents after games, already plotting the evening parties, Mike was holding his baby while his girlfriend beamed beside him. To Mike, he lived a party, albeit a more serious party, but one that gave him twice as much enjoyment as one-night stands and huge next-day hangovers.

Mike was maybe 5'8" if he was lucky to be measured by a blind man. He was stocky and quick, not fast, but able to stop and turn directions on a dime. Mike spent hours a week in the weight room during the season, knowing that his upper body and leg strength were huge assets. He was one of the most dedicated players because he couldn't loaf during practice and sleep during film. He lacked some of the athletic tools of other players, but he made up for it with grit and determination. The knock on him was his size and, with his anemic academic record, the place to be after high school was City College. Football was the key for him to get through college so the two years he would spend at home gave him the opportunity to stay close to his family.

Learning his first year about college football, and losing, Mike's sophomore season was crucial in determining if he would go on. He knew he could play at the next level, even Division One, but he needed film to prove it and statistics to back it up. Mike was beyond just getting production. Mike sincerely cared about the team and his teammates. I lost count of how many times Mike pointed out mistakes I made while running routes against him in practice. We would talk on the field and in the locker room as he explained the defense's reaction against a formation. "Now Doc," he would say, and then start into a detailed explanation of my mistake. Mike would make a great coach.

Mike was also a great father. His daughter and girl friend lived with her parents and Mike lived at home, but he would drag his weary body over to her house every evening and spend time with both of them. Sundays were precious to him. It was a free day—no school, practice or games, just a day to be a normal father and somewhat of a normal boyfriend. There were quite a few players that had children. Some were like Mike, dedicated, but more often than not, most were unconcerned or oblivious of the seed they planted and helped bring into the world.

The offense, buoyed by the kickoff and flooded with adrenaline, rushed onto the field. One player with the number #3 on his red jersey huddled with Chuck for last-second instructions. His lanky body towered over the shorter Chuck and, with a final word, he turned and, without hurrying, trotted toward his team loosely arranged in the middle of the field. If ever there was a vision of salvation or an image of Messiah in shoulder pads to lead a group of mediocre college football players to the Promised Land, it was the black human catapult that went by the name of J.T. Stone. Just turned 18, six foot, four inches and 180 pounds, the power of the golden arm masked the boy inside. He was used to the fame that came from his high school exploits in basketball and football splashed weekly across the local newspaper.

J.T. moved with the grace of one who knew what his body was capable of. He was aware of his athletic impact on people, but his reserved, quiet demeanor placed people at ease. J.T. knew he was the man for the next two years, even before entering City College. From the beginning of the 1995 summer football practice, the offense was geared around his ability to launch 60-yard missiles as well as grease 25-yard frozen ropes into the teeth of the opposing secondary.

Wrapped up in J.T. was the quintessential dilemma faced by all California athletes, especially with the strength of its 64 junior college football programs. So many high school seniors are like J.T. Marginal or borderline in school, they face uphill battles in the college classroom and, even though each may bring awe-inspiring talents to the field, what is the use if they can't read or write a simple sentence or add two positive integers? Their first stop is not College Station or South Bend, or Ann Arbor, but West LA City College or LA Valley or Bakersfield Community College. Keyshawn Johnson, the star ex-USC (now New York Jet) wideout, is a perfect example. Bouncing around California junior colleges, he finally pulled his act together at West LA City College and on his own incredible talents, and an otherwise weak West LA squad, ended up with two years of scholarship at University of Southern California.

J.T. knew he wanted to play professionally. It was what he had dreamed about all his life. He wanted passing records and to be famous. Sure, he was famous around Santa Barbara County and he had a lot of visits from schools, but he had to look at going to City College as a necessary step in his evolution as a player. If USC, Washington State, UCLA, even quarterback U, Brigham Young wanted him; they would still want him two years from now. His SATs were bad and he didn't want to go Prop 48. He wanted to play right now, not a year down the road. Plus, Chuck was an ex-quarterback and he was a good one at that. Coach kept telling him that the offense was perfect for his abilities and a good training ground for the pros. He thought J.T. could throw for over 3500 yards a season and set California passing records. J.T. thought about that a lot; that's averaging 350 yards through the air per game. That should make colleges and pro scouts stand up and take notice. Make lemonade out of lemons.

J.T. knew he would think daily for the next two years about where his career would take him after City College and he could not stop thinking about playing for BYU. He knew if he played there, he would go on. Didn't all the their quarterbacks get drafted? He only occasionally would think about being a black non-Mormon pioneer. Really, have you ever heard of a black quarterback at BYU? Could he adapt to wearing certain clothes and all that religious stuff and handle being in a very small minority? There weren't a lot of blacks at his old high school, Dos Pueblos, but he had all of his homeys around him. Plus, it snowed a lot there and got cold.

Coach kept telling him to get into summer school after he graduated, take classes, get his feet wet. He would even help J.T. But J.T. wanted to cool his heels. Didn't want to think about school. He just graduated from one school and he wanted to take the summer off. His parents split during his last year and he was confused, thought he would make some money and help out around the house. Coach kept telling him he needed to get through in two years. Get his degree before his spring semester of his sophomore year, so he could go on to a D-1 school and get in on their spring ball. Learn the system so he could step right in during the Fall. But he still had a red-shirt year to play with, so what was the rush. He had heard Coach talk about last year throwing wonder Jarrod

DeGeorgia enough. He wasn't going to make the same mistake, not graduate and make grades so he had to go to some small D-2 school stuck out in the middle of nowhere fucking Nebraska.

Jarrod DeGeorgia was the cannon that preceded J.T. at City College and ruled the offensive roost for the 1993 and 1994 seasons. Jarrod was the quarterback the first year I played. He was also a first class pitcher on the City College baseball team and was drafted by the St. Louis Cardinals in 1994. Outside of being quarterbacks, Jarrod and J.T. were as different as salt and pepper. Jarrod was white, a little over 6 feet, chunky and slow afoot. But, after two years at SBCC, he was seasoned and tough as nails. Jarrod played for Division Two Wayne State College in Nebraska after leaving Santa Barbara.

DeGeorgia had torn the conference apart his first year (1993) throwing for a conference leading 2807 yards in 251-of-426 attempts. His season highlight was a 32-of-63 425-yard performance against Moorpark. The game also underscored DeGeorgia's penchant for interceptions, throwing four. He also led the conference in that statistic with a season high 17. So for the entire world to see, our 1994 season was easily billed as the DeGeorgia Air Show. Behind a porous offensive line, he continually took a beating each game. He would get up slowly after each sack and set his jaw and stick his helmet back into the huddle. He was also a quick learner and, by the time the 1994 season was a third over, he was second-guessing Chuck on play calling and the offense became a factor of who was more adamant on the selection. Chuck would signal in a play to Jarrod who usually ended up half way to the sideline. At the same time, Jarrod was suggesting his own play. They would glare at each other and then, like two lawyers, argue back and forth as the play clock ran down. Frequently, Chuck would bow to Jarrod's selection and then Jarrod would hustle out to midfield and the rest of the offense. He would spread the gospel by committee and then, in his trademark, gravelly Rod Stewart-like voice, bark out the signals and take another 5 step drop, all the while avoiding the incoming rush. If Chuck would win out, Jarrod could still audible at the line and throw his favorite route, a 93 bomb down the sidelines to one of his fleet receivers.

For most players, an incident, a game, even just a play comes to characterize the player's personality and with Jarrod, it was no different. The Thursday before the LA Pierce game, the second to last of the season, Jarrod badly sprained his ankle slipping on his porch. Of course there were rumors that he did it playing basketball that same evening. To this day, Chuck still doesn't know the truth. Jarrod was determined to play and, fortunately, our game was Saturday evening, giving Susan, the trainer, a second day of treatment and a second day for Jarrod to overdose on Advil. The team doctor looked at the ankle prior to game time and told Jarrod it was advisable that he not play, but if he wanted to, go ahead, "if you can stand the pain, you can play."

Sue taped the ankle, put on a huge steel brace, and then taped over the brace and sent Jarrod out into the fray. Not having much mobility to begin with, JD moved like a pregnant walrus, limping between and during plays and was an open target that was buried several times by the Pierce pass rush. Hobbling between sacks, Jarrod played brilliantly completing 30-of-42 passes for 424 yards, five TDs and did not throw an interception. We outlasted Pierce 52-43 in an offensive slugfest. After leading by only a 14-10 score, both teams went into overdrive and the game came down to whomever had the ball last would win. We did and we did.

Chuck went out to see Jarrod in Nebraska early in 1996. He came back saying that, after replacing the starting quarterback, Jarrod had thrown for 2000 yards in only the five games he started and made the All-Nebraska team. In March of 1996, Jarrod returned to Santa Barbara while on spring break. He was soon going to be looked at by a NFL scout and was enthusiastic about his senior year. "Man, Doc, the game is more complicated at this level," Jarrod told me while we stood in the gym and watched the spring football class play basketball on a rainy day. "Every play has four or five variations on it that I have to determine at the line of scrimmage based on the defense. Our receivers were great, all 4.4 or better speed. Simon Banks would have been our possession receiver, and you know how quick Simon was."

J.T. realized that he had a big act to follow for the 1995 season and it wasn't just making the adjustment from high school to college. No, he was confident of his ability to handle the next level. It was more the specter and records of Jarrod DeGeorgia that would haunt him every game, completion, and interception.

J.T. barked out the formation and the players spread out to their positions like a wave. The four receivers formed bookends to the interior linemen. Even with their numbers obscured, as they turned into the center of the field to get the signals from J.T, I knew who they were. Ryan set up closest to the Bakersfield sideline, on the other side of the field from us, and was average in height, but not in build. By just looking at him, you could tell he was a player. He ran to his position and set up, poised to dash off the line. Ryan was already in motion as he stood still.

Just inside of Ryan, flanked in the slot, was Eric. Eric was five inches taller than Ryan was, but not as stocky and moved slow when he wasn't running. It wasn't that he was unconcerned or aloof, it was that he got there when he got there. He looked in at J.T. and I knew that he was chomping on his mouthpiece, turning it over and over. I had seen him do it a hundred times in practice and games. It was his only concession to nervous energy.

Eric Mahanke and Ryan Capretta grew up a town apart, separated by maybe 10 miles of the 101 as it crossed the coastal range before dropping into Santa Monica. Eric was from Newbury Park and Ryan hailed from Agoura. Eric was taller by a couple of inches, Ryan was stockier; Eric was part Mexican, Ryan all Italian. Ryan was faster, Eric surer handed. They played against each other in football and basketball all through junior and senior high school and were stars of their respective teams. Their senior years they were at the top of the conference in receiving and receiving yardage. Each was featured that year on the ever-popular *Friday Night Football Focus*, a roundup of all the area's prep football games every Friday during the season. They were used to the accolades and fame that settled on them like a blanket that last year of high school. Until they both showed up for summer ball, neither one knew the other was going to be there. Eric had the better summer and was tabbed as one of the starters from the beginning of Fall practice. Ryan filled in as a second teamer, an unfamiliar position to be in, considering his stellar high school career. From the start, each worked hard, running the routes, memorizing the plays and soaking up the offense like a sponge in water that had been laying in the desert.

Eric loved the passing offense at City College. That meant getting the ball a lot. His only worry was there was only one ball and four receivers and there were some damn good receivers vying for playing time. One thing was in his favor the first two weeks of the season; three of the four starters were burners and speed demons, Torlando leading the bunch. None of these burners were possession-type receivers. Run the precise route, get the necessary yards, find the seam, settle in and make the sure-handed grab. That was Eric's forte. He wasn't fast, but he was tall and big and made a good target for J.T. He was a sure thing on the short stuff and he could catch the ball in traffic, put it away and get some yardage. Yeah, if he could fill that niche, he would get his catches and help the team. No matter how good or fast your receivers are, there was always the need for the third and seven reception, money in the bank.

Early in the fall, Ryan couldn't figure out why others were playing in front of him. In high school, coaches rewarded hard work with playing time and docked those who didn't put out with little playing time. It wasn't like that those playing ahead of him weren't good. Players like Torlando were all world, but Ryan knew that all-world only took you half way. Torlando and some of the others showed flashes of brilliance during fall preseason, but they didn't work hard and Ryan wasn't used to that. He would talk to Eric, who was starting, and they would commiserate about Ryan's plight. Eric would keep telling Ryan to stick in there, he would have his chance. "Be patient, it's a long season."

In the beginning of the season, he had some difficulty holding onto the ball. He had to work through it. There was pressure on every route in drills, every play from scrimmage. And those first two weeks receivers' coach Dudley was charting everything thrown in drills and scrimmage. The ball didn't feel quite right and he couldn't get away from that feeling of every catch being the one that would make or break him. But he was determined to make good and it was a long season. He just needed to bide time and continue to work hard in practice. By the fifth game, he was installed in the starting lineup.

Closest to our sideline, #88 turned to the referee standing just steps from us, wondering if his feet were behind the line of scrimmage. The ref nodded and Dave Weismiller turned the other way to listen for the cadence. His arms dangled by his side, loose and relaxed and his back was straight, legs braced behind, ready to explode out when the signal came. David Weismeiller had missed football since high school. Had missed it a lot. Going into summer 1995, it was two years since he played on a mediocre run-oriented Diamond Bar High School team as a skinny 150-pound wideout. In high school, he was like Eric; not the most athletically gifted nor the quickest, but he knew his assignments and routes cold and was a thinking man's player. And he started. But that was awhile ago and he still dreamed about football. "I couldn't help it," he said. "I would wake up thinking I was still playing. That I missed out on something and I needed to get it back." It wasn't just the immediate rush of snaring a pass and turning it upfield that he missed, although that was a big part of it. It was the camaraderie of the players and being part of a team that he missed the most.

David applied at University of California, Santa Barbara when he graduated from high school, knowing they didn't have a football program. They, like so many schools, had simply run out of money for a money-consuming sport. Put to a referendum, the students voted the sport out and now there sits a beautiful stadium with a seating capacity of 18,000 that is used by the poor schools' fall sport, soccer.

David drank beer and took classes his first two years in college. He was way successful in one and just passing in the other. He could never shake the feeling that he was missing something in his life. He worked at the Campus Rec facility and one of the student supervisors who had played for two years at City College and talked about playing frequently, whetting David's appetite for the sport. He went over to talk to Chuck about it at the beginning of the summer and started playing with us at the start of summer ball. He was rusty and out of shape but, even in his early practices, he worked at polishing his skills with dedication. He was quiet and unassuming, and instead of becoming just one of the many guys who tried out and gradually faded away when fall practice started, David started fall practice as one of the 21 receivers vying for a position. He learned the plays, took his turn in the rotations, and waited. "I knew that I would get my chance," he said. "I wasn't disappointed that I was third string. It didn't matter. What mattered was that I was playing again. I knew that eventually I would get my chance to play. Looking around me at the players like Torlando, at some point, they were going sit awhile. And I was going to be there, ready." David's body wasn't quite up to the task and minor, nagging strains and muscle bruises added to his unease as time ticked away. He swallowed those up like he did suds on the weekends. He received therapy and had the trainers wrap his body in ace bandages and would limp through whatever his body allowed him to do during practice. And he kept coming at you like slow-moving lava from a volcano.

David and I shared the sidelines during the first few games of the season, waiting out turns, hoping for blowouts, one way or the other, so we could get some playing time. But the games were always close and we would huddle, willing the starters to score so that we could also take part. Ironic as it may seem, we wanted the receivers who stood in our way of playing to excel so that we then could get in and play. Such are the rationalizations of second teamers. Against Compton, the halfway point in the season, Dave played in two key drives at the end of the game and threw a vicious block on a defensive back. That earned him, along with the academic and personal problems of Lee, the receiver ahead of him, and my inability to capture the confidences of Chuck and Dud concerning my ability, a starting berth against Hancock. Dave finished the season as a starter. David's personality matched his field personae. He was quiet and methodical in his performance, running the right routes, making the correct blocks, and when he did have the occasion to catch a ball, he was in the right position.

Briefly, David stepped out of his role against Glendale and contributed two huge catches in the fourth quarter. No matter who you were or how much you played, David's performance that game was inspiring and, for a moment, he loomed as large as Torlando and became the symbol of the receivers. "It was great," he said. "The balls were there, I made the catches, hung on and we scored. This is the reason I kept playing. To feel and be a part of this. It was worth the pain and struggling. Don't let anybody tell you differently." I felt some envy toward David, but mostly I felt attached when he was on the field. He had come up the hard way to earn his starting spot and he symbolized all that was right about persevering and hard work.

J.T. purposefully moved up to the center and then took three steps back and set up in the shotgun formation. He looked up and down the line and as he glanced over at our side of the field. His gaze stopped on the receiver set in the slot, inside of David. Benjy Trembly, all 190 pounds of him, seemed to be more crouched than any other receiver, but that was misleading. Benjy was also only 5'9" in his cleats. With the jersey being cut off, unable to be tucked in, a little roll around his midsection creeped out over his belt. Benjy wasn't fat, nor was he even overweight; he was basically a six-foot person stuck in a 5'9" body.

From a distance, without his helmet on, Benjy looked older than his 19 years. Benjy was one of these guys who were more than halfway on the road to being middle aged and he wasn't yet out of his teens. His face was young looking. Deep blue eyes rarely were serious. His head was shaved and the fuzz indicated a receding hairline. But up close, Benjy looked younger. There were a number of freckles scattered over his face and a mischievous gleam to his blue eyes. His powerful legs fell off behind him, digging into the turf, waiting, anticipating the first steps off the ball, the first contact with his defender.

Benjy Trembly was steady as paint. He wasn't flashy or smart, but he knew the plays and could fill in wherever Chuck wanted him; running back, receiver, defensive back, holder for field goals and point after attempts. He was also J.T.'s backup. He loved going two hours north to the family house on Lake Nacimiento and tearing around in their speedboat. He wasn't simple or shallow, just uncomplicated. He didn't drink, smoke, or do drugs. He had a job at a gas station.

Benjy was from the small beachside town of Carpinteria, ten miles south of Santa Barbara on the 101. Teenaged males from Carpinteria were a special breed. They didn't want to leave. They would hang out, sitting on the beaches, surfing, driving around and find jobs to keep them going, but wouldn't eat into their "time." Benjy played quarterback and receiver at Carpinteria High School and then came to City College and took some classes and sat out a year. He went to City College for one reason: to play football. Benjy had no aspirations to go on after his two years of playing were over. He wanted to be a fireman like his old man. College was to serve his desire to beat heads for two more years.

Benjy loved to hit on the football field. He loved to block and feel the concussion and watch the other player crumple to the turf. Catching the ball was fun, but butting heads was the ultimate. Hearing the air blow out of a guy, rendering him useless, was bitchin'. In preseason, one play defined Benjy to the rest of the team and coaching staff. In the last scrimmage with California Lutheran University, Benjy filled in for J.T. at quarterback for the last two series. On one broken play, he took off straight up the gut and ran over and through a safety. Watching it on film Monday after the scrimmage, there was a murmuring of awe that filtered through the darkened room as we watched Benjy plow through the defender. Chuck rolled through it a couple of times and, although he questioned Benjy's sanity, it was obvious that he appreciated his kamikaze spirit.

Not a pass, but a hit in the Santa Monica game, made Benjy's season. Trying to sit on a two touchdown lead with eight minutes to go in the fourth quarter, Chuck sent Benjy in to block on a fourth down, outside receiver screen, where the slot guy cracks back on the linebacker, freeing up the screen. Benjy decleated the backer (knocked him off his feet) and Twuan picked up the first down. Benjy came off the field high as a kite and the receivers went berserk. Following the "block," Benjy was always in the game when a crucial block was needed and, although no blocks stood out in importance or style like the Santa Monica block, it was hard for Chuck not to shove Benjy in. If once, why not again?

Benjy was always touching somebody, affectionately slugging people in the arms or putting his hands on arms or shoulders to make a point. It wasn't that he was effeminate or touchy feely, but he wanted you to know that he was there. Benjy was insecure about his abilities and about how people perceived him. He was always telling players about his good plays and other plays that he contributed in the team's success. "Doc, did you see my block?" he would say as soon as he got back to huddle or to the sidelines. "Did you see me lay the db out? or "What about the catch? Did you see me scrape it off the dirt?"

It was a child's response to the multi-dimensional interactions that took place on the field at the same time, as if Benjy had to lobby for his efforts to be noticed. And it wasn't just to the players. Many times Benjy would sidle up to Dudley and fill his ears about a catch or block. He never complained about where he was placed. He just wanted to be part of the performance. Where other receivers talked at you constantly about catches and yardage, Benjy was like a puppy, seeking approval for the block he threw or the tackle he made. Finally halfway through the season I told him that all I hear is about his plays and successes.

"You know, Benjy, there are other people on the team as well," I said. "Don't get bigger than the team." "Am I really that bad?" he asked. But he got better.

Still, Benjy saw the world through Benjy's eyes. But of all the players, Benjy would talk to me about his life and what he wanted from it the most. Benjy wanted his life validated and, somehow, I was the validator. For an hour and a half on the bus back from our scrimmage against Cal Lutheran, he talked to me about love and life according to Benjy, going to great lengths to assure me he was the uncomplicated man-child that he seemed to be. "All's I want is to have a family, have a good job and have my recreation," he told me. "Same as football, I want the experience that I won't have the chance to go through again. You know me, Doc. It isn't the stats or the catches, man, it is the team; the players that we hang around with and the game itself. I just want to enjoy it."

The line was set and receivers motionless, except for the nervous twitches of the first play of the game, as J.T. began barking out his signals. J.T.'s bark was not very loud, and from experience, I knew the outside receivers were straining to hear the cadence. Behind J.T., the lone running back shifted from behind to the side of the quarterback, a white strip of towel from his belt dangled in the afternoon breeze. Half crouched, Twuan Hill came to a stop and set up with his hands resting on both knees. His quick movement didn't hide the fact that Twuan was bowlegged and his short sleeved jersey didn't hide the fact that Twuan was black. His helmet did hide the fact that Twuan's head was shaven and had a looped earring that gave him a rakish, pirate look. From inside his facemask, a gold tooth glittered in the afternoon sun. Twuan was a human cannonball and just as explosive and quick when he fired out from his position. He was Benjy's height and weight, but there the similarities ended. Twuan ran a 10.7 100 meters and Benjy was lucky if he covered that distance in a day. But that was the great thing about football; there was room for everybody.

On the defensive side of the sidelines, just down from me, I heard a familiar voice yell, "Come on Twuan, lay some hat." I didn't need to look to know who that was, but I did anyway. Chris Hill, Twuan's cousin, towered over those around him. His helmet was by his side and small rivers of sweat rolled down his face. Around 6'4", Chris was the starting safety and, with two or three other players, the heart of the defense. His athleticism was legendary. Chris had been the best high jumper on the track team last year and just missed making the state championship meet. Chris turned and I caught his eye, the ever-present infectious grin spread across his face. His eyes laughed and were alive with the excitement of the upcoming battle.

Chris and Twuan called the projects in East Smyrna Beach, Florida home. Two hours from Miami, East Smyrna Beach didn't have huge gang problem of other urban government housing. At least not the number of gangs. The projects weren't federally funded, but everybody called them the "projects." Mostly blacks lived there with a few white families, but not many. The kids would play in the streets and crack houses blended in with homes filled to the brim with families, a reality that one accepted. You didn't think twice about walking around, day or night. Everybody knew who the dealers were. How could you miss them as they stood around waiting for their customers? Big groups of neighborhood people acted like police watching out for the innocent and the children. They tacitly accepted the cancer of drugs that was kept in remission, but never allowed to grow too much or too big.

Chris grew up in a three-bedroom apartment along with his parents and four Hill children and his father's best friend's son. "We never had a lot of money when I was younger. My father worked four jobs while my mother worked at K-Mart to make ends meet. My father never liked to owe nobody. Always liked to pay cash for everything which is why we lived in the projects for so long."

Twuan and his parents moved out of the neighborhood when he was younger. They were scared of the projects and sought sanctuary and a slower lifestyle in the country. The day before Twuan and Chris left for California there was a big raid on a crack house next door to Chris' apartment. Twuan was sheltered from this reality by his parents' protective fundamental Pentecostal beliefs. Twuan and Chris' fathers sang together in a gospel choir and the church was a big part of their lives and their children. "It was kind of funny," said Chris, "my Dad being so strict and us living in a place full of crime and drugs."

The Hill cousins were as different as night and day. Chris was happy-go-lucky and always the clown with a quick joke or a story. Twuan was darker, moodier and was always off kilter. When he was in a good mood, he was a little too loud or boisterous. When he was down, he was like a black hole, sucking the energy around him. The cousins came all the way to California to be stars, grab the statistics and return to play for University of Florida or Florida State. They came to Santa Barbara City College because they spent more time in high school on the field then taking care of business in the classroom. They waited till the last minute to take their SATs and came up yards short. Twuan and Chris's talent had reached a comfortable plateau and stopped growing. Dreaming of the big time, Twuan and Chris found it hard to concentrate on the Ventura Colleges and Los Angeles Pierces. Twuan was well aware he was one of the engines that drove the offense. While watching the weekly replay shows of his runs and catches that aired on the local Santa Barbara cable station, he could easily envision himself twisting and turning through the secondaries of the Southeast Conference. Didn't the coaches see his importance, thereby releasing him from some of the responsibilities that were expected of him? He wasn't here to win. He was playing to build a reputation so he could move on and up. When you got right down to it, showcasing your talents was junior college football. Winning was for those no-talent players that would never see a field after their years here. For Twuan, it was just get me the ball and hitch your wagons to my horse.

Chris loved the sensations of football from his high school days, the hitting, the cheerleaders, and the smell of the popcorn. Everybody was close; you won and lost together. You came out on the field pumped up and bathed in the lights, screaming at the top of your lungs and you could do no wrong. The friendships were just as fun as the game. He played with his mother's sister's boy, Twuan and Mike Hives, his other cousin. It was family. The coaches listened when you came off the field and then sent in plays. You were something at school and the crowd turned out in numbers, big numbers. High School football was king in Florida and the players were royalty.

Football in Santa Barbara ranked near the bottom of things to watch and or get involved in. Defensive coaches didn't need Chris' advice that first year; they knew it all. They played him out of position at linebacker toward the end of the year and he played tentatively. To Carmen, his coach, Chris was able to play out of position because he was so good, but if Chris didn't feel comfortable and was frustrated, then where was the fun. The number of fans that showed up to watch the games were even less than the visiting teams brought to their high school games. All he, Twuan and Mike knew were each other. There were no longer the close friends that made the game fun. Twuan had to compete for playing time with established veterans and it took him too long to become a part of the offense. It was surely different and at times, it didn't even feel like the same game that they had had so much fun with back home.

After their first season at City College, they were one year older and experienced college football players. They had a full year of classes under their belts and spent the summer between seasons taking a full load of summer school classes back home. Chris was returning to his job working in the school's Learning Resource Center and they were going to have too much fun partying. After living a childhood of religion and Sundays of feeling the spirit and talking in tongues, the boys were far removed from their extended families. The sky became the limit to their behavior and often the sky wasn't that high. Twuan was the lover and the girls were plentiful. At times it was almost as if they were circling, waiting for a chance to land. Twuan and Chris knew this season was going to be the one that catapulted them into Division 1 schools. The team might not be any better than the mediocre 1994 5-5 team, but they were going to go to town.

Chuck had frequently talked to both over the summer, telling Chris he "was the man this year on defense," and wanting Twuan to be the same on offense. They were naturals for the roles, Chris more than Twuan, because he was more outgoing and could laugh at himself as well as letting others laugh at him. He always lapsed into the role of a southern black, complete with the slow drawl and self-effacing personality. For kicks, he would shake his head from side to side, his lips whapping on his cheeks. On the field, Chris was a leader, vocal and demonstrative, whereas Twuan was pure emotion, firing off the ground after being brought down and then pumping himself up, fists shooting towards the heavens. Exuberation for the game was something they carried with them across the country, something so interwoven in Florida football. More often than not, exhuberation was a thinly-veiled promo film to underscore their respective talents and they played the stars. Twuan had scored several touchdowns this season and, after each, would do a victory dance that invariably brought a penalty for excessive celebration. Twuan didn't care; it was his time to shine and he was earning it weekly.

Ironic as it was, City College featured an all-white starting receiver corps and a black quarterback. It was an irony that never really surfaced in public discussions between players and it wasn't due to few blacks on the team. Half of the receivers were black and the leading receiver, Torlando, was black. Over the season, it just worked out that way.

I felt the presence of the rest of the receivers as we clustered around Dudley in anticipation of the first play. During the game, when the offense had the ball, the receivers not on the field would follow Dudley up and down the sidelines, like ducklings chasing after their mother. It wasn't because we wanted to. It was a result of Dudley telling us at the beginning of the season, "If you want a chance to play, you better be right next to me. If I turn and can't find you, then somebody else goes and you lose your chance." After a couple of games, even when the pecking order became clear of who played and who didn't, we still followed Dudley, always knowing that it took only one opportunity to make good and nobody was going to chance missing it.

I turned back from meeting Chris' look and pushed closer to the action on the field. I really didn't need to push that close to see because the player in front of me only came up to my chin and if I had wanted to, I could have picked him up and moved him to the side. The player was light, but not frail. Lee Green should have been out there in David's spot. He could run rings around him and once he made the catch, he was off to the races. Lee had been out there in David's spot, but Lee's personal life intervened in the middle of the season and he was relegated to coming off the bench, which he did more frequently than the rest of us non-starters.

Lee Green was a good example of contribution without statistics. He was from Clovis High, just outside of Fresno and an exception in that he was black from a mostly rural school. He, like David, attended cross-town University of California, Santa Barbara and City College. Since UCSB was on the quarter system and didn't start till October, they both were able to juggle their time and for only a month, had to deal with classes at both schools. For Lee, his time was further diminished as he also worked at Jiffy Lube in the early afternoons and on weekends.

Only 5'6" and 140 lbs., Lee made up for his size in hustle and speed. Even at the end of the season, when his time commitments caught up to him and he was forced to come to practice late, or occasionally miss altogether, and demoted from the starting unit, he still saw playing time. He never complained, just kept going 100% in both practice and games.

J.T.'s muted signal calling floated across the field. We all knew the first play was going to be a pass. And the second and the third. So did Bakersfield, if they had done any scouting whatsoever. They were probably counting on a receiver screen that Chuck had opened with the last two games. But the receiver that Chuck loved to isolate on for that play wasn't even on the field. In fact, he wasn't even in the cluster of receivers huddled around Dudley.

Arthur Williams was at least suited up, but he lounged indifferently in the back, behind the crush of players near the sideline. Arthur had a dislocated shoulder and had difficulty raising his arms above his head. Susan, the team trainer, had told him that he shouldn't play. He thought he could and was pissed off that the coaches were taking her diagnosis for now. Arthur longed to be in the game. In fact when he was in the game, which was frequent, he felt he was the offense. Arthur knew it would only be a matter of time before the coaches gave in to the inevitable and his desire to play and stopped listening to Susan. He would still be a factor this last game. Arthur was deceptively quick and ran with a graceful lope and, much like Torlando, could leave defenders frustrated, reaching for a part of Arthur that just a second ago had been within grasping distance. He wasn't physically imposing, maybe 6', 160 pounds, but he could jump to the moon and when the ball settled into his hands in full stride he was off to the races. Arthur knew he was funny, he could leave people in stitches. With a carefree grin, a gold tooth and a large gold chain with his football number dangling on his chest, Arthur was usually on top of the world, messing with people's minds, telling jokes, playing the clown. It was his way of playing off pressure. Arthur trekked all the way to Santa Barbara from Daytona Beach, Florida on the advice of Twuan and Chris and, from the day he showed up, was penciled in as a starter. Thirty minutes of practice was all that was needed to see that Arthur was going to play a major role in the offense.

Half an hour was also all that was needed to show that Arthur was going to be less than productive in practice and one practice was all that was needed to highlight Arthur's problem of holding onto the ball in traffic. When he did hold on, and it was usually a catch made more spectacular than needed to be, nobody could touch him. At times, Arthur lacked the concentration needed to blot out everybody and everything except the ball and his hands. This problem was never more evident than in his first three games, dropping as many as he caught. However, Chuck instituted a wide receiver screen that utilized Arthur's unique talents and, in several games, Arthur broke for long gains on the completion.

Perhaps realizing his worth to the team, Arthur quickly fell into the habit of cruising on autopilot through practices and scrimmages, increasing the frustration of those playing behind him in the rotation. To those non-starters, it wasn't fair that Art, with his questionable hands and lack of practice ethic, joining Torlando and Twuan in that category, was getting large amounts of playing time. But then, football is like life; fair is a place to ride Ferris wheels, not a code to fight for playing time by. Arthur was well aware of his stone hands. It went along with everything else he was going through, being 4000 miles from his mother, family and his friends. For the first time in awhile, he had to battle for a starting position. Plus, he was on his own and, at times, it was scary. He knew he could play better and others did, too. All one had to do was check out his highlight tape. But the pressure was high and Art knew he needed to adjust. Arthur was also aware that he fueled his performance on emotion and intensity. He played better when his joy for the game surfaced, when the intensity and adrenaline coursed through his body and his feet felt as if they were streaking on air. It was hard to duplicate that in practice day after day. Everybody knew what he could do. Practice was for fine-tuning, not life and death.

He knew his hands were going to come around. It was just a matter of time. His problem was partly due to the fact he came in late and learning a whole new system and position in a matter of weeks was going to play havoc with his mind and concentration. More than occasionally, Art would break one and be long gone and then he felt, even knew that he should be starting. His playing time was less than Torlando or Twuan and he would continually bitch and moan on the sideline when taken out, blaming Dudley and Chuck for not seeing his potential and letting it flower.

"It's going to be a hitch to Dave. Just watch. J.T. loves to throw to his right," the receiver next to me said as the ball was threaded back toward J.T. from the center. I nodded, eyes glued to the field. Not surprisingly, the accent of the receiver was thick and German. Stefan Kratzer loved American football and had loved it since he played it in his native Germany, starting five years ago. Unfortunately, Stefan had also played more in Germany. This season he had barely seen the game from the field. But like the other second and third teamers, he continued to be part of the City College receiving corps. For them, the game was not much different than the scrimmages that daily made up the important part of practice. The only difference was that nobody really cared what they did on the sidelines at practice; they were a part, but not really.

Each practice was the same; down on one knee, resting their weight on helmets placed strategically in front of them. Stuart, slight, black, and a shaved head, was passing the time in conversation with Jeff, almost identical in stature and ability, except he was white. The flow of the conversation had neither beginning nor end. It was free form and at every practice it sought another direction. Kratz and red-shirt freshman Troy listened in and occasionally offered their thoughts. As the words spilled out, their eyes followed the scrimmage unfolding in front of them. Out on the field, Drone, another second teamer, and I milled around Dudley, waiting to be inserted for a series or two. Every now and then we would glance back to the sidelines and see the four looking out at us. Those on the field were one step closer to the reality of playing time.

Kratz couldn't figure out why he was sitting and Torlando and Art were playing. He knew he wasn't half as talented as they were, but deep in his German heart, he played each play in practice like it was the Super Bowl or an escape over the Wall and it tore him up to see those two loaf through scrimmage. He didn't know how long he could be motivated to go like a banshee when there wasn't any return.

While Kratz sat and fumed, Troy just waited for the time when Dudley was finally going to see that he blocked 100% better than Art or Torlando and was fearless when it came to going over the middle. Like the others, he rushed to fill in positions during the seven on seven passing drill at the end of practice and he chased that maniac old anthropologist/ receiver through drills. It just took one shot, a catch or two in a game, a block and he was in. Just a foot in the door was all he wished for. Until then, he wasn't a quitter. "Stick it out," said his Dad, and he was going to, if it killed him. He wondered if inactivity was the same as death.

Jeff and Stuart were best friends and roommates. They loved football and they were closer to the game now than if they had been playing pick-up in a park. Stuart, from an inner city San Francisco high school, didn't play his senior year in high school. Most of the time, he was watching out for his friends, many who were into drugs. Stuart was going to succeed in college and maybe even play a little ball. He was set to bite the bullet on this year, stick around and learn the system and come back big next year. He would enjoy the experience of college. So the time passed and he got no closer to scrimmaging than where he kneeled, but he could bide his time. For now.

At times, Jeff's mind was miles away; 300 miles to the north exactly, where his girl friend from high school went to college. Football helped him balance his life and he enjoyed being out here with the boys. Like the rest, Jeff harbored fantasies of stepping up and playing a hero's role. He was ashamed to admit it, but he had dreams in Technicolor where he was high stepping it to pay dirt. He felt better knowing the other guys dreamed the same dream. His girlfriend Tracy listened to his complaining about the team and said the right things, so he kept coming out. He had decided to red-shirt this year, releasing him somewhat from having to come out every practice. If he was still going to play next year, why waste one now?

During practice, the image of Drone, hands on hips next to Dudley was common. Drone shuttled his thoughts between anger, bitterness and acceptance of lack of playing. His anger and resentment against Dudley were never far from the surface. He didn't understand why he wasn't getting the chance to see some time. He knew he was on par with Capretta and Benjy, even with Art. He came out every fucking day, not like some of the others. He was reliable and put out in practice and he loved the game. That's all he and his older brother, Kon, a running back on the team, talked about; football and, of course, women. Drone had talked to Dudley early in the season, more like confronted him after practice, and right on the 50-yard line. "I just want to know why I am not getting a shot," he had asked. Dudley hemmed and hawed, said some pretty noncommittal things like "keep working, have patience." Drone said to me later, "Dudley, he don't know shit."

As this last game unfolded, Drone was no longer a part of the team, nor was his brother. Both had quit the team in a rage with two games to go in the season. Set against his black skin, braces gleamed when Drone laughed. His brother, Kon was named after Constantine, the first century Roman emperor, yet spelled with a "K." Kon was one year older and a smaller, stockier model of Drone. They both had attended and graduated from Hollywood High School. Their parents lived outside the school district, but the boys lived with a relative who lived inside the district boundaries.

"Shit, Doc, " Drone told me on the bus down to one of our games, "Hollywood was just like you expected. Lots of money, drugs and car phones. The girls were something else." Kon went to Boston College his first year, but the aid he received didn't help much and he made his way to USCB after sitting out a year. He was on track to graduate with a degree in political science and was picking up general education requirements from City College to be eligible to play.

They were as close as two brothers could be. The bond was visibly expressed in the tattoo that each wore on their right upper arm. Drone's name was spelled down the arm, while Kon's name intersected at the "O," forming a cross. During practice and games they stood together and their shouts of encouragement floated across the practice field or the game when one was on the field. Kon had played primarily on the kick-off and kick-off return teams and Drone was quick to praise Kon as he came off the turf. "Fuck it," Kon told me once. "I should play, you should play. It's that simple. I am getting tired of this fuckin' shit."

"I know, I know," Drone filled in. "Let's stick with it, see what happens the next game or two."

Drone had a graceful, fluid-like stride when in flight and a tendency to leave his feet for balls otherwise reached with outstretched hands.    That was plainly seen running fly patterns under J.T.'s bombs. Kon was only 5'8", but 180 pounds. His short, muscled legs ground furiously when he carried the ball which, over the last two seasons, had been exceedingly rare in games and even infrequent in practice. Kon started the year as one of the possible starters at the lone running back position but, after the first game of the season, Twuan was inserted at running back and Kon was demoted to infrequent periods of spelling Twuan and special teams play. The coaches said that Kon was a step slow when hitting the hole. He didn't always make the right decisions when he got into the secondary, and lacked some of the kinetic creativity of Twuan or Torlando.

During practice and games, each wore a black silk scarf under their helmets. Walking around the gym or locker room, even on campus, their baggy shorts or jeans hung low, boxers puffed up over their pants, perilously close to sliding down their thighs at a moment's notice.   In an offensive scheme that features four receivers and one back, Kon was destined to receive little playing time. Somewhere along the way, Kon and, by association, Drone, had made Chuck's bad list and suffered from it.   Kon was an extremely hard worker, yet also extremely outspoken and, in football, authority is seldom questioned and when questioned by players, authority labeled this breach as malignant and questionable. Kon had a lot on the ball, intelligent, but he was like many of us; a step away from playing, or in other words, by the fate of playing at this time for Chuck Melendez, his abilities were not what were needed by the offense.

And then there was me, much different, but still the same. I led practice drills, gave team speeches that were filled with words of wisdom, motivated others and myself through effort and found myself usually getting into the game for a series or two. More for my efforts on the practice field and leadership skills, Chuck had named me team captain three games and I had actually started the Glendale game and played about a quarter's worth. But like most of the "scrubs," I had yet to catch a pass and become a statistic in the 1995 Vaquero season, even though I had dropped a couple in the Glendale game. For me, maybe more than the others, my quest to become a number in a record book was paramount. I was soon to step out of world that in a few short years would only be able to imagine in a slumbering daydream. I wanted some acknowledgement of my trials and tribulations. At times, the recognition I sought became a small metaphorical altar to self-importance that I wanted to trumpet to those around me. Time was now telescoping. Whereas 24 months ago it seemed to crawl, now only three hours remained and my quest still lay unfulfilled.

By the end of the season, the non-starters were all head cases wondering when our time was coming to play, at the same time dealing with the fact that our time was coming very slowly or not at all. To Drone, he should have been playing yesterday; for others like Jeff and Stuart, good things come to those who wait and learn.

The ball found its way into J.T.'s large hands. He dropped back one step and looked to his right...

**KIST**
*Stone quickly to the air from the 20 fires from the pocket, complete to the 40-yard line to Dave Weismiller. On the reception, first down for the Vaqueros. Gain of 11 on the play. David Weismiller having a fine season has turned it on as of late. Six catches coming in with ome touchdown. Bakersfield linebackers up and showing blitz but don't come. Stone pumps once from the 30, fires for Twuan Hill over the middle. He has it at the Bakersfield 30! Down to the 24-yard line! And Twuan Hill gets up fired up from the tackle. A big gain for Santa Barbara. 36 yards. First and ten Vaqueros!*

# Chapter 5

---

## The Tools of My Trade: Ethnography on the Fly
### with a Jolt of *Gonzo*

**S**hit! I felt myself slipping on the 15-yard curl as my cleats tried to grab the LaPlaya Stadium turf, throwing off chunks of million-dollar Santa Barbara real estate. I found myself going to one knee, momentum breaking down as I tried to handle the abrupt change in speed. I stabbed the turf with my outside foot and pivoted, straining to whip my head around and locate the quarterback and the ball. The ocean breeze whistled through the ear holes in my bright red helmet almost as if my ear was pressed up against a seashell listening to the mythical ocean. Only it wasn't mythical; it was the Pacific, and the surf pounded Leadbedder Beach a football field away.

The quarterback's arm was already scything through the salt air and I picked up the perfect spiral from between the goal posts as the ball exploded off his hand. I sensed Lohse and Safrak, the two defensive backs, on my back and right side, struggle to adjust to my pivot as they turned back toward me. The ball was low and I went down to get it, even as my body fought to retain some balance. I felt the ball, briefly smelled the worn leather, as it slapped into my hands, inches above the turf. Almost simultaneously, both defensive backs slammed into me as I was preparing for the impact with the ground, wrapping me up like a bear crushing an unfortunate tourist in Yellowstone. The two collisions, with the defensive backs and ground, jarred the ball from my hands and it innocently dribbled away, unaware of the forthcoming carnage.

In the next second, I was to feel the pain of doing anthropology the hard way, that of very active participation. In the upcoming weeks, following that next second, I was going to be constantly reminded of the sacrifice of mind and body to dig myself into the culture of college football every painful step of the way, every waking moment.

My body bounced off the ground and rolled to the left as Lohse rolled with and then over me, stretching my right quad down. Safrak rolled in from the other direction and pinned my left quad to the ground. I screamed in response to a white-hot pain that shot through my right groin as the muscle ripped from the bone (Susan the trainer would tell me 20 minutes later). I stopped rolling and ended up on my back. I closed my eyes to the pain as it railroaded up and down my inner thigh like a New York subway. I opened my eyes and looked up into the helmeted pterodactyl features of Lohse and Safrak. I could see their faces through the face-bars, tinged with dirt and sweat and dominated by the whites of their eyes.

"Doc, Doc are you all right?" Lohse asked anxiously. "Shit, I don't know," I managed to croak through the waves of pain that crested through me. "Let me lay here for a minute or day." Through the haze, I heard the voices of the other receivers, just ten yards away, but coming from what seemed like Los Angeles. "Come on, Doc, shake it off. Get up, Doc, move around." I could tell Jerome's voice anywhere. The grass felt like a wool blanket. It was comforting to feel the prickles through the pain. The backs reached down and pulled me to my feet. I stood for a second, wobbling as the pain went from horizontal to vertical. I tried to jog back to the receiver's line, but had to stop after a couple of strides. My right leg refused to follow my brain. Oh shit, my mind kept repeating over and over, there goes the next month of the season. I somehow made it back to the safety of the receivers' line.

Chuck turned to me as I limped past, his brown eyes hidden by his sunglasses, "You all right, Doc?" he asked, concern dripping from his question. I shook my head. "It's my groin. It feels like it's on fire," I told him. I made it to the back of the end zone and tried to stretch it out, but all I got was more pain. Dudley, all 6"2 and

250 lbs. ambled over, his expression also hidden by shades. "So what, you finished for the day?" he asked. Listen you idiot, I wanted to scream, probably for the entire fucking season. But I didn't and managed, "I don't know, I'll tell you in a minute."

The drill dissolved after a couple minutes and the team went into formations. The second play I hobbled up to Z, the inside receiver on a four-receiver set, thinking that for some asinine reason I could go if I just ran through the pain. I got maybe five yards off the ball and my body broke down. "Doc, get off the field and into the training room," Chuck screamed from the opposite side of the field. I hung my head and started slowly toward the training room as the next play was called.

I remembered pain like this once or twice before in my life. The last time was eight years ago when I pulled my right hamstring 30 meters into a 100m time trial at the University of Illinois. I was thirty years old and just into my fieldwork on black sprinters. Only two months of training to be like a collegiate sprinter had not prepared muscles to withstand the sudden spurt of acceleration. From the Illinois track to the training room in the stadium was almost a mile, most of it across a field. It took what seemed like an hour to make the journey, hopping as I went. Now I only had to go across the field, out the stadium, and up a short gentle hill to the PE complex. Time, again, chose to stand still as each step brought more pain. The muscle began the natural act of internal swelling and bleeding in response to a very unnatural trauma. I still had an hour drive to Point Magu tonight to teach a twice weekly 2 1/2 hour ethnic studies class to the Navy. "Doc, just what the hell are you doing," I wondered aloud as I began hopping up the hill.

I leaned back in my chair, trying to crack my back. It was late and I was just finishing my field notes from that earlier practice after coming back from the Navy class. It was 10:30 p.m. Shit, another hour before it was time for more Advil. I used to eat Ibuprofen like it was popcorn, but I changed over to Advil when it wasn't working. Four or five times a day ripped into that constant inflammation. I felt another shot that afternoon, along with the pulled groin, a banshee-like kamikaze hit administered by middle linebacker, Ian McDonald, that almost caved my chest in and laid me flat for minutes. I only remember Ian's demonic glazed eyes as he pushed himself off me and maybe only half imagined the spittle that hung around the corners of his mouth.

My mind had crept along all night. Occasionally the gears meshed and a whole thought escaped the cerebral prison. I bet myself any money I had a slight concussion as well as a busted groin. I paid the price for this afternoon, just as I continued to pay the price for the past days and weeks with interest. I paid for that weasel McDonald's cheap shot, a hit after the whistle had blown during scrimmage while I was looking the other way. I knew I was waking up tomorrow wishing I was buried in an all-body cast. McDonald threw the shot put and discus last spring while I sprinted for City College and he kept tormenting me. "I'm going to rip your head off next fall, Doc, just you wait," he would say. I saw Ian bite the head of a small lizard he found on the field during two a day practices in August. He just ripped it off and ate the head and then tied the headless corpse to the laces of his cleats and practiced all day with that thing flapping with each step he took. I knew I was in trouble after that. I decided to hell with the waiting period and was on my way to my kitchen counter to drink a glass of milk and eat some Advil before cranking some more on my notes. What I wanted was some high-grade Darvon to take the constant throb away but, lacking a needed prescription, I was content to hammer at it with whatever I could get over the counter. I was ecstatic that I was even able to move after the groin shot.

I still had to write up my nightly fieldnotes and describe the individual battles that waged on our small battleground and decipher the meaning of each fight. It's a code; a violent battle of churning legs and arms that, to unlock, I had to get inside everybody's head. I yearned for a blackboard to help with my keeping track of players and personalities. Chart them like pioneering and iconic anthropologist Bronislaw Malinowski did when he was writing fieldnotes 80 years ago in the South Pacific. There were no more blackboards at City College, just the white vinyl boards that you mark on with magic markers. Instead of getting chalk dust all over your hands and clothes, I left class with black, blue or red streaks on my hands and arms and high as a kite. Using the markers was like burying your head in a bag of glue and sucking like a Hoover vacuum cleaner. That was probably why I missed the board so much and ended up looking like I was

Katherine Hepburn using charcoal to write her memoirs. I paced at least a mile around the classroom during lecture, spending most of the time by the open windows to get away from the board and breathe fresh air.

I looked out the window. There was no moon tonight. No light filtered through the palms in the front yard. But I knew there were stars. The air was usually very clear this time of year, the evening offshore breeze blowing out all the gunk that LA sent up the coast during the day. It was easy to look and get swallowed up by the vastness of the sky. The real rush was to go the block and a half from my apartment to the beach at midnight. I would walk down the crumbling, officially closed, Thousand Step stairs to the beach, whip out a blanket and, preferably with a warm body, fall back on the soft fabric and forgiving sand. I would open my eyes and kiss time good-bye for an hour or two. Occasionally, spits of light dug across the night horizon and then the sky became an overexposed snapshot. When the moon was full, the Harbor and Channel were creased by the moonbeam as it formed a corridor leading out into the Pacific. The solitude of the beach contrasted with my hectic and violent existence during afternoon. All day long, testosterone-addled football players surrounded me. I took classes with and taught to young southern California co-eds, their tan bodies inviting to a middle-aged man retreating backwards in time. I was constrained by the ethics of my profession and the population of females I spent my time around was destined to be the wishes I made on stars. More than frequently, I wanted the company of women my own age, but it was so hard to step out of my life, where football and school claimed their precious territory of time and monopoly of interest.

Bronislaw Malinowski, for all his human faults and eccentricities, was somewhat of a hero to me. Trapped in the Trobriand Islands off the coast of New Guinea during World War I, Malinowski made the best of the situation facing down frailty, lethargy, loneliness, alienation and a heightened sense of mortality to write what is still considered a classic piece of anthropology fieldwork. For the first time to western anthropologists, his research produced an exhaustive and complete description of a foreign society. His story was just as compelling as his research.

The man plied his pioneering ethnography while trying to keep his racism and Eurocentrism suppressed. Those feelings he kept for his diary, visited often during the many hours he spent on his back racked with sickness. Give the guy his due, every anthropologist, from the stiff upper lip British to the American evolutionist, felt that way. However, here finally was a white man, not just a trader or missionary, trying to understand how the "natives" thought.

Given the context of a white European male studying black and brown people, Malinowski was also an unmitigated racist and chauvinist. He kept a diary during his research, posthumously published by his wife, and it details the other story of his research. He had erotic fantasies about the female natives, spent months underneath a mosquito net recovering from malaria, hating the natives and wishing them ill fortune.

I scarfed the Advil and decided to screw the notes and headed for my bed that was bigger than a football field at 11:30 at night. My mind was reluctant to slow down, even though my body had gone to the dogs. I reached over and dropped a Gordon Lightfoot tape into the small boombox on the dresser. I needed some soothing folk tunes to take the edge off the rap music that constantly blared at me in the locker room. If it wasn't the actual music, it was Twuan or Jerome or Chris, wrapped up in their own Walkman, adding their voice to the music that, luckily for me, they could only hear. When these guys were plugged in, what emerged was a cacophony of sound, lyrics from many different artists, swelling in intensity and laced with the emotion of the street. Each song was an anthem that mixed hope with despair and the message was more than just the quick staccato images hurled out by the artist. It was also the interaction of the listener with the beat. With Gordon, I tried to open my mind up to the deeper thoughts of the day such as the 90s insensitivity displayed by Chuck. Reacting to a busted play, he would scream that it was an abortion while the 5:30 p.m. recreational joggers and walkers, many of them women and children, circled the track.

I was caught in a methodological freefall. Sport and anthropology have always mixed like vinegar and oil. Sport wasn't good enough to be studied like the old standbys of religion and subsistence patterns. My style of ethnography was not like the traditional research method. One must actively experience everything, and experience was best translated using a shotgun approach; experience and behavior were caught in a snapshot, frozen by the flash, and the field research became an immensely long roll of film. It was an exhaustive and emotionally draining process. I had to purposely lose the identity of anthropologist and become, for all practical purposes, one of the boys. Many ethnographic monographs failed to give the reader the flavor and intensity of living for that moment, many times over. All right, educate, but at the same time put the reader right smack dab in the middle of everything. It was like making a feature length film. I didn't direct it, but just lived the story line and, like white water rafting, I battled the rapids and the frothing waterfalls and eddies that were football and was always just a second away from becoming river bait.

In the need to be able to bring this story home, I looked to the frantic and electric voice of the original *Gonzo* journalist, Hunter S. Thompson. The man cracked balls the size of Brazil in his work on the Hell's Angels, hung with heavies from Tom Wolfe to Ken Kesey and then got down and dirty with presidential candidates. My God, the guy actually thought McGovern was going to whip Nixon in 1972. That was voice! Early on, Thompson tested the limits of journalism, deciding on intense participation and an overthrow of conventionality. In a 1967 *New York Times Magazine* story Thompson wrote on the Hippie community of Haight-Ashbury and the psychedelic drug use, "...but the vicious excesses of our drug laws makes it impossible, or at least inhuman, to document the larger story. A journalist dealing with heads is caught in a strange dilemma. The only way to write honestly about the scene is to be a part of it. If there is one quick truism about psychedelic drugs, it is that anyone who tries to write about them without firsthand experience is a fool and a fraud."

To report on life was an exercise in stretching the bounds of normalcy. "Gonzo journalism is based on William Faulkner's idea that the best fiction is far more true than any kind of journalism," said Thompson. His classic book on chasing the American Dream to Las Vegas, *Fear and Loathing in Las Vegas*, with a 300 pound whacked out Samoan attorney and a trunk full of drugs was just that–fiction that was too real, too much like life to be fiction. When Thompson wrote, "We had two bags of grass, seventy-five pellets of mescaline, five sheets of high-powered blotter acid, a salt shaker half-full of cocaine and a whole galaxy of multicolored uppers, downers, screamers, laughers...Also a quart of tequila, a quart of rum, a case of Budweiser, a pint of raw ether, and two dozen amyls.... But the only thing that worried me was the ether. There is nothing in the world more helpless and irresponsible than a man in the depths of an ether binge..." the line between fact and fiction blurred, but so highly believable and weird not to be true. Thompson deep-sixed what he saw as the confines of journalism because you couldn't fit the story into the journalistic formula; real life was way too exciting. "My idea," Thompson wrote in *Fear and Loathing on the Campaign Trail*, "was to provide a big fat notebook and record the whole thing as it happened, then send in the notebook for publication without editing. The way I felt, the eye and mind of the journalist would be functioning as a camera." It didn't hurt that Thompson was wired before being wired was in. What created this wired approach was immediacy and intimacy. What kept it going was the natural frenetic and wild pace of the story and the nuances of life that didn't survive the editor. In Thompson's quest for realism and the bottom line, he was part of the story because necessity dictated it. "True Gonzo reporting needs the talents of a master journalist, the eye of an artist/photographer and the heavy balls of an actor because the writer must be a participant in the scene," he said.

What truly made Thompson *Gonzo* was not his reflection, not what he brought to the show, but what the show brought to him. He was after the frenetic urgency of politics, marathon running or drug running. In *Fear and Loathing on the Campaign Trail*, he described his work as a "high speed cinematic reel record of what the campaign was like at the time, not what the whole thing boiled down to or how it fits into history." Neither leaning upon his self-importance or the need to get in touch with his own self, Thompson busted his butt to follow the story where it led. Thompson didn't want to weave a grand tapestry of historical significance. He just wanted to keep on the river raft of Americana and ride it till it bashed him up against the rocks of mortality or shot him like a cannon through the rapids of social depravity and hedonism where he would ultimately discover that the end of the river was just the beginning.

Ever since I started this wild ride into the social morass that is college football, I thought *Gonzo*. I tried to record, picture, and live the stories of people that ran rampant through my consciousness in the primal arena of testosterone and mano a mano battles. It was this combustible explosion that ultimately gave me the panoramic view of sport and culture, almost like the Dali Llama sitting on top of the highest peak in the Himalayas. The view included the stories of last night, the kegs of Saturday night, the pot, the sex, and the long arm of the law. In other words, it was the coming of age in a secular-driven American religion called college football.

Deep down, I knew I wasn't true *Gonzo*. I didn't have the personality of a renegade that could say, "fuck it" and go about doing whatever anti-establishment, anti-social thing I wanted to do. But then again, I didn't want to. The trip I was taking needed consciousness and it banked on balancing different roles and getting the most out of each. This wasn't the Hells Angels or the wired out political junkies and hacks that required Thompson to seek alternate reality just to get by. This was a culture of pain, of performance, of timing and perseverance, and of sacrifice. Dropping acid, eating mushrooms, or doing ether was not the gig here and now. Beer and some pot took the edge off and soothed the overloaded mind and out-to-lunch body. To me, what I was doing was *Gonzo* enough, even if it paled next to the master.

Three different times in the last ten years I have joined a circle of athletes. The first was ten years ago working on my M.A. thesis on black and white collegiate basketball style at Iowa State. The second period was my three-year fieldwork that ended six years ago producing a dissertation and book on black and white collegiate sprinters at the University of Illinois, and now this two-year continuing study with college football players. For each period, my friends have tended to be the same people I compete with and against. In effect, three times, I was a window looking into the lifestyle of college kids. Each time the faces and personalities moved on, only to be replaced by another group with different faces.

Early athletes I played, and still keep up with, are now married and settled down and working, making money, and being successful. I feel like a high school teacher who watches kids walk in and walk out of his life and are gone, only to return in memories or at reunions. Things never really change that much. Kids ten years ago are like kids now, who are like the college student I was two decades ago. But I am getting older and even though the sporting experience and feelings of competition never really change, I have changed.

I have a 12-year-old-son, an ex-wife, been through several relationships that have not worked out over the years, partially due to my "obsession" with sport and participant-observation, taught college for three years and lived life experiences that many of these players will not experience. Even now, I hear the voices that question my sanity, even the voices behind my back that condemn my choice of study. I rarely see my Illinois-bound son, except for some time in the summer and at Christmas. I talk to Parker, my son, every week on the phone, sending him articles and stories of my team, trying to infuse our conversation with the happenings of my season. I am too far away and the crackling of the phone reminds me of the tenuous thread that connects us. I want him to know that what I am doing has merit. It isn't just a lark, but then I also want him to know that what I am doing is special and that I am unique.

The relationship I am in now will fail much like the others before. She is slightly older than I am; blonde and just beginning to fight the ravages of a lifetime spent under the California sun. Her warm body and talents as a masseuse provide sanctuary for my tired body and softens the brutal truth of my own mortality that hits the hardest when the violence of practice and games was hours old. It is all I can do to show up to her apartment at night, plead for a backrub, and fall asleep while her expert fingers knead the pain and consciousness out of my body and mind. She is happy to oblige, but is used to dates and weekends away. Her idea of fun is not me stumbling from her bed at six in the morning, more alive than when I stumbled up her stairs the evening before. After the novelty of the coupling wears off, she will soon wonder why I teach classes at three different community colleges. Why I drive an hour each way at night after busting my ass at practice. Why I have a Ph.D. but can't pay for her movie or her dinner. I can hear it coming, as I have heard so many times before from other women. "Why don't you just grow up and get a job?" she will ask, and it won't be long till her fading footsteps echo a retreat. Often now, I look at my life through the eyes of an 18 year old, or seeing my accomplishments as too bizarre and out of the ordinary. And then I feel uncomfortable playing the role of "Doc." I am 38 and sometimes I let the numbers roll off my tongue resting from the 40s we run or jogging back to the huddle after catching a slant. I know I am experiencing the cultural dysfunction of being a fish out of water. I see all the faces around me, not yet really touched by life, not marked by the responsibilities or hardships of surviving outside of the comfortable existence that is childhood and adolescence. And then I know the awful cruelty and emotional pain of growing old in our society. It goes beyond the body aging. Aging collides with the youthful rebellion of body and spirit, of mind and soul. My mother calls it maturity and wonders if I have ever had any. Same-age friends set in a life of working and family vacations and holidays tell me it is inevitable. My athletic brothers, 33 and 31, denying some envy, want to know what I am going to do when my knee blows out, and Parker may come to understand my reasons when he is my age, but now just wonders why.

Here in Santa Barbara and in southern California, there are a few ageless hippies, surfers, artisans and the "young at heart" who see the future as next week, or the next wave, or the next joint. I wonder if I fit into one of those categories. The Nike maxim of aging, "Just get by." But through all this, I don't stop and wonder if spending a year playing basketball, three years running track, now two more playing football so I can describe the cultural reality of athletes was worth the time or the life I could have had chasing another dream. It is there, too obvious for me to see. There is a purity of challenging your body and mind to accomplish the unthinkable. Here it is different than in Des Moines, Iowa. Age is an enemy and a sure sign of weakness, and people fight it tooth and nail. Daily, I witness the sure signs: sun-streaked or platinum blond hair, face lifts, boob jobs, and liposuction. There is an art to just getting by.

This is the Southern California body culture where the body becomes an easel to the very visible art of body perfect and the individual struggle for identity in an ocean of conformity. Nowhere else in the country is the shape and tenor of the body placed on exhibit as much as it is here. Notwithstanding Hollywood, which seems to drive its own engine of body art, human flesh parades on the streets, in the parks, at the beach. In

Santa Barbara, it is the life of the tanned and beautiful, the rich and famous. Some come to gawk as they walk up and down State Street and Cabrillo Boulevard and then take these images home to Peoria or the rest of America and rationalize their envy by saying everything out here is plastic and superficial. "Aren't we glad we live where there is real life, seasons, life and death," they tell their neighbors. Those who live here, for the most part, have to buy into this body culture or suffer a fate worse than dying. Death ends existence, vanity is a lifelong search.

For most of the football players, their bodies became an extension of their life on the field. The shape and tone of bodies and the decorative symbols that adorned the many arms, biceps, and backs of the players I called teammates expressed the culture of violence and aggression, teamwork and individuality found in football. So many of the players had tattoos, and not the cutesy butterflies or odes to Moms, or even dolphins or other coastal images, but the ones emblazoned with jersey numbers, statistics, individual revelations of greatness, symbols of death and naked power. One Mexican-American player's entire back, from the small of his back to the wings of his shoulder blades, was an altar and a collage of ethnic spirits. Images were placed on rippling muscles to get the most effect.

In her fascinating work with female Chinese athletes, Susan Brownell discovered that the female body has become a means of challenging the traditions and autocratic authority of the state and culture. There is no direct confrontation, no tanks and soldiers coming face to face with modernity. Through gaining glory for the state, the female athletes live and express gender identity and growing power through their body. They become stronger by controlling their body. To Brownell, sport renders a space where Chinese society can contest government and tradition that would bring punishment and possibly death in a more political field.

These two coastal California cultures, one of body beautiful and the other of bellicosity, wash together in the multi-cultural space of southern California and allow a forum, away from the harsh publicity of politics and causes, to trumpet nonconformity. As long as individuality isn't sacrificed or challenged, beauty and the beast co-exist in the larger ocean of body culture. Firm and globular breasts, lifted faces and miles of tanned flesh together with

70

etched images of skulls and crossbones are similar to the Chinese females track athletes' wearing of bikini briefs in running and pumping up their bodies. All are expressions of a more benign, but still visible, battle of soul and control.

I can run rings around most of my teammates. I do more stadiums, faster than my receiver mates, at the end of practice. I storm through the drills during practice and from this banzai attitude, I feel good and buy into this contrast of body beautiful and the beast way too easily. But that good feeling is lost when I try to explain to others. On one hand, I am hanging on for dear life, sucking the most I can before dropping off the face of the earth. It is not ironic that most athletes see their careers that way. In sport, you live in the present. What you did matters not one whit, if you can't produce today. Another sound byte from Nike: *Life is too short, play hard.*

This was my *Gonzo* ethnography. Jump on the wagon, lose yourself in the action, express it, record it, watch it, and ask way too many questions. Listen, hurt, ride that bull till it bucks you off, climb back on and hang on for dear life while your knuckles turn white and the wind peels back your cheeks. Lick your wounds and, in the process, discover why anybody would risk fucking their bodies and minds for the rest of their natural born lives just to compete on a grass field for 10 Saturdays, for four months, for one year.

It was third and ten and I was split in the slot, running a Cat 65, an eight yard up, out and up. The ball was snapped and I exploded off the ball, cutting on a dime, shooting up the sidelines, trying to track down the 50-yard cannon shot for the winning score.

# *Chapter 6*

---

## The Ghosts of LaPlaya

**KIST**

*This is certainly the start Vaquero fans would hope for. Try to take the lead and take some of the assault out of the Renegade attack. So J.T. two quick plays, has it down to the 24-yard line. The game less than a minute old and the Vaqueros driving on first down.*

The sideline was going crazy. Lightening had struck not once, but twice. Players were pounding each other on the back and Chuck had ripped off his headset and was trying frantically to get J.T.'s attention. Dudley was pumping his fist in the air and screaming, "Take that Bakersfield. Fuck you! We got ya now!" Even Joe had stopped stalking the defensive sideline and was shouting encouragement. God knows what Carmen, up in the press box, was yelling on the other end of the phones.

On the field, Vaqueros were stomping around. Twuan was running a little circle and his arms were raised high in exultation to the grandstand. He didn't care at that moment that most were Bakersfield fans. They had red on, they came with their own television cameras and radio crew that were recording Twuan right now, and they were going down to defeat.

J.T. had turned back toward Chuck to get the call. Chuck, the headset draped over his arms, was frantically searching in his mind for a play. At that moment, with adrenaline sweeping through his body, I was sure Chuck was not standing on the sideline but, instead, rocking in J.T.'s cleats at midfield right here in LaPlaya Stadium, twenty years earlier, his arm on fire from connecting with his teammate Dudley for another long gain. He had a big future resting on his golden arm. He was on top of his own little world. So was Dudley, a scholarship to USC already in the works for the 1977 season.

Now the ghosts of LaPlaya, of Chuck, Dudley, even Joe, were riding high again in the Vaquero saddle. From the uneven turf, ex-Vaquero players, now Vaquero coaches that had lost their youth and shape, were once again stalking the grass. The years were ripped away like leaves from oaks in the middle of an Iowa thunderstorm. Twenty years, one generation, a different time, different faces, but the same old rivalry; Bakersfield versus Santa Barbara.

City College athletic director Bob Dinaberg remembers the 1976 season that Chuck starred as a quarterback with his favorite receiver, Steve Dudley. Bob should know. He was the head coach and Carmen DiPaolo was the defensive coordinator. "It was different then. We filled LaPlaya for every home game. City College was in the middle of a 10-year dynasty in the Western States Conference. Chuck came out of Dos Pueblos High, the hottest arm around and Steve Dudley was unstoppable at Santa Barbara High School."

Together they made magic for that one year. Chuck heaved long bombs to Dudley and almost scored at will. Shuffling through old grainy black-and-white stills from the college newspaper, I picked out shots of lean and mean players and long sideburns. They were young and immortal. Warriors with futures so bright as to blind them from the reality of life outside the friendly confines of Santa Barbara. There was one of Chuck, almost unrecognizable, the field general surveying his troops, barking out signals, frozen in the flash, confident. Another one shows Chuck, his arm cocked, waiting expectantly in the pocket a second before releasing a howitzer down field. "Chuck was a big time thrower," said Bob. "I basically underestimated him. He was one that, in almost every statistical category and situation, achieved more than I expected."

Where Chuck was the consummate leader, Dudley was an All-American. "Dudley was as good as we have ever had here," Bob said. "Nobody could cover Dudley man on man." Chris Pagliaro, offensive coordinator in 1975, now academic advisor at City College told me, "He was just too fast and too good. He just tore up the conference." Following that year, the two parted, Chuck going to Weber State and Dudley to USC.

Seven years later on the same City College turf, Joe DiPaolo, coached by his father, terrorized conference foes for two years. "Joe was small and very active as a linebacker," said Bob. "He led the conference in tackles and assists. He was that good." Switched to outside backer at Weber State, he made all-conference two years running and still holds tackling records 15 years later.

But that was then and, two decades later, the Vaqueros were beating on Bakersfield's front door, demanding to be let in. Chuck couldn't hurdle the intervening years and win the game on his arm. He had to win it with his mind. And he had to have the help of two other LaPlaya ghosts. J.T. may have the arm now, but Chuck was the man. Chuck screamed at J.T. to get his attention in the surrounding delirium. He gave him the play, snapped his headset back on, gathered up the seemingly miles of extension cord and started to coach.

Chuck and I looked at each other over his desk one morning in early April before the start of my second season. The late morning marine layer that hung over the beach and City College darkened his office. The Spartan furnishings, a desk and two chairs and a bookcase, did more to emphasize the emptiness of the room than the austere taste of the college.

"So what do I need to do to get ready for next season?" I asked. Chuck, who is fourth generation Mexican American (his great-great grandfather was Benito Juarez, the famous Mexican President), leaned back in his chair, as the creaking sound a chair makes when too much weight settles in, drifted over the desk. Over 80 lbs. heavier than his college playing days of 175, Chuck was a large man. His short black hair and mustache added to the brown of his complexion and spoke of a Mexican ancestry like the hue of earth tones that predominated around Santa Barbara in the arid hot months of summer and fall.

Befit a man of his position, he tried to look serious as an answer formed in his head. Over his shoulder, I looked out his window to the beach and the frothing surf, active due to an incoming spring storm. A mist gently moistened the pane. As the droplets of water collected on the glass, I thought of the surrealism of the moment. The context of our relationship constantly amused me. The irony of ages and similar academic duties gave this meeting a Salvadore Dali-like feeling where everything is not really as it should be.

"You need to improve on your whole game because you lack the experience a lot of players have," Chuck said. "You need to improve on your ability to catch the ball and you need to improve on your strength."

Tell me something I don't painfully know already, I thought. Hadn't I just spent the last 14 months involved in football starting from scratch in a game that demands much of its participants, surviving on Advil and licking my wounds nightly from the sanctuary of my apartment? Chuck continued, oblivious to my mental musings. "Your speed is good; still, I think you need to improve on that," he said. "There is a difference between football and track speed."

Chuck was right. Coming off the spring of 1994 when I ran the 200 and 400m for City College, sprinting on turf was a shock. Thinking all I needed to do was strap on cleats and outrun four defensive backs and three of my receiver mates to the ball, I was rudely awakened to the hidden dimensions of stopping and starting, cutting and pivoting on a natural carpet. "I know you are a real good sprinter," Chuck said, "but at the same time you don't get a whole lot of separation when you are running your deep routes. You need to apply your sprinter's speed to the football field."

Images of last season flooded my mind. Trying to decelerate and cut on a 10-yard out in practice while being mugged by a defensive back was everything track wasn't; being on your toes and flying off the curve on a 200m was the high of sprinting. In track, to succeed you ran away from people. In football, you eventually had to run over somebody. Stay low, Chuck would tell me over and over again at practice. "Get low, real low, don't stand up. You are just waiting to get clobbered by the defensive back." But I told him that I was fighting a lifetime of sprinting where you stood tall and lifted.

Chuck lowered his hands and formed a steeple. For a moment he was a Mexican Buddha pontificating on the metaphysics of receiving. "I think you are doing a good job. You spend enough time at it, your routes are improving, as is your catching ability. But you still have a long way to go," he said. "You still need that experience of catching the ball while being laid out, the experience you get only during the season."

I had been hit and beat enough times in practice last season to know the feeling, but not enough in a game situation. I had to be ready for the violence when it came. When adrenaline surged through the defensive backs like a runaway Amtrak train and they lit you up like the neon lights on the casinos in Vegas.

"To do that you need power and you can only get that in the weight room, " he said.

I knew only too well the need for power. Last season I played at 155 lb. and paid for it dearly on the field. I wasn't about to make the same mistake twice. Since January, I had been lifting three times a week. I wanted to play at 170 this next season. "One of my concerns is that I want my receivers to be where they are not going to get beat up by the defensive backs," Chuck said. "I want them to be the initiators on offense. I want them to be assassins."

"Come on Chuck," I interrupted his next thought before it got untracked. "Unless I juice up and jump on the steroid train, I am never going to be that big or even approach that big. Besides, being too heavy will take away from my speed." It sounded good. A compromise between size and speed demanded explosion and power not bulk.

"I think all that I am asking you to do is to become as strong as you possibly can in four months and as powerful as you can get," Chuck said. "I think it will really help you catch the ball. I would tell any guy this, not just you." Chuck stopped and looked at me. "Does this help you?" he asked. "Do you have an idea of what you need to do?"

I nodded. I knew what I needed before coming in to to see you, I thought, but I wanted to hear it from your lips. As an anthropologist and as a player, I needed to experience this conversation just as I was a player trying to put his game in order. Come on, Chuck, coach me. I am a player. I am filling a role, a position that requires performance. What anthropologist Victor Turner saw in performance was the reconstruction of culture on the stage of reality. Of everybody I came in contact with, players, trainers, coaches, Chuck was the leading performer, not only in accepting my ongoing study, but taking part as an active member of my football world.

"I have to put myself in the position of the players," I tried to explain to him. " I have to maintain some objectivity. That is one of the benefits, as well as one of the drawbacks, of the type of research I do. I get to the point that I don't know who I am."

"You mean what role you are?" Chuck asked.

"Exactly, where do I fit in," I said. "I am trying to take in as much as possible and understand as much as possible, all the while just trying to be one of the boys. Let's face it. You know last season I had a hell of a time learning just how to be a football player, let alone play like one."

"I know," Chuck said. "But it's all a part of becoming a better player." That seemed too much like a well-worn cliche or the Army recruiting ad, "Be all you can be."

"Some things I never saw before," I told him. "I did things I had never done before and then I had to get used to being pounded on, beat up and spit out. You don't get that in track. Now for next season," I told him earnestly, "I am more prepared. I have a better understanding of what my body is going to go through."

"That is why physical preparation is so important," Chuck said. "That is why you want to be able to punish somebody, to push and control the defender when you can. Remember, football is a war, a fight, a struggle of strength and power and fitness!" he said.

Football as a Darwinian agent for natural selection? Gee Chuck, why not? Only the strong survive. In the analogy of genetic adaptation, football provides a mechanism to not only survive, but to be successful. Yet when the environment changes and the player leaves the confines of the field, can he adapt and respond to the change in the situation? Was this the storyline I was going to see? Deviant football players run amok on the field of life, using strength, power and explosion the only way they know how? So what Chuck, are football players machines with a predisposition toward violence?

Chuck continued, "The game is survival of the fittest, the strongest." I was smug in my call. "For you, it is a problem of beefing up, but it is also because there are certain instincts you don't have because you didn't play when you were young." Chuck could never let a reply go without a nudge about my age. "These instincts are big-time advantages for other people."

Come on Chuck, a genetic predisposition toward football? A gene to sack the quarterback, one to take your man deep, or deliver a frozen rope on a 15 yard out? My mind was beginning to wander, conjuring up caricatures of helmeted blood dripping rhino-men ripping into each other for the possession of a small severed head of a juvenile kudu. Too much assigning Richard Leaky to my students in Physical Anthropology last season, or was it semester? "I have to say that I am really looking forward to next season," I said. "Last season, it was K-12 for me. This season, it is time to enter college," I told him. "Hang with it, Doc," Chuck said and smiled, his dimples played out across his wide brown face. "The year has yet to begin."

Chuck was optimistic about this upcoming season. And why shouldn't he be? He had, probably, a more gifted passer coming in to replace the MVP of the conference who was moving on. The team was a little thin at the offensive line and had only two sophomores on offense coming back; one of those was as old as Chuck, but Torlando could beat you by himself. The defense was returning a solid nucleus and he could always count on the DiPaolo connection for shaping up the boys on defense. The secondary was going to be awesome.

Already Chuck was thinking ahead to the Bowl game that they were finally going to get. On the down side, his life was chaotic. It wasn't like four-year schools, where assistants did all the work and the head coach just assigned responsibilities. At the junior college level, the assistants were part-timers with full-time jobs and everything was left to him to accomplish. He had to recruit, find housing and jobs for his players, make sure they were all enrolled, nursemaid and hold their hands. He spent hours a day on the phone and he never got a break to go fishing for salmon in Oregon or for the sea bass that he reeled in from the surf. It was April and he should be enjoying the freedom from practice.

Chuck was still a bachelor at 38. He didn't have time for a relationship. There was time for the nights out after games at O'Malley's, a local bar, with Steve Dudley, when Joe and Mark Johnson, the running back and special teams coach, would join them and they would sit back and let the game drain from their minds and just drink. Then Chuck would occasionally and wistfully remember all the girls that wanted to date him when he was the big star quarterback at Dos Pueblos and City College. He had to beat them off like flies, but now it was different. Sure, he had put on too many pounds and, to make it more difficult, the woman had to be able to adjust to the pressures and time commitments of his coaching. Maybe it was better that he wasn't involved now.

Football was in his blood. He loved to play. He had stayed a little over one semester at Weber State but, as he told me, they really didn't want a Mexican-American quarterback. He joined up with an old coach from high school who had the head job at NAIA Eastern Oregon State College and led the nation in passing his senior year. He thought for sure he would be drafted, but he wasn't and he made the mistake of not retaining an agent and lost out on the NFL. He passed up a chance to play in the Canadian Football League and stayed on to be a graduate assistant at his alma mater.

"I should have been more aggressive," he told me once. "It was a one-shot deal, and I thought then there would be other chances at the pros, but there wasn't. I will always regret that." He transferred to California State University, Humboldt, where he coached and finished up his Master's in physical education. Now coaching filled his addiction for the game. The highs were high and made up for the lows that came with losing. He had tried to make it in business after he left his graduate assistantship at Humboldt State. There were no teaching jobs and he came back home to Santa Barbara. The baseball position opened up at City College, Chuck had also been a standout pitcher when he wasn't throwing the pigskin, so he went after it and was hired. His teams were mediocre, but he was coaching and he filled in as quarterback coach for Baldwin, the coach before Chuck. Finally, a full time position in the physical education department at City College opened and he grabbed it. The dream became reality as Dave Baldwin left. Chuck dropped baseball and was appointed the head football coaching jobs and his life was never the same. He was never more alive than when he was plugged into the headset, wrapped up in the game, calling plays, urging his players on, feeling the same adrenaline rush he felt when he played, his soul on fire with the drive to win.

Dudley was right on Chuck's shoulder as Twuan finished pumping up the Bakersfield crowd. "What did you call, Chuck? What was it?" he shouted over the din of celebration. "Screen to Twuan," Chuck yelled over his back. Dudley nodded his approval to Chuck's back and, before being asked, turned to his flock of receivers that were obediently gathered around him like puppy dogs and simply said, "Screen to Twuan." To the Vaquero formation forming on the field, he hollered, "Got to have it, got to have it!" And then he put his hands on his hips, braced his legs, as if he were physically involved in the action. Bring it on, goddammit. His stance echoed volumes.

Thirty-eight-year-old Dudley was light years from Dudley in his prime. In 1976, he was skinny, fast and had an Afro. In 1995, he had a gut, short cropped hair with streaks of gray, but the same spindly legs of a sprinter and hands of velvet that made him a scholarship player to USC the year after leaving SBCC. Now the legs didn't work as well because of only sporadic activity, but the hands came out to play when he threw with us before practice. He spent all of the 1994 season nursing a hamstring injury from playing centerfield in a parks and rec softball game.

After spending the last 16 months with Dudley, I came to like him and, at the same time, wondered whether he was head coach material. In other words, he was the perfect assistant coach. Often, I listened to him agreeing with whatever Chuck said, or he would agree with what I would say or, in fact, what any of the receivers would say. He would make a joke about a player; then, after the damage was done, he would say, "no, no, seriously, he is a good guy." Dudley had a smile and laugh that was infectious and contagious and I couldn't help but laugh with him when he messed with our heads.

During the 1994 season, receivers walked all over Dudley, playing hurt, playing when they wanted to, sulking and talking back. In fact, during one game, Dudley was attacked and punched by one of the receivers for not playing one of the receiver's friends. In each game, when the defense was on the field, his voice carrying in the night chill, Dudley would gather us together in a casual circle like hens and throw his own verbal darts. "What the fuck are you guys doing?" he would scream. "Get your head out of your fucking ass and catch the ball. Bring it together, receivers. Come together or get the fuck off my field. Now get back into the game!" It never failed one of the receivers would mutter, "Fuck Dudley." Or "Man, I don't need this shit," one would say to nobody in particular.

Dudley, his ears roving antennae, would pick it up and bark, "Shut the fuck up!"

One evening, I got a chance to unravel the life story of Dudley off the field. I met up with him in O'Malley's, a State Street bar, and the unofficial Vaquero hangout for both players and coaches, the first weekend in July. It didn't hurt that Colin Flynn, the strapping defensive line coach, was also one of the chief bartenders. O'Malleys' was a college sports bar hangout with a full wooden bar stretching the length of the room and a faded brick wall interior. Casey, a defensive lineman from last season, and I walked into the bar that night and it took a while to accustom our eyes to the dark interior and the blue haze of smoke that draped the room like a curtain.

Five TVs and a big screen projection blared the numerous sports that one can get on a late weekend summer night. State Street was a zoo jammed with tourists and City College and University of California, Santa Barbara students. The bar was just as crazy. One thing was certain; on a weekend night, O'Malleys' had its share of long-legged California blondes with even tans and bare bellies. Casey and I just cruised down the length of the bar, wading through the morass of five deep standing between the bar and the back wall, knocking breasts and butts along the way. The juke box blared 70s tunes.

Without too much difficulty, I spotted Dudley as he was the only black in the sea of blonde and tan. His was singing away to the juke box, his eyes bright with a pitcher of Bud that he was working on by himself. "Doc, what the hell are you doing here?" he shouted over the din. "Searching for a beer, what else?" I replied.

I plopped down next to Dud, my elbows resting on the mahogany bar. I grabbed Colin's attention, slapped his hand, yelled for a beer and then gave him five dollars. Colin had never been married, was the father of an infant daughter whose mother lived in Las Vegas and worked full-time as a bartender at O'Malleys. Colin was big, over 6'4" and 235 lbs., but he had played at 250-lbs. He had short, curly brown hair and freckles that gave him an impish and puppy dog look that college-aged girls drooled over. Occasionally during those two years I played, Colin would take trips over to see his daughter. Once the mother and Colin tried to patch it up, but Colin was never serious about getting back together.

Colin's status as Lothario was well known and his trysts with women were legendary among the players. Because of Colin's live in the present attitude on life, never to bed, sleep-till-noon lifestyle, and his preoccupation with working out, most of the time with his players, he was successful in establishing a unique rapport with the team. Many looked up to Colin and what he represented; a life that many 19-year-old males could only imagine in their wildest of fantasies, behind the bar, with several TVs constantly blaring out sports, quaffing brews while serving an adoring female clientele that leaned over the bar exposing cleavage while giving their drink orders.

"You know Doc," Colin told me once, "I am not in any hurry to get out of here. I have a good job, make lots of extra cash in tips, have fun with the ladies and live in Santa Barbara. What else could I want?" In stark contrast to Colin's carefree life was that of Don Hopwood, fellow defensive line coach. There were many similarities between the two. Don was just as big, had played at about the same weight as Colin, but was slimmed down from his playing days. Both had been defensive standouts at Santa Barbara City College and both had gone on to successful college football careers, Colin at Sacramento State and Don at UCLA. Now both were back coaching at their alma mater. That is where similarities ended.

Whereas Colin's life seemed to be uncomplicated, Don's life was anything but carefree. More than any other coach on the team, Don's life was a picture of tenacity and perseverance, a rocky road that ultimately led to the successful confluence of higher education and life experience. Don didn't graduate his first time around, playing out his eligibility at UCLA and then making several runs at the NFL, the CFL (Canadian Football League) and the now-defunct USFL (United States Football League). In between, Don married his high sweetheart and had three children. He moved his family to San Juan Island, a place with four seasons, well away from Los Angeles. He ran heavy machinery at a gravel pit, dove for sea urchins and spent years dreaming of what could have been. During his stay on the island, he got shots with the San Francisco 49ers and the Boston Breakers of the USFL, but both ended in disappointment and frustration. He and his wife brought a boat and property to build on and then, less than a year later, his wife of 12 years ran off with his sea urchin diver, leaving him with three kids, a stack of bills, and a dream that finally went the way of his wife.

"San Francisco actually called me while I was still up in Washington," he told me one October practice as we watched the sunset over the last few plays of special teams scrimmage, "and asked me if I wanted to come back and I told them yes. I was at work and I thought to myself, the next day I am going to be playing in the NFL. They called me at 5 p.m. and said they had made a trade for another player. I know that if I had been in San Francisco I would have gotten a look. And it is a story thousands of other guys have: I could have done it, but it was politics."

Don eventually ended up back at Santa Barbara. He moved in with his parents while undergoing a custody fight. He enrolled in UCLA to finish up his degree a decade after he left, so sure of his future being absent of playing football. "Not playing is that dream that never got fulfilled," he mused as I asked him about missing out. "Yeah, it bothers me a lot. It took a long time to get over it and I didn't and so I turned 30 and then I realized it is probably too late. Up until then I was really hoping, at some point, to play. My dream was to be the oldest rookie in the NFL. I turned 30 and decided it was over." Don now has a bachelor's degree from UCLA and works for Nordstroms while raising three teenagers. He spends a few weeks every summer touring and playing football in Europe with ex-college and pro players from Santa Barbara, rekindling his lust for the game and admitting inside that he is way past his prime, but making the best of life's offering.

Colin slid the beer over to me. I grabbed it and swiveled back to face Dud. "So what's up, Dud?" I asked. "Nothing much, just drinking my beer and watching the women." He wasn't kidding. Dud had strategically placed his stool facing the door so, anything that walked in, he would have a clear view. In between the music, Dudley's off-key singing and a couple of students of mine coming up to say hi, we finally got through the pleasantries. Casey left to go "cruising for babes" in a neighboring bar.

By this time it was close to 11 p.m. and the people were wall to wall and rubbed their elbows, thighs and other parts around us like a high tide. A blonde in a low-cut dress passed in front of us, with ample cleavage spilling out. Dud yelled that Chuck would call that a "low rider." In spite of myself, I laughed at his stab at ethnic humor. Through Chuck and Dudley, I had pieced together a skeleton account of his college and brief pro career, but I figured this would be a perfect time to start putting the flesh on the bones. I knew that I was in when Dudley slopped the last of his beer down, pulled out a package of cigs, which surprised me, "Don't tell Chuck about this" he warned me, and shouted "Whiskey, I need whiskey!"

He slapped the bar, catching Colin's attention and demanded a whiskey, straight up. He then took out a bill, wadded it up and, after slapping down the cash for the whiskey, shot the bill across the bar to the tip bucket against the bar length mirror. It dropped in and bounced back out and skidded across the floor. He turned to me and said, "I should have played basketball, but nobody let me. It was football or nothing else."

"So how long were you at Southern Cal?"

"Man, Doc, I got some stories for you, but I can't tell you 'cause you still are my player," he said.

"Shit, Dudley, it is not the same and you know it." He wasn't going to shut up. He just needed to put some rationale behind it. "I was at SC for a year, the year with (Paul) McDonald at quarterback, Kevin Williams at wide receiver, Ronnie Lott, man, I used to have to go up against Ronnie Lott everyday, Clay Mathews. Man, practically the whole team was drafted. That's the year we beat Notre Dame, UCLA, Michigan and Ohio State in the Rose Bowl. John Robinson was the coach. But Doc, it was really fucked up. Man, I had to get out of there after a year or I was going to go down with a sinking ship. The NCAA was starting to nose around, wanting to ask questions."

"How much did you play that year?" He held out his fingers and curled his index finger to touch his thumb. "This much. I was faster than Williams, and better, but down there it wasn't how good you were, but how much you could talk. And Williams and the rest of the receivers were from LA. Who are they going to play, a kid from LA or one from Santa Barbara?"

Dud took a hit off his whiskey while I pulled from my Bud longneck. "Man, I got three stories for you, Doc." I nodded and waited. This is what I came for. "I remember going in to one of the coaches office and him taking three envelopes out of his desk, just jammed full of hundred dollar bills. Man, almost everybody was on the payroll. I must have got paid $2000 that year and I am pretty sure I was at the low end of the totem pole. Man, it was drugs, sex and money. I went face to face with Robinson once, we were this close."

"So give me another story, Dud," I prodded him. But it was a wasted line. He was ready for the next one before I got it out. "I gave Ronnie Lott a lick once he never forgot. Man, this is true, too. Ronnie, God and me know its true. He's got the scar, probably, to prove it. He had to cover me everyday because I played on the scout squad. One day, I caught the ball and turned and met him head on and my face bar hit the top of his nose and flattened him. He went down and they had to stop the play and come out and help him off. They just picked him off and moved the next guy in without stopping. It was like that. They just used your body and when it was finished or hurt or done for, they just threw you away. After that, Lott kept telling me he was going to break my face."

Dud was getting animated and it seemed natural that we should be sitting here on a Saturday night, pounding whiskey and a Bud, pinned in by California flesh shouting about football. Kind of all-American-like. And July 4th was just a couple days away. "You know Clay Mathews, don't you? he asked me. I shook my head.

"Just like Jeff Fisher, who is now head coach of the Oilers, Clay wasn't shit when he was playing. Man, I don't begrudge him his job. He got what he earned but, shit, the world is sure a funny place."

"So what about Mathews," I asked, trying to keep him on track. I didn't think I could pound beers with him and stay cognizant.

"Well, Mathews couldn't cover a curl for the life of him. So one day, after practice was over, Lindsay, the receiver coach told me and this other receiver that we were going to have to run curls so Mathews could learn to cover them. So for an hour, we ran curls. I wasn't going to let Mathews touch me. He kept getting more and more worked up, kept saying he was going to fuck me up, but he never did. So a lot of times after practice was over, I would try to sneak off the field, but just before I would get out, I would hear this 'Where's Dudley' and I knew that it was more curls with Mathews."

"I got to go take a piss. Save my chair." Dudley disappeared for about five minutes, so I pulled more on my beer and watched the crowd surge. I leaned back and tried to remember those USC games I watched on Saturday afternoons when I was a kid. There was always something magical, even mystical, about the Trojans. Fleetwood Mac serenaded me with *Tusk*, their song that is accompanied by the Trojan Marching Band while I pictured the first USC game I watched at age ten. It was the classic showdown between Gary Beban and the Bruins and O.J. Simpson and SC. It was exciting football, complete with passing, broken field runs and the game decided in the waning moments by a blocked extra point.

*Sports illustrated* columnist, Dan Jenkins would write about that day, "It was, of course, too Hollywood for belief. That UCLA's glamorous quarterback, Gary Beban and USC's glamorous halfback, O.J. Simpson, could emerge in the same city, in the same conference, as the best players of 1967, was improbable enough. That they could also wind up battling for the national championship, the Rose Bowl bid, and the Heisman Trophy, all on one unbearable Saturday afternoon, was strictly from the studio lots. But there it was that Saturday, the Trojans against the Bruins before 93,000 in the Los Angeles Memorial Coliseum and millions more on ABC-TV's national telecast, a game played for more trophies, titles, and prestige than any single college contest ever."

Even a ten-year-old boy could damn well understand the high drama that lay in every single down that climactic fourth quarter. Like every other boy that was awed by Simpson, the players became much larger than life to me, like the huge balloon Disney characters that floated high in the sky during the Rose Bowl parade. Now here was a whiskey guzzling ex-Trojan finally assaulting those tightly-held childhood idols. I could handle the greed and corruption in football mega-programs like University of Miami, Florida State, even the much-deserved death penalty slapped on Southern Methodist University; but USC, the Trojans of my youth? Tell me it ain't so, O.J. One by one, Dudley was slowly pulling my tightly-held myths away from the Trojan mystique and I was not letting go too easily. But the Buds were helping lubricate the process, greasing those cherished myths like ball bearings. If Dud got $2000, what did O.J. get, the Taj Mahal?

The smoke hung even thicker, creating an indoor smog alert. Through the haze, I saw Dud coming back from the johns in the back as he slowly picked his way through the mass of humanity. By the time he had made it back to his throne, he was singing along with Elvis on the box. I waited till he was done and shouted, "So what is the third story about SC?"

"It was the girls man, they were all over. I had two, three girlfriends at a time. I had one that would pick me up in her Caddy after practice. She would wait for me. She was Italian and her Daddy was connected with the mob. You know, the mob and SC were like that," and he crossed his fingers. "But her Daddy didn't like the fact that she was dating me, so he called me up one day and told me to leave her alone. Break up with her. So I called her up the next day and told her I was breaking up with her. She said, 'My Daddy told you to do this, didn't he?' I told her no, cause that is what he wanted me to say. But I got away from her fast. I wasn't about to get messed up with no mob characters."

I looked at Dud as he slowly shook his head and smiled, his eyes bright with remembrances. "You just wouldn't have believed it, Doc."

"So I made it to the Cowboys," Dudley continued, "after my senior year at Eastern Oregon, where I went to join Chuck, after I transferred out of SC. Didn't play very much, but what I saw there was even worse than college. Guys like Landry just manipulated you. Did I ever tell you that Landry and I were face to face once, just glaring at each other? Landry got what he deserved when they let him go. It was only fitting that he be treated like he treated the players."

"So, Dallas made SC seem like a convent?" I asked him. "Man, I was from a small town, Santa Barbara, and Dallas was everything Santa Barbara wasn't. It was wild."

"So how long did you play in the big D?" I asked.

"They let me go after that year and I was picked up by Seattle, but I didn't want to play for that team of slaps so I quit and began coaching at Eastern Oregon with Chuck."

I wondered about the relationship of Chuck and Dud. In the last three decades, they inextricably seemed to have been fated, or even destined, to be together, almost joined at the hip. I remembered talking to Chuck about it this spring and how at times he felt responsible for Dud, but then Dud also added a bit of familiarity and security for Chuck. Relationships that last over time are built on trust and the feeling that, the world may change around them, but they will stay the same.

"Dud, how come you left SC and went to Oregon?" I asked.

Actually I was more interested in how Dud could have been in school, actually three schools, for six years and not graduate and played four of those years. He still is over a year shy of his degree. "Well, I went to join Chuck at Eastern Oregon State College because I knew I wasn't going anywhere at SC. He had left Weber and sold me on the school," Dud shouted over the music and buzz of the bar.

"Wait, how were you able to play the next year after transferring without sitting out a year?"

"Eastern was an NAIA school and I could play immediately. But, check this, several times during the beginning of the season, there were questions raised about if I was eligible, but nothing ever came of them. All during this time, Chuck was leading the nation in passing and I was first in receiving. They finally pulled the plug after the eighth game and I was out for the rest of the season, but I still had over 60 catches."

"Why didn't you keep on playing and go to Canada?" I asked.

"I was burned out and, besides, I had a chance to coach at Eastern with Chuck."

These last words were screamed and I knew I was not getting much more out of him that night. Besides, I was starting to feel the Buds I had downed while following Dud's football odyssey. Dud had come back to Santa Barbara after his coaching stint at Eastern, maybe just to follow Chuck back. Dudley had a good job with UPS, but left in a dispute with management. Since then, he had a series of jobs, nothing really permanent except coaching, and that was only part time. He was still at least a year away from finishing his class work and I was still amazed how somebody could go through six years of college and still be that far away from a degree, any degree. However, my amazement was tempered as I learned from my association with higher learning in California that, at least at SBCC and UCSB, kids did not feel that it was their duty to finish as quickly as possible.  In one of my physical anthropology classes I taught at Ventura College, a girl had taken the class over for the third time.  And when I looked around me, I understand some of that hesitation.  Why leave too early the surfing, the weather, the babes, and paradise to face the jungle of the real world?

J.T. took the snap directly from center, faded back and flipped the ball to Twuan in the right flat.  He barely touched the ball before being laid like a carpet for a loss by far too many Renegades to count.

**KIST**

*Flat pass to the near side. Not well executed at all. Hill flattened at the 26-yard line by a host of Bakersfield tacklers led by Troy Richardson, 5'9" 160 lbs., freshman db from Greenville, North Carolina. We will call it a loss of 2, will bring up a second down and 12 from the Bakersfield 26-yard line.*

"Shake it off," Dudley screamed out to nobody in particular.  "Let's get the next one.  What's the next call, Chuck?" And so it went.

A Bakersfield blitz leveled J.T. the next play and we were third and long, going backwards every play, out of range of our place kicker. "We got to go for it," Chuck said, as much to himself and the guy up in the press box, as to anybody else. "Throw a 93 at 'em," Dudley shouted at him, inches away.  A 93 was a streak pattern by all four receivers, "Somebody's got to be opened." Chuck flashed the call to J.T. and we watched the play unfold, the line hold, J.T.'s plant, his perfect spiral, Eric's outstretched hands in back of the endzone, the ball settle on his fingertips....

**KIST**

*J.T. with plenty of time, pumps for the endzone, fires and incomplete! Wow! In and out of the hands of Mahanke. Hard to tell whether it was knocked away or just dropped. Double coverage for Bakersfield in on the play. Ty Thatch the corner was there along with Watkins. Pretty pass by Stone, but it goes for naught.*

...and roll harmlessly off on to the turf.

"Aw shit, fuck it, goddammits" rolled up and down the sidelines as the field goal unit trotted onto the field. Eric was one of the last off the field and, as he came to the receivers huddled around Dudley, his masked eyes asked for understanding. "I had it right here," he said, pointing to his hands. "Right here. I had six." Chuck was pissed off. He knew that was a chance we couldn't afford not to convert on. Against Bakersfield, those chances never repeat themselves. Now all that was left was a possible three from a field goal. Fuck!

### KIST

*First incomplete and Chino Moreno will come out to attempt a 52-yard field goal. Ball will be spotted at the 42 by Trembly. The snap is good, the kick is low and no good. Had the accuracy, it was straight, but only about halfway up the cross bar and lands at the back of the endzone.*

On the defensive side, Joe disgustedly took off his own head set and marched off down the sideline as far as he could get from the offense. His legs churned in his frustration. "Okay, defense ready," he shouted. "First team in." With his broad back turned toward us, he couldn't help thinking that nothing changes. The offense sputters in crucial situations and it is left up to the defense. Fuck! Bakersfield is going to score their points. Nobody can stop them, just slow them down. The offense has to match them score for score and blowing a sure thing opportunity is not the way to do it. He slapped the head set back on and reconnected with God; in this case, his father and ex-coach.

"We're ready to roll, Dad," he said into the phones.

It's not hard to pick Joe out of a crowd; 6'2", over 200 lbs., thinning black hair swept back from his forehead. A goatee and moustache spoke volumes of his Italian-American ancestry. He moves in an easy athleticism that is a reminder of his football playing days.

"Were you good enough to play pro ball?," I asked him once. "I thought about going to Canada, but finally felt that I was too small. I was only a 190-pound outside backer. I would have had to juice up, get to 220 at least."

"Were you fast enough to play safety?"

"Yeah, I could run 4.7s consistently, occasionally getting a 4.6," he said. "But I had the mentality of a linebacker."

"Any regrets?"

"Nah, not really. I was all burned out after that fourth year, so I stuck around and coached."

Joe wore many hats at City College. He was the head defensive coach, an instructor and physical education facilities manager and also the good son of Carmen DiPaolo, long-time defensive secondary coach since the 1970s. If Joe was all Italian-American, Carmen was Mussolini. He was Joe's height and ramrod straight, showing signs of military, but was more a testament to Carmen's playing career as a two-way player at UCLA in the early 60s. He went to the Rose Bowl in 1962 and was teammates with Bob Dinaberg. His gray hair was frizzy and stuck out on the either side of his ever-present baseball cap. His face was lined with character fissures and he spoke in clipped, no-nonsense sentences. Carmen used to live in the next block down from Joe and his wife and two young boys. I would pass Carmen still working in his yard on the way to the store where his brown pickup truck/camper was parked in front, ready to make a quick getaway fishing.

Joe wanted the world, or at least his world, to think he was simple and another replica of a conservative college football coach. His ability to communicate with players was through the physical language of his authoritarian personality and his family background. Joe was the consummate outdoorsman. Picture him in his camouflage gear, holding a shot gun in one hand and three dead ducks in the other, surrounded by three other guys in the same gear, but with less ducks.

If Joe is simple, his Dad was basic. Carmen was earthy, black and white, there were no shades of gray. He had been coaching at City College for 25 years and gave the impression that he had seen everything that came down the pike. He was never without a baseball cap and shades. He was gruff and acidic, uncompromising and the line between normal social discourse and anger blurred instantaneously. Anger lay dormant, hiding in his commands or coaching and in a second, his shouts and yells would shoot across the field and you were left wondering, was he pissed off all the time and you just didn't catch it?

Watching the Northwestern/USC 1996 Rose Bowl at Joe's

house, Carmen regaled me with stories of playing in the days of only leather helmets and his experience in the 1962 Rose Bowl. "When I got to UCLA," he said, "everybody played with one cross bar. If you were special, you know retarded, you got the bar straight down the middle. Everybody played both ways and you only came out when you broke a leg. It wasn't like it is today."

It was very easy to picture Carmen playing then rather than now, almost as if time forgot Carmen and trundled ahead. Chuck loved Carmen DiPaolo as a coach. "He brings intensity and emotion and experience to the game and, besides that, he is funny," Chuck said.

"Coach Carmen is the best," said Casey. "Once, when the offense screwed up during a game, Carmen bolted from the press box and started attacking the chain link fence behind it, beating it, yelling 'Fuck' over and over again. Scared the living daylights out of some fans back there buying hot dogs."

"Is your Dad going to coach forever?," I asked Joe. "Nah, when it isn't fun anymore, he'll hit the road," he said. "If Chuck leaves, would you be up for the head job?" I asked. "I can't be head with my Dad still here. At one time, my Dad was going to be head coach and I was going to be the defensive coordinator, but he decided he didn't want the head job and I couldn't get the head job. So we said, screw it; neither of us will coach. Then Baldwin came in the picture (the head coach for four years before Chuck came on last season), and I gave in and coached while Dad sat out a year. Right now Dad is not really involved that much, so the stress doesn't get to him like it used to."

I have seen both get pretty worked up. I asked Joe a question once during a game last season and he just stared right through me. One of the defensive players yanked me out of your way and said, "Doc, you better watch it. It's not a good time to try to talk with him. He will bite your nuts off."

"I try to keep it in perspective," Joe said, "but Dad takes it more to heart. It could easily eat him alive. I grew up watching him deal with losing. After a loss, he would go under for days; depressed and all of that."

To hang with Carmen was to revel in a wealth of stories and experience. It was like wallpaper in a 100-year-old house that peels and exposes layer after layer of yellow, cracking parchment-like paper. Only in places where it is sloughing can you get a picture of what the interior used to look like; and then only in fragments. Players bitched about him playing favorites or that he never built them up, only tore them down. They said they play in fear instead of wanting to perform for him. But when all is said and done, one was never in doubt where the players stood with Carmen. And we all know where Carmen stood, in the defensive backfield during practice, just out of reach of the play. His arms folded across his chest, white golf shirt and black coaching shorts symbolic of his personality, he barked commands and delivered criticism from the hip.

"Where the fuck is your mind at? If you can't play any fucking better than that, get the fuck off my field!" he screamed at some poor unfortunate defensive back. To watch film with Carmen and Joe and the defense on Monday afternoon, following a Saturday game, was to feel like a B-17 bomb crew in WW II, flying through curtains of flak put up by German ack ack guns. To get out with only one or two hits and still flying was considered divine intervention.

Once the lights went down and the film started, players sat in the dark wondering, not if, but how soon the first barrage would be thrown up in their face and sighs of relief were audible when the film ended. The lights came back on and the players were no longer invisible, they were naked and the flak was not blanketed, but laser-like, pinpointing and rarely did it miss the mark. A number of times I snuck in the back under the cover of darkness and listened while cringing in a vicarious nature. I sweated, fatalistically wondering if there was something out there I did that Carmen or Joe would jump on like walking the sideline wrong, tripping over the cord running from Joe's headphones or just getting caught in his path as he stormed up and down the field.

If the game wasn't so charged, Joe and Carmen would be hysterical. Carmen was up in the press box and Joe on the sidelines joined by an electronic umbilical cord. "God dammit, Dad," Joe would shout into the phones, "the play was fucking messed up from the beginning when Ian (middle linebacker) got cut by the guard!" One could only imagine what Carmen was adding to this dialogue, but then Joe would reply after a moment of silence digesting Carmen's sage advice, "Dad, what the fuck are we going to do about that fucking guard?" Silence.

"I told Ian about last time off the field. Okay, I'll try again," Joe would respond. Then Joe would signal in the defensive alignment for the next play, his arms flapping in some mysterious code known only to the middle backer. And up in the box, Carmen would wonder what the fuck Joe called and the exchange would begin again. "Dad, I called loose double cover" Joe told the headset. Silence.

"I called it because they got to go for it, Dad."

"Of course, I know they have to get 5 yards," he would say, "but..."

He wouldn't get a chance to finish as the play went off and the opposition would get a first down on an out. "Fuck! I told Ian to stay home, Dad," Joe complained.

And so it went, the Abbott and Costello of City College.

Joe was looking forward to this year. Finally he had a solid nucleus to build on and that would make his job so much easier and enjoyable. But deeper, Joe was unsettled. He was from the old school of coaching where discipline and sacrifice was everything. It mattered if you played hurt, every player has to play hurt. It was part of the game. It mattered if you listened and then executed properly. It wasn't so much who scored or the compilation of statistics as much as if the team did what they were supposed to. If they did, City College would win. It was that simple.

Chuck was different than Joe. He cared about statistics, about passing yards and receptions and leading conference categories. To Joe, the AirChuck offense bred that kind of thinking. Then there was how Chuck, and even worse Dudley, handled the receivers. There was no accountability. Players came late or didn't even practice. They sulked when they weren't in and bitched when they didn't get the ball. If that happened on defense they would have their ass on the bench. During the games, the receivers yelled at the coaches and even one game last year, one of the receivers attacked Dudley on the sideline and then only had to sit a game. Football was a game of emotion, but you had to control it or it would ruin you and Joe saw that happen too much. There were too many free spirits on this team, and most of them were on offense. Maybe it was something about playing defense that made them different than the receivers. It was the team that stopped the opposition; all 11 players made it work. An interception or fumble, even a sack was not just an individual effort, but made possible by everyone playing a part.

Chuck talked a lot about the mistakes he made his first year in handling players and he was going to change, be more hard-nosed. It was about time. Joe could only do so much. His part was to keep the defense in line and mold them into a successful unit. Chuck was the head coach and he needed to set the terms from the beginning.

Joe watched his defense set up for the first series of the game. Even with their size, they looked small. "Come on D, dig in," he yelled. He got down in his usual crouch, bent legs, his hands on each knee, as if the lower he got, the closer to the action he was. The ball was snapped and the huge Bakersfield back tore through the line and into the secondary.

"What now?" he said into the phones to God. "How the fuck are we going to stop Gray?"

**KIST**

*Bakersfield's Nathan Sparks at the controls. Hands off on first down. Big gain. That's Mike Gray, the featured tailback out to the 44-yard line. Great line surge. We will give him a gain of 13 on the play.*

Two plays later, Gray, his legs pumping, arms driving, carrying Vaqueros on his back and hanging onto his legs, powered to inside the Vaquero 20. Joe took off down the sideline, following Gray's progress, screaming directions as he moved. Players on the sideline, used to Joe's game sprints, took steps backwards creating a path.

**KIST**

*On third and short, Gray is exploding to the 35, 30 inside the Vaquero 20 and is dropped at the 15-yard line. Mike Gray running to the right side. Two runs for big gains and that one there down to the Vaquero 15-yard line, a 26-yard rip off by Mike Gray. So two carries 39 yards early on Bakersfield now threatening. Gray to the*

*10, five and Mike dropped at the 4-yard line. Tackle made by Jeff Moore, the middle linebacker. Another gain of 11. First down and goal for the Renegades.*

Joe watched helplessly as the Bakersfield offense ripped huge holes in his defensive line. The running back Gray was even bigger than his linebackers. His guys have got to be quicker. Beat the Bakersfield blocks and stand Gray up and hope for reinforcements. Not even Carmen can come up with advice.

**KIST**

*Sparks under center, two receivers split to the left. Gray and Lane the setbacks and on play action, Sparks fakes to Lane and now is going to take it himself, to the 10, 5 and he is in! Touchdown Bakersfield!*

Chuck stood hands on hips, watching the Bakersfield celebration on the field. If only they could have scored he thought. The defense was going to have to do a better job than this. The sidelines went quiet. Players and coaches alike were stunned with the ease that the Renegades exhibited marching downfield. What nobody wanted, but more than a few expected, was in first gear. Bakersfield was just getting started.

**KIST**

*The confetti flies in the air. This large contingent of Renegade rooters here on the home side celebrating the TD. Nathan Sparks on the play action fake to Shawn Lane and takes it himself. From four yards out. With 8:01 to go here in the first quarter, Bakersfield jumps out in front 6-0. Now Chad Hathaway will attempt the extra point. Jordan Richards will hold. Snap is down, kick is on the way, it is good. With 8:01 to go, Bakersfield jumps out in front 7-0.*

# Chapter 7

---

## Into the Fire
### HellWeek Images: Aussies and Pussies

**H**ell Week.  It was the beginning of the football season before classes start and the normal student returns to campus.  It was a time when players really wondered if they wanted to go through four months of football.  It was a time for survival.  It was an intense period of introspection, competition, and running your body into the ground.  It was two practices a day, two-and-a-half-hours each, plus an hour meeting in between with your team, be it offense or defense.  You lived football, and other things more mundane such as family, relationships, and current events took a back seat or were not even in the car. But you learned a lot about yourself and others, too.  The week slowly unwound in a series of half-remembered drills, scrimmages, and newly learned plays and formation.  More and more was piled on till your head was busting with knowledge.  Emotion flared in a second as heat and exhaustion took its toll.  Players that just days ago were acquaintances, or just a name with no face, now were the most important people in your life.  Some became friends, some were tolerated, and others hated.  For better or worse, you were "married" to these faces and names for four long months. Coaches became more important than parents were. Your performance became dedicated to pleasing them. Their approval was more than important, it was vital. Images that lived past the next play stood out like a photo album, the stark black and whites stained and creased by the constant pain and sweat.

The game left no room for grays or for pondering the vagaries or inconsistencies that were found in real life. Football compressed everything into a 100-by-54-yard rectangle. Outside the stadium, life may go on although, as a player, you wondered if the old adage applied to those who were not watching your game: "If a tree falls in the forest and you are not around, does it make a sound?" As you exhausted your body, a coach's face seems to continually loom just inches away, screaming about what you were doing wrong, rarely about what you did right. Half the time, they were breaking you down to where you were close to being only a physical extension of their minds. And they spent the rest of the time rebuilding you into their image of a football player.

Football was a goddamn violent game. To make the breakdown and buildup game work, primal feelings were appealed to by using graphic images of manhood. And this was accomplished by using stark, polarized dichotomies. Football was we versus them, we either win or lose, we played well or we sucked, we beat the guys or we got beaten. Football was a game played by men, for men. Either you were a man or not a man, or if you weren't a man, then you were a "pussy."

"The sub world of the American athlete," Todd Crosset, ex-collegiate swimmer at Texas, former assistant Athletic Director at Dartmouth and now professor of sports management at University of Massachusetts, Amherst, said in *Sports Illustrated*, "is one in which the ancient virtues of manhood, of the brave, cool, tough, dominating, and aggressive male, are celebrated."

If this wasn't strong enough, sport became a chameleon, transmuted into the larger culture of males, "a closed culture, shot through with incessant messages of male supremacy." Tearing down required using images and labels that were graphic and overstated. For a coach to come face to face with a 250-pound lineman on a practice field just after he had been humiliated in a blocking drill and assess his performance in a sensitive way and say, "Tom you missed your block, now let's try it again with verve" was not going to enter the brain with as much power as having the coach stick his face two inches away, pull on the poor, unfortunate player's facemask and scream at the top of his lungs, "Smith, you fucking idiot! You got beat by a fucking pussy and that makes you a fucking faggot! Now get your fucking ass back down there and block his dick off and do it right this time!" On the second appeal, the brain of the player would have been worked like a cattle prod and the correct blocking technique would have been vividly imprinted.

If there was anything socially debilitating to a college macho football player, it was being labeled a fag, a queer, a butt pirate. You could fuck sheep or jerk off until you were blind or blue in the face or both, but to be called a fag was a fighting word. It simply was the kiss of death. The nature of this generational regard for women was not specific to this team, these athletes or even this situation. I have witnessed, even taken part when I was younger, in talking the line, and not just in locker rooms but in dorm rooms and bars. It just wasn't jocks; it was males in general.

In football, the means of one's success, how good you really are, depended on mastery over the opponent. How much could you "make him mine." How much could you make him bow and then rub his face in the dirt at your feet. "An athlete," continued Crosset, "cherishes nothing more than control over an opponent and nothing lifts him higher than the sense that he has attained that control." Being gay is too close to being a woman. "Particularly in contact sports," he said, "things feminine have served as symbols of things to be avoided. Part of the male athlete's identity is not to be a woman. Women are degraded. You don't want to be the skirt-of-the-week. You don't want to be a wimp, a sissy. To be a man is not to be a woman. Women are not to be respected. Women are despised."

It was not so much the content of this message that was important, but the actual use of the dichotomy to reinforce perception. The construction of a football player's macho identity at the expense of women was not just a function of players. If nipped in the bud by coaches, it would become just locker room talk. But many coaches condoned such behavior by legitimizing such an attitude. Dave Meggyesy, ex-Syracuse University and St. Louis Cardinal linebacker, in his eye-opening book, *Out of Their*

*League*, writes of the power of the coach to exploit this masculine fear of being labeled a "woman" to promote the necessary violent and oft times sadistic behavior in football.

"[My coach] said I was 'afraid' to stick my nose in there," wrote Megessey, "as he always put it, adding that I looked 'almost feminine' in making the tackle. This sort of attack on a player's manhood is the coach's doomsday weapon. And it almost always works, for the players have wrapped their identity in their masculinity, which is eternally precarious for it not only depends on not exhibiting fear of any kind on the playing field, but is also something that can be given and withdrawn by a coach at his pleasure. Most coaches...give their players a tantalizing hint of what it might be like a man, but always keep it just out of reach."

I can't remember how many times I was called a pussy for missing a block or dropping a ball after a hit. Suffice to say it was many. Not so much from the coaches, but from the players. When it came, it was meant. In the moment of execution, I was stripped of my person and identity and all that mattered was my ability. Did I block, did I catch? A man did, a pussy didn't. I remember times when, under my breath or out loud, I chastised a teammate for being nonchalant or not going all out and called him a fucking pussy or worse. In the heat of the moment, I bent under the weight of the culture. In the heat of the moment, screaming "pussy" at a player never felt more right.

In her fascinating book on high school football, *Dreams of Glory*, Judy Oppenheimer, mother, recounts a coach's preseason speech to his players. It is a perfect example of the dichotomy of manhood and the feminine other, perfect opposites and foils for the knife-like emasculation fostered by coaches. "Gentlemen," the coach said, "I want to talk to you about something important for each of you to know, what makes a pussy. Are all of you pussies? Do you want to be a pussy? That's what we gotta know right now. A man is born a fucking pussy. You either are a pussy or you're not; there is no other way. Now, we saw that in wartime. In Nam. In wartime, the pussies come out, they show themselves. Non-pussies kicked ass; they killed some gooks. In football, gentlemen, you're either a fucking pussy or you're not. It is as simple as that. You think about that right now. Any of you want to be pussies? Do you?"

How many psychologists have looked at this comparison in

Freudian terms resting on the contrast between the vagina and the penis? The perception was of one, supplicant and open, the other, strong and ramrod stiff, waiting to penetrate and take over. Or did it rest, perhaps, on the ancestral relationship of our early human ancestors where sexual dimorphism (males often were two times the size of females) was based on behavioral necessities of risk management on the savanna falling on the larger shoulders of the males and the biological necessity of childbirth and child care burdened by the females?

Every semester, I have polled my students on their perception of contemporary male-female relationships and every semester I have been surprised by the number of both males and females who felt there was some preordained template that divided males and females and produced gender differences. Was it any wonder that this view was exploited by coaches, who were also fathers, and bought into by players? If most of us bought into this belief, it wasn't a stretch for the coach to harvest motivation and reap the benefits of this behavioral and cultural opposition.

In our sensory-laden world, we are constantly bombarded by sense information. To staunch the flow and channel information into a manageable format, we decode the information based somewhat on a binary or at least an opposition-oriented feature. Black or white, hard or soft, rough or smooth, and after each contrast, another sub-contrast is made and so on until finally that unit of information is assigned a category.

Why should football be any different than other facets of human experience? It is the fascinating part of anthropology when we can decipher the enormous amount of variation in these rules and tease out the similarity or universals that are common to all societies and culture. In football, the coach takes this perception, whether right or wrong, it does not matter, and bends it to suit his need. You want to be a pussy, then you can't play football. To play football, you can't be a pussy. It is interesting that Oppenheimer's son's coach put it in somewhat of a biologically deterministic way, either you are a pussy or not; it is that simple.

Oppenheimer wrote of another coach who thought of this dichotomy as a romantic and one overlaid with the more fundamental notion of good versus evil. "I guarantee you," the coach told her, "if we went back to renaissance days, the Knights of the Round Table, those knights would be the best football players... with the women in the stand waving handkerchiefs, the men on the field with their gear going into combat."

Mariah Burton-Nelson concluded that males see their own domain being chipped away by women and their demand for equal rights. So they fall back on time-honored assertions of masculinity and tradition when men were men and not pussies. Griffin painted a picture of an age-old dominant masculine power play controlling the membership of gender. If you were not a man, then you were a woman, a fag, and a pussy. There was no sitting the fence, you were in or you were out. To each, sport socialized males into a masculine world; taught them how to be men and the natural order of the world, men dominant, women, submissive. In fact, Griffin saw sport operating on five levels to provide males with the proper blueprint for life, the masculine way.

I am not condoning the message or content of what I have heard or been called. It is indeed crude and debasing but, then again, is it just the nature of football which solicits such behavior; or is it more a function of the human need for establishing control, whatever the instrument? Due to the need of an autocratic or dictatorial framework to mold a hundred or more players into a cooperative and successful unit, football, along with other sports, has always looked for simple dichotomies to use as control mechanisms. In the 1950s and 1960s, as discussed in Jack Olsen's classic book on race and sport, *The Black Athlete*, blacks were used as the foil. You didn't want to be a nigger. Hell, blacks didn't want to be a nigger. "Man, quit playing like a nigger!" Even more current than the traditional dichotomy of man and pussy is that of being labeled a fag or queer.

In an irony of contemporary American society, Casey, last season's defensive and offensive lineman, and I went to movies every now and then with a good friend, who happened to be gay. The commonality of our association was all three of us were inveterate movie freaks and we held court on the movie business without reference to my friend's choice of sexual preference. What so many people would chose to identify James as, gay, was lost in the subterfuge of animated conversation about acting and plots. However, not to sketch an idealistic picture of social harmony, surrounded by the familiar environment of the field and players,

Casey was not hesitant to return to a more comfortable homophobia.

The most debilitating and successful method was labeling a player's identity in front of peers and coaches. Numbers controlled, not the message. Being called a fag by a teammate demanded a quick denial and immediate counterstrike on the attacker, taking into question his masculinity, the size of his penis, the ugliness of his girlfriend or his mother and a German shepherd. But it never went beyond verbal bombs or escalated into anything except words and laughter. It was always done in front of an audience and played like off-Broadway. The hoots and howls of the listening players registered the hits and misses of the two combatants. The ferocity of the verbal sparring and the heat of the attack weren't really surprising. It was the physical aggression of the game turned from the hit of a backer to the mind fuck of an opponent.

Chuck introduced his vision of the world according to Chuck that first Monday of Hell Week. It was a vision that dripped with the voice of authority and the message of autocracy. A football team lives and dies on the willingness to acquiesce to a higher authority than each player. Listening to him lay down the sacred code of sacrifice, I knew that the battle was as much Chuck following through with the "word" as applying it to 90 mostly eighteen and nineteen year olds.

"Okay, let us get some rules straight," he barked to the offense sequestered in a PE classroom. Joe was doing the same to the defense in another room, but I would have laid money on him getting his message across with more success. "What we are trying to do is get some discipline. You treat us with respect, I am going to treat you like a man. Now when you start acting like little kids, I am going to treat you like little kids. We want to have a great deal of fun out here. One of my goals is to go 11-0. I think we have the talent to do it. As long as you guys have pride in yourself. Last year we threw the ball for 3100 yards. We ran it for 1000. This year we want to set the state record which I believe is 3800 yards, which is also the national record. We were 600 yards short of that. I want that record this year. Plus I want one of my running backs to gain at least 1000 yards. I want to run the ball for at least 2000 yards. I am shooting for 6000 yards in offense.

"We are going to go no huddle so we can have a few more

drives each game. Hopefully our defense is an ass-kicking defense that will turn the ball over to us. I want some records. We broke just about every offensive record last year. Let's do it again. There is no reason we can't. We have a lot more talent this year. We have much better offensive line, our speed on offense is going to be better. We have all the ingredients, but it is going to come down to how hard you guys work.

"I have already talked to some of you guys earlier. Let's not have a bunch of bullshit this year. No bullshit talk. We want to work and have a good time, if you don't get off the field. Get the job done or get off the field. I don't like a bunch of bullshit."

The 1995 season was underway.

"I want to hear whether it is zone or man, god dammit," yelled Dud, as we huddled under a postcard clear blue morning sky. "I am getting tired of hearing nothing. Now get your shit together, receivers." We were about 35 yards away from the end zone. It was an hour into the first hour and half scrimmage of HellWeek. I had already caught two passes and had one roll off my fingers. The defense was juiced up and the hitting sounded like cannon thuds. Roars of encouragement to teammates echoed down from the defensive side of the 50-yard line. The biggest thuds originated from Down Under. Chuck had been blessed this season with two carefree, robust beer swilling, pain-tolerant, Australians. They had been recommended by a former SBCC running back who was playing professionally in Australia. Through several phone calls over the course of a couple of months, details had been ironed out and they had finally arrived.

A couple of days before the beginning of Hell Week, Chuck and the two Australians appeared at the top of the grandstand while I was working out. Even from the field, 72 bleacher steps away, they were huge. "Come here," Chuck yelled, when they made the climb down, "I want you to meet these guys." I filed over and was dwarfed by the new recruits. They were Phil and Rick, a running back and wide receiver. The wideout was built like a brick house with bulging biceps, blonde stubble that passed as hair, a goatee and a devil-may-care attitude. The running back was slightly smaller, but still big with dark complexion speaking of a possible South Pacific origin (later I would find out he was Tongan) and his head was shaved bald, like a Marine.

We shook hands around and made small talk about Aussie football, rugby and the difference between rugby union and rugby rules. Their football team in Australia had visited the States and played two high school teams in New Mexico and one in Arizona and were beat in all three games. Their accent was thick and very unmistakable and I knew from my experience with Australian and English accents in a college setting they would never have to have to worry about the lack of female companionship. Girls seem to melt in the face of the linguistic onslaught and are powerless to avoid it.

The next day after meeting them on the field, I stopped to see Joe and Chuck in the PE building before going out to the track. "Did you see the size of that Aussie receiver?" I asked Chuck. Playing coy, he answered, "What do you mean?" But the glint in his eyes didn't lie. "Come on you know what I mean, he is huge."

"Yeah, he is isn't he and Phil, the running back is pretty big too."

"Where are they now?"

"Upstairs, in the weight room," he said. "Trying to bench a house. We may have to get more weights for them. One thing I do know, they are going to make out big with the girls. We took them over to a good friend of mine's house to see about lodging and the daughter, who isn't bad looking, was trying to get them to talk. 'I want to hear them talk,' she kept saying. I am sure they can get a bouncer job and they will have it made. Every girl is going to be climbing all over them! All they have to do is talk."

I went down to the field to run the length of the football field strides with Rick and Phil. We warmed up with a couple of laps and then started on our strides. Rick showed some speed once he got rolling. Right after the first stride together, Phil asked if it was all right if he stripped his shorts off and ran in his jock; pure Aussie.

Chuck and Joe came down to the track to supposedly check out the condition of the turf and grass on the field. But I knew what they were up to, coming out to see what the Gods of the Pacific brought them. Five more field-length strides and the Aussies were panting and wheezing. "We spent too much time in the weight room these last couple of months," gasped Phil, who had a degree from James Cook University in Marine Technology/Biology. Rick was from a farm and had been a physical fitness instructor in the

Australian Armed Forces.

Since I was intensely curious to see how they caught, I brought out a ball and we began throwing it around. They couldn't catch. They had awkward hands and looked like they hadn't gone through a high school program yet. They caught the ball against their chest, cradling it protectively. "This is how we catch the rugby ball, against our chest to keep it out of the hands of the opponents," said Rick. It was hysterical to see them throw the ball like a rugby pass, underhanded and with a flick of the wrists. It didn't take Chuck and Joe too long to see the state of their hands and Joe went away drooling over the prospect of having Rick on the defensive line as he left the field. "Christ, we aren't used to getting the ball in any kind of fashion," Phil explained. "Our quarterback back home could only accurately throw it maybe 20 meters at the most."

As we were leaving the field, Rick looked a little pale which was something for him since he was white as a picket fence. Two steps onto the track he vomited. One second he was walking, the next second, while still in stride, out it came. Almost like spitting. Ten steps later, out came the second installment. As relaxed as the first. He vomited two more times up the steps on the way to the locker room, out it came. Phil and I walked in, but Rick stayed outside to clear his tubes. "Don't worry about him, that's the way he is," Phil said.

That evening, Casey and I met the Aussies downtown at the Brickyard, next to O'Malleys, a bar with 52 microbrewery beers on tap. We drank for awhile, discussing the merits of American versus Australian beer. Australian beer was strong and American beer "drinks too easy" was the final consensus. We talked about the wicked nightlife in Queensland and their stories of working till six in the morning as bouncers. We watched life parade up and down State Street and followed hips and breasts with our eyes and exchanged glances of approval. That's what they do in Australia.

We moved down the strip to a surfer bar with live music. Above the swell of the music, Phil and I talked, or shouted, about the similarities in our different societies between the Aborigines and the Native Americans. Phil was darker, and compared to Rick, represented stark contrasts in race. "What is the situation with the Aborigines? Is it like our handling of indigenous peoples?" I yelled to Phil sitting two feet away from me.

"In Australia, you can make enough to live on and never work," he shouted back. "There is no real problem with the Aborigines if they work. I mean, there is no problem with me regarding prejudice as long as I work to support myself and stay off of governmental aid. The problem is that many of them choose not to work."

"Yeah, but if it is like here," I countered through the surf music, "whites came over, took over the country, committed genocide, most of the time in the name of God, finally imprisoned the pitiful remaining souls on reservations. They eradicated the traditional Native American society and culture and then sat by as the remnants became alcoholics and drug users with a collective self-image as high, or low, as the homeless you see wandering around State Street and the beaches."

I had a few beers by now and, fueled by Budweiser, was starting to see the world in a way that was a throwback to my graduate school days. After a Friday seminar we would walk over to a bar a block down the street. It became an unofficial classroom to guzzle brew and talk of worldly things, events and theories and idealism that would only surface in an alcoholic haze and nowhere in the real world.

"I mean there isn't that much of problem for us," Phil said. "We don't tend to judge people by color as much as what they do."

"It sounds too perfect to me," I said somewhat facetiously.

"So why did you wait so long to play football?" asked Phil.

"I never played until last year and now I am writing about my experiences as any good anthropologist does," I explained. "It's just like my study and book with the black sprinters at the University of Illinois."

"So what are the differences between black and white sprinters?" Phil said.

"Well, I didn't look at the physiology, I looked at the cultural differences."

"I know that, just what were the differences?"

"All the sprinters thought of themselves as sprinters and not black or white sprinters. It was those outside the group that split them up according to race."

"That's how it is in Australia," Rick chimed in. "Nobody gives a fuck what color you are. If you are a bum or jerk-off, that is what people care about. I mean, if you are a fuck-up and an Aborigine, then you are a coon and if you are white and a fuck-up you are a bum or an asshole."

"This country puts too much emphasis on color," Phil added. "I mean, look at Oprah. Everybody is getting on the show. The blacks claim that people don't know what it is like to be black. Shit, in Australia you never hear that crap. Everybody is considered fucking equal. I went to this party the other night and this fat bitch kept asking me what I was. I told her I was Australian and she kept saying, 'no, what really are you' and I kept saying I am Australian. Back home, because I am darker doesn't matter except if I am a fuck-off. She just couldn't understand that."

"Yeah, even when we call friends and shit like that, coon ass or asshole, it's just our way of talking to each other," Rick said.

Maybe later, on a long bus ride to a game, we could explore this more, I thought. Not in the midst of a gaggle of 21-year-olds working the bar for pick-ups and potential mates for the night.

J.T.'s unassuming and quiet voice somehow cut through the background noise of the scrimmage as he faced the ten of us, his back to the defense. The lineman were in the front row, reaching for their knees, sucking air and the four receivers and running back were holding hands stretched out in the back row. He called the play and said break. The rest of us broke hands and clapped and then spread out to our positions, three receivers to the right, a lone receiver to J.T.'s left.

My heart pumped a little faster as I settled into the second of three slots. Finally, I get a shot at a something longer than a six yard out or hitch. Drone was out to my right running a 15-yard curl. I was a doing an eight yard up, out and then up. The success of the play was whether the defensive back would bite on Drone's curl and leave me one on one with the corner streaking up the sideline. Ryan was set to my left and staying at home to block, and I could barely make out Troy's eyes through his helmet as he lined up on the opposite side of the field.

The defensive back was playing off about six yards, and I knew the play would be a success if J.T. would throw it. On the second hut, we were off. I rounded my cut, took one glance back and then set sail up field with a step up on the back. For a second, I thought J.T. would hit Drone, but he cocked his arm and let fly. I reached back as I hit the end zone and adjusted a little to my inside and grabbed it as I fell back into the corner, my feet hitting just inside the line as the back landed on top of me. My first TD pass in two seasons. Who cares if it came in a scrimmage? I felt the high as it bruised my insides trying to get out and celebrate, but I played it cool, jogging back to the sidelines cradling the ball. The strong silent type.

Players came up to me, giving me high fives as I made my way out of the end zone up toward the huddle to give the ball back. J.T. came out and gave me a high five. Colin Flynn slapped my hand and said "awesome." Dud looked at me and smiled his big toothed smile and said, "You just gotta believe he is going to throw it. Don't doubt it."

"I didn't doubt it," I said. Except for that fraction of a second. I got more fives and "good catch" back on the sideline. This game isn't bad at all, I thought, as I crested on the wave of andrenalized performance. How quickly does success wipe away the pain of HellWeek.

The evening sun hadn't set just yet, the Friday of Hell Week, but it damn sure felt like the day was done as I painfully folded my legs into my 1979 RX-7, held together by a prayer and Duct tape. My right knee was still cold from icing. Susan thought I had some tendinitis setting in. A chill had settled in on the beach and around campus. It was 7:15 p.m. and I was one of the last leaving the parking lot. A couple of cars down from me, Chuck was leaving too, climbing out of a shirt and into another as he stood outside his white Toyota pickup. Maybe he doesn't go home, I thought, or maybe he doesn't want to. Football is his life right now.

Five days and nine practices were over. On Monday, I couldn't wait for this day to come. Now I was too emotionally and physically worn to give a care. But, then again, that is Hell Week; kick your ass, stomp on your face, burn your lungs and crush your spirit. I don't know anybody who likes it. Plenty that get through it and figure the rest of the season is a snap. I got in the car and drove the few feet down to where he was finally in a purple shirt, buckling his pants.

"So what, do you think we will be better this year?," he asked me, coming towards the side of my car. This was the first time I had a chance to talk to him this week without the swirl of activity and drills.

"Much better," I said.

"Why?" he wondered.

"Because right now we haven't had the dissension like last year and everybody so far has come to practice."

"Yeah, you are right. No clashing of egos...."

I stomped into Casey and Thiessen's apartment that night. "What's wrong, Doc?," Cliffie, the Hawaiian offensive lineman wondered from the same position he no doubt was in the night before as I grabbed the can of Bud thrown my way. Now I catch, why not on the field? "Come on Doc, you can tell us. We are all football players here."

"I want to play and I am frustrated," I said. "Troy is ahead of me and filled in for Torlando today."

"Just because you don't start doesn't mean you won't get any playing time," Casey said.

"Yeah, Doc. You're the man," Thiessen chimed.

"Quit whining and keep playing," Casey added. "That is the nature of football. Fighting for positions."

I looked into Mike Hayes' eyes, only somewhat hidden by the helmet, seven yards away. We were facing each other in the scrimmage of the second Saturday of the infant season, just six yards off the right sideline. He was lying back in a three-deep zone and I wondered what he thought I was going to run. I knew the route. J.T. barked the two huts and I exploded off the ball, breaking down at seven yards and came back to meet the ball off my hitch. I grabbed the low ball and instead of cutting back outside, used my forward momentum and continued across the field, right to left, looking for an opening. Not finding one, I tried to outrun the pursuit that was coming in from all directions. I failed. Four guys hit me seven yards deep in the secondary right in the line of Chuck's vision as he stood watching the play unfold from his station in the backfield. The first backer on the scene stood me up and the other three came in like sharks in a feeding frenzy, smelling the sweet scent of blood and sensing the fear of the captive.

As I picked myself off the ground, my mind still reeling from being mauled, I heard Chuck's shriek from a distance. "God dammit, Doc, don't take it across the middle! Make one move then get up field. You are going to get your head taken off by a backer. I don't want to have to visit you in the hospital!" It was the last play of the second team's second scrimmage. I shuffled off the field. I had a bad feeling about my performance in the scrimmage and the last play didn't help matters much.

All week, I was the first one off the bench and filled in for one of the starting four and was playing on the second team when not filling in on the first. I wondered how that was going to change, especially after the lights went down in the team room on Monday afternoon when we watched the video from the scrimmage. Film does not lie. Stark naked on the screen, no where to hide, we watched ourselves perform and always wondered why we couldn't have run the play the way it should have been, or catch the ball that slithered off our fingertips, or else popped the backer that would have sprung the back.

That night, not even a bottle of wine and grilled shark and a night stroll to the beach with my masseuse friend could erase the premonition of being moved down the ladder of playing time. The season had just begun, but only two weeks remained before the first game and time was running out to prove your mettle and grab a starting spot. I lay awake at night wanting sleep to desperately come. My mind would run over Xs and Os, patterns and missed opportunities and obsess over what I couldn't change and fretted over what I could have changed. I wallowed in this animal that had completely taken over my soul that only lost its grip when I taught or enjoyed my morning cup of coffee surrounded by the java culture who could care less if I missed a block or dropped a slant.

Obsession. Such an ugly word. A grip of emotions so powerful it leaves you locked in a vice of worry and misplaced passion. Like a tiger that can't quite bite its tail and filled with what ifs. At night, however, obsession feasted on your mind like a vulture on road kill, picking at your eyelashes, cheeks, even the brain that oozed gray liquid from the shattered skull.

It was a nightly production for me, always the same stage and the same actors; the familiar drama of the turf. It was the passes that dribbled off my fingers. The blocks I threw on phantom defensive backs that, surprisingly, weren't in the same spot where I threw the block. They had already gone around me like grease on a skillet.

At times, I was panic stricken while terror ground me down into a quivering mass of jelly. The make-believe game that hung in the balance was lost as I dropped the ball in the endzone. Other times, the path to greatness unfolded in slow motion, each agonizing step a nightmare of indecision and too-late adjustments. Never mind the passes I did catch, the things I did right. It was the crap and frustration that lingered below the surface, festering like an overripe boil. The plays ran again and again in my wired mind like the images of game film that Chuck repeats over and over again on Mondays, pointing out mistakes with the precision of a laser. No matter how I laid, on my back, the side or on my stomach, the images didn't change and were even more debilitating because I knew how the play ended. But the film ground inexorably on and on. Obsession.

"Catch the fucking ball, Doc," Thiessen's yell would echo in my mind, as several passes eluded my frantic clutches. "Put it behind you, Doc. Relax, be smooth," Dudley softly said. I broke on a slant behind the deep drop of Thiessen. J.T.'s bullet popped in my hands and I don't break stride as I turned it up field. God, that felt good. I could do it. Momentarily my self-confidence built as I started back to the huddle. A glow of satisfaction warmed me and I wondered why couldn't it stay.

And then, just as quietly, the film changed once again. The play started the same. I angled at 12 yards for the corner. I looked back at my break and saw the ball clearly. I reached out to pull it in and the ball hit the heel of my palms and dropped to the ground. "Catch the fucking ball, Doc," screamed Thiessen. "Fuck you, Thiessen," I yelled back. But he didn't hear the yells from my mind. I knew what I needed to do. Over and over again, only to have the same result.

Toward the end of Hell Week, on my way out to the field for practice, I ran into Rick. He had the red shirt of the defense on and I knew right away that the great offensive experiment had failed. You have to have hands to catch the ball. "Coach (Joe) said if I went to d-line, I could probably start and get a lot of playing time," he said. Already he was picking up on the lingo. "I really wanted to stay on offense. Man, I really love to catch the ball and run over people. Now, I guess I can still run over people, but I will never see the ball."

"Think positive," I said, "maybe you will cause a lot of fumbles."

He put his helmet on and the face bars all but obscured his infectious grin. I knew it was still there, but you don't smile on defense, especially the line. This season's big question was, could you bottle up the manic personality of an Aussie by sticking him on defense? From the beginning, my bet was on the Aussie.

Since getting here, the Australians practically lived either at the Safari nightclub on State Street or in LA on the weekends. It sure wasn't at their studio apartment that was only big enough for a bed, couch, and a table. Phil was going great guns. He was strong and tenacious, even though he ran standing tall. Nobody seemed to be able to pull him down. His only problem was a tendency to become disassociated from the ball. He napped in the locker room before practice; his large Australian body sprawled every which way. I wondered how he could sleep without a gas mask sucking on 100% pure oxygen. The smell of sweat, dirt and rank bodies overpowered the locker room.

As Hell Week ended and classes began, I wasn't moving up on the depth chart. My negligible blocking skills didn't help, especially when I missed blocks during scrimmages with coaches standing over the play. I was getting frustrated, so I approached Dudley after practice one evening after leading the receivers through our ritual of stadiums and push-ups and sit-ups following scrimmage.

"What am I doing wrong?," I asked. "I know the offense backwards and forwards. I want to get in there more!" Earlier that day Chuck had told me, "You'll get in, but until we see some improvement in blocking, there is no way you will be in there on running plays. Use practice time to work on it. You aren't the only one who isn't blocking well. I am going to get after Dud to work you all more."

As I waited for Dud to come up with something, I wondered if he felt comfortable telling a 38-year-old man why he isn't playing more than some 18-year-old. Dud's shades hid his eyes so I couldn't really read his face as to what he was thinking. "Look it, keep working hard," he said. "You work the hardest of any out there. You are doing good. You are on the second team."

"Shit, Dud, so are six others. That's not saying much."

"Work hard at running your routes. Keep coming back on your curls. Work on your blocking. We are looking for blockers."

We turned toward the dipping sun and started off the field, dodging a couple of recreational joggers and baby stroller as they whizzed by on the track. "Doc," he continued, "it's a long season. Have patience. Football is a violent sport and it takes a lot of players to fill a team."

We parted as we finished climbing up the short flight of stairs leading into the locker room. "Later, Dud. Thanks for the time. You know how I am. What can I do to get better?"

"Get Casey to buy you a beer. Relax! Stay healthy."

# Chapter 8

## All in the Name of Character

Offensive line coach, T.K. Walter, all 6'2" and a fluctuating 250 pounds, was a screamer with a fearsome bark, gentle bite and quick laugh. His eyes sparkled with merriment, but mostly his mirth was self-directed. He had a moon face, a crew cut, chopped off index finger from a football injury, and was always trying to lose weight. Even on the hottest days, he would show up to practice in a long sleeve City College Football sweatshirt. He would lift and play basketball during the spring with the team. He was the only coach on the team that did not spend part, or all, of their playing days at City College.

As he prowled the sideline during the game, one of T.K.'s favorite lines was to yell out loud to anyone within earshot, which was usually on the other side of campus, "It's time to build character, it's character building time. How bad do you want it!" He was concerned about his players; not only about their performance, but also about their lives. During the season, he rewarded the offensive with a barbecue every week at his house,

115

trying to build some camaraderie. "You wouldn't believe how much I spent on meat," he told me after the season was over. "Those guys ate like horses."

During the game T.K would roam the sidelines looking for disconsolate players to cheer up. He was loud, profane, and expressive and spent much of our games with his face inches away from his players, fingers pulling on the cages, screaming and swearing at the top of his lungs. "God dammit, Mike [Hives, the 350 pound tackle], you got to move your fucking feet and get a piece of that guy! Quit pussyfooting around out there and get your fucking head back into the game."

T.K. was from the hills and coal mines of Western Pennsylvania. Many college and professional players were formed in that crucible of poverty and black lung, much as coal itself was born from the pressure of tons of earth eons ago. "I saw Joe Namath play in Beaver Falls," T.K. remembered, "In fact, that was one of our biggest rilvaries. Football was king there. You played football or you were nothing."

Of all the coaches, I liked T.K. the most. He was earthy and crude at times but, underneath was a sensitive individual. Most of all, he saw that there was life beyond football. T.K. had left in the middle of the last week of the season to go hunting. He had made these plans months before and he wasn't going to break them. But somehow that didn't bother his players. T.K. had lived and died with them all season and he delivered a stirring speech to the team the day before he left.

T.K. always insisted that football built character. To T.K. it was the coach's job to not only teach his players the fundamentals of the game, but also to reach below the surface of the X's and O's and rub the player's face in the lessons of life that, to T.K., were so easy to see. "Sure, football is violent and sometimes dehumanizing, but dammit, Doc, it does build character." he said.

One evening after practice, T.K. and I stood on the field and argued back and forth about the social worth of a game like football. I was on the steering committee dealing with gender equity in the college athletic department and there was the real threat that, besides eliminating some male sports, there was going to be a cap placed on the number of football players. "Come on Doc," he said, "football needs the numbers to operate." One of the solutions being considered was to cap the number of football players at 60.

"T.K., the last two years, we ended up with less than 60 players at the end of the season. This year we started with 92 and now we have 55 players. Capping isn't really going to effect us."

"Now it won't, but what happens if we build this program up, like it should be. Now I have a daughter, too, and I want her to have all the opportunity she can if she decides to go into sports. But I think football is a different story. We can't run a program on a cap on players and right now it is hard to get by on the budget. Shit, look how much we get paid! Peanuts! We are doing this because we love the sport and we believe in it and what it brings to the kids. From football I learned about discipline, about goals, about cooperation and playing with others that were different than me. I happen to think football is a sport that helps build character and is good for the players to go through."

"I think football builds character," Joe said. "It prepares the player for the competitiveness of the world outside. Makes them strong inside as well."

Chuck also sang the praises of a violent sport. "Look at what football gives you. It prepares you for life because everything you get in life is in football; teamwork, competition, overcoming adversity, celebrating victory and fighting through defeat."

A local high school football player suffered a head injury during a game in 1996 and was rushed to the hospital and a head operation. A week later, he was released. At the local coaches' roundtable the next Monday, all of the coaches said that scores and game highlights take a back seat to the "welfare" of the player. The Carpinteria coach said even though there is danger in such a violent sport, "I love football a whole lot because of the things it can teach you. Something that happens in sports can give you a perspective on what's important in life. It gives us such an opportunity to learn how to live with one another. It's a great thing."

In *Dreams of Glory*, Judy Oppenheimer writes of a high school coach who believed that football taught you to attack life. He told his kids that football "teaches that you don't have to be the biggest and the strongest and the best to be the most successful." On the flip side, once *Sports Illustrated* columnist and author, Rick

Telander wavered, writing that his teammates at Northwestern, many now doctors, lawyers, and executives were not always proof that football made a better male. "All we proved was that Northwestern kept up its entrance requirements for this football team and we deserved to be in college," he wrote. Then there is the other side of the coin, where the good players had serious problems with society, even after leaving the sheltered campuses. For example, Telander used the case of Barry Switzer's Oklahoma Sooners to illustrate the problems that he had with players running afoul of the law on and off the field. One Oklahoma City newspaper flirted with the idea of promoting a Sooner all-time All Criminal Team. Oklahoma is no longer the only butt of jokes; it is the University of Miami and Nebraska, New Mexico State, Texas Tech; it is shootings, assaults, rape that has become commonplace in college football and also in other high-profile college sports.

The 1994 and 1995 Vaquero teams had more than just one or two players that had prior experience inside the big house. Just before the start of the 1996 season, six players from the surrounding Los Angeles County were either arrested or had some involvement in criminal activity. Jerome, along with his half-brother Josiah, was arrested for breaking and entering. Four probable starters in the secondary worked out deals with the District Attorney. Jerome and Josiah both had to serve time for parole violation.

It would be easy to follow Telander's path and place the blame on the game, but the sad fact is it wasn't the game that brought this behavior out at City College. It was something more insidious and reflective of our society, including social inequality and teen violence. Even in Santa Barbara, gangs and gang violence were common. Many of the players, especially those who came up from urban LA, were from a high school background that was steeped in violence. If anything, football and education were an attempt to give direction and provide alternatives to what many teenagers in the Santa Barbara area gave in to; a future of too-young marriages, alcoholism, drug abuse, and senseless violence. Many of the players came from rigid and strict high school football programs, and the transition from high school to college ball was easy.

Throughout the season, Ryan, Eric, David and Jeff bitched that this year was their first season of little authority and less still of

118

accountability demanded by the coaches. "It's only Coach's second year and he is still pretty inexperienced when it comes to discipline," Benjy said one day during a round table discussion with the some of the receivers about the team. "Yeah. He has to learn discipline," said Ryan. "The biggest thing is discipline. If you don't discipline your players, they won't respect you. They will run all over you if they want. The past couple of games he is getting better. He hasn't been taking that much of a "oh, I am hurt," bullshit from players. He has been kind of getting on people. He is learning. He has a lot more to learn, but he is a good coach."

"He will be that much better when he gets a few years under his belt," Eric chimed in.

"He needs to be more of a disciplined coach than a player's coach," Benjy said. "That is because he already has set up in our minds as a player's coach, as a guy who is going to kick back and joke around with the players. He shows signs of it, but it is too late now. He can change it for next year if he realizes it."

"When we went out for Hell Week, the first speech was about discipline," Ryan added, and I finished, "and remember all those rules that never made it past those walls."

"Yeah, but after that I knew what was going to happen," said Eric. "He set himself up for a fall."

"He has to do a little more coaching and less looking at the girls that run around the track during practice," Benjy chimed in.

"He needs what you were talking about earlier," said Eric.

"What's that?" asked Benjy. "To get laid," I said for him.

Granted, the lessons learned from football were predicated on a game of controlled mayhem, but to many of these players that was the only expression of life's alternatives that they could relate to. It took a strong male image to get them to not only abide by the rules of a team, but to exert discipline and control. Outside control was one of the missing elements in their lives. Conformity to regimentation and a strict adherence to rules became that missing or never before experienced control. Even school was the representation of conformity seen in classes, homework, grades and the need to take and pass a certain number of units to be able to play. College football was a process of deconstructing, constructing and reconstructing the mind of a teenager. Each year, for the coaching staff, the prime directive of the preseason was to establish an autocratic hold over 100 players.

Football was a strange mix of spontaneity and repetition, of creativity and imitation. Instinct on the turf was needed. When Torlando let his body take over and react to the opposing team, it was a thing of beauty and wonder. But, on a sweep, when the left side of the offensive line worked as unit, filling a lane, downblocking and then leading the sweep, it was also a thing of beauty; a meshing unit. Instinct is something that can't be taught. Cooperation and filling a role can be taught, must be taught, for a team to be successful. As tradition dictates, individuality only works within the concept of team. That is why coaches perceived independence as a cancer that must be exorcised and replaced with a sense of dependence on the coach, teammates, and on the team.

Using what every player has been conditioned to respond to, threat and fear, couched in the inherent violence of the sport, coaches rid the players of independence. Coaches, like drill sergeants, tear down whatever independence or individuality is visible and replace it with an overpowering sense of blind obedience. Coaches use the authority of their position to break you down, then build you up. "It is a strange ritual of the profession, handed down, I assume, from latent boot-camp influences, on the sport, as though the coaches are militaristic potters and the players mud," wrote Rick Telander.

At age 31, my brother Stephen enlisted in the Army Reserves. With a college degree in journalism from the University of Iowa, six years of newspaper reporting, and two years of teaching high school English and Journalism, he embarked on a completely different life experience. Before he departed for Fort Benning and 12 weeks of boot camp in January of 1996, we watched and laughed several times at Bill Murray's *Stripes* so he could become acquainted with the experience of complete subordination. During my last phone conversation with him before he was bused down to Fort Benning, I questioned for the umpteenth time his motivation. Finally exasperated, he blurted out that he was looking forward to losing control and independence. It was the experience of being forced to "be all he could be," both physically and mentally that attracted him. "It is the manly thing to do," he said. "I look forward to the challenge of being tested physically, but also becoming a part of well-oiled machine."

He survived boot camp and was singled out for his excellence. My mother flew down for his "graduation" and was duly impressed, but Stephen had lost some of the idealism he set out with. "I got quickly tired of the constant process of tearing you down and being insulted and demeaned and then facing the consequence of others' fucking up. The drill sergeants enjoyed humiliating us and nobody was spared their sadistic ways. I ended up hating one of them but, you know, I never really lost respect for his position."

Tongue in cheek, Chuck yelled too often, "Don't question authority. Just do what your coach says." Drills were designed to not only condition and teach, but also implicitly reinforce the power of the coach. If a drill was not done right, it was done again and again until it was. Punishment was physical and felt, therefore feared. Punishment was also mental; to be verbally undressed in front of your peers, your teammates, including those who were competing for your position, was painful to observe and excruciating to be the object. But punishment was necessary, for everyone. Simply, in a Skinnerian sense, the sting of the proverbial whip lessened with time and "reins" continually had to be readjusted, pulled tighter and then loosened. Performance increased when the process of readjustment was finely tuned; not too much, and not too little. The success of the coach is based on interpreting the correct ratio and then applying it to 100 individuals.

At some point, drill sergeants and coaches love to be hated because, in a weird sort of way, hate expresses and validates success. Oppenheimer's son's coach said, "You break' em down, so they bond together against you. That's how you get unity on the team. Then, bit by bit, you bring them back up.'"

Chuck's speech to a sequestered offensive unit at the beginning of the season was a hint of his philosophy. "We do it my way or you don't do it." Too quickly it became clear to the receivers that Dudley didn't have the personality of a whip artist. He lacked bite and, at times, even the bark. For Twuan and I, the returning players, the summer hiatus didn't change Dud and he came back his usual mellow self. It wasn't that Dud was blind to what was needed. He had been a part of successful football programs. It was the fact that Steve was unable to put into practice what he, himself,

121

had been a part of. He was too laid back. While Joe and Chuck lived and breathed football, Steve treated coaching as a job, enjoyable as it was, but one that had its place in his life. And it wasn't that Steve didn't get involved or caught up in the excitement of the game or feel the frustration of a loss. He was as animated during a game as Chuck, but during practice he would hide behind his shades and, often, I wondered what he was thinking or focusing on.

On the other hand, Joe was much like a younger Carmen, both in bark and bite. If Joe was going to live the game, his players were going to put forth the effort and play his way or hit the beach. During practice, he was constantly roving and watching and when he yelled at a player, the player listened. If he didn't listen, if he didn't put into practice what Joe wanted to see, if he dogged a drill, he was out of that drill, scrimmage or, worse yet, the game. During the two years I played, there was not one player on offense that was either kicked off the team or suspended, except for Mike Hives and Joe kicked him off. But on defense, it wasn't surprising to see or hear of a suspension or expulsion.

Joe turned maniacal in his approach during a game and was consumed by the intensity of the action. One did not plead for more playing time, nor did one offer more than a passive query concerning a different approach than what Joe called for. "Joe is the same way that Carmen is," said Mike Hayes. "They are both good coaches, they know what they are doing. My first year, I didn't like Carmen at all. He would tell you right before the game how to play. Then he would sit in the stands the whole game. I like him more now because I am not afraid to talk to him. Last year I finally said, 'screw this.' I told him, 'I want to play and I don't know what it will take to play, but I will do it.' I told him over and over again. He would say 'you will get your chance.' And when I got to play I tried just as hard as I could. I did pretty well at the end of the year last year. Both Joe and Carmen expect you to do well. That is why you are out there. If you screw up, you are out of the game. You have to make a super pick (interception) to even get a word of praise from them. Like last week when I got that interception, it was the first time Joe said good job to me. What kind of coach is that? I mean Joe and Carmen are like, okay, this is what you need to do and that is it. No questions asked. You can't tell Carmen anything."

Joe fits the mold of football coach to a tee. When talking to any of the players, after they said they hated him, most would grudgingly admit that respect lay at the foundation of their relationship with him. "I respect Coach Joe," Casey told me. "He thinks everybody is dogshit. He doesn't show favorites. You could be the star, but if you showed up late for practice or loafed, he will kick your ass. Drone told me that even he respects Coach Joe. He said, 'Coach Joe feels everybody sucks and he isn't afraid to tell you.'"

Coaches always run the risk of crossing a fine line between being a classy coach and becoming a Mussolini wannabe. The safeguard against that is the concern a coach will show toward his players off and on the field. Coaching football, even at the collegiate is a learning process, whether it be the fundamentals and tactics of the game or experiencing the social interaction that comes with four solid months of playing and living with too many other guys. Even beyond that, football instills a sense of respect for those who work hard and disdain for those who don't. And this starts with the coach (es). It is not just establishing stringent rules and doling out punishment when those rules are broken. It goes way beyond that. Respect becomes just as easily a sense of pride and feelings of satisfaction when goals are reached. Respect for the team and respect for self.

Chuck was continually preaching about reaching for goals, striving for perfection and, win or lose, coming off the field knowing you have played your best. Of course, none of us lived in a fantasy world, thinking that victory was only a way station on the way to the development of pride. To win was the ultimate goal. To lose was only made more palatable by the effort expended. Chuck never hesitated letting the player know he appreciated his efforts in practice or after a game. Of course it was a hell of a lot easier to say when the thrill of victory was still flowing through your veins. "Against Santa Monica," J.T. said, "I made a lot of mistakes. Even when I made those mistakes, he was supportive. He just doesn't look at the bad points. I look up to him for guidance in my career. I think he can help me get to the place where I want to be."

Players spend their energy on the field and trudge off after practice and games depleted, only to come back the next day.

Coaches live football. Practice is only a small fraction of the energy they spend on the game. They spend their weekends breaking down game film and watching film from the next opponent. They spend hours before and after practice blowing off steam talking about players and strategy. They vicariously experience old playing days and are forced to remain behind a white line during games that are the most intense periods any of them will ever experience. Adrenaline shoots through the coach's body for 3 1/2 hours and the only outlet is to scream, jump up and down a lot and swear. Players bleed adrenaline through playing, hitting players and running themselves into exhaustion. Coaches don't have that luxury of physical release and are still going 100 mph two hours after the game. The more time you invest, the higher you fly in victory, the harder you fall in defeat.

My involvement with football laid me open to alternative lifeviews but, much like my brother, I found myself voluntarily giving in to the chiefs and Indians mentality. Football was not a "feel good" sport. It reflected much of what goes on in our culture and, to a much larger extent, what shaped and constrained society. Like social norms and pressures, football was based on toeing the line, "play the game" so you can play in the game. My life in academics prepared me well for the two years I played. For all the talk of ivory tower and the purity of science, academics is a game of jumping through the right hoops, sucking up to the right people and listening, listening, listening. You were "guided" in your research, you were at the mercy of a chairperson and research was as much political as it was the fruition of a creative, independent thought. For all its foundation in objectivity and an age-old scientific methodology, the power of academics was subjectively tied to agendas, personnel and school of thoughts. The pursuit of knowledge was an idealistic dream. Much like anything mired in society, the actual realization and direction of that pursuit was controlled by the vagaries of human existentialism.

To step into such an anti-intellectual, physically ordained spectacle such as sport was not a stretch at all. Instead of listening to the wisdom of the power that controlled my professional life's destiny, I was listening and following the wisdom of an earthy, profane, sometimes raw coaching staff. For me, it was the wisdom pleasantly devoid of agendas and backstabbing and convoluted paths of personal gain that so fuel the machinations of academic departments. On the field, under the glare of perfectionism, words were sparse and the few uttered were loaded with meaning and emotion, ripping through bullshit of give and take. There was no room for alternate views of reality. There was only one way and that was their way. I accepted the crap ladled out to us that was piggybacked on the Xs and Os of the game, such as the socialization of a masculine identity and the reinforcement of perceived gender inequity and all the other "social functions" of sport that seem to support the current gender order. It was nice to see the future so clearly and set with simple objectives like win, play hard and win some more.

I didn't buy into all that the feminists scream about, but I encountered much of gender dysfunction that was easily seen and felt during my time in football; the debasement of women, gays and the ritualistic tearing down of a player's identity. Like any individual with half a brain, a very independent mother with a master's degree and three sisters who could best me at sport and get straight As, I knew the real gender order and I was somewhere near the bottom. It was the game, the bonding of same-centered souls, the high of victory and even the low of defeat that dragged me through the human sewage of chauvinist pigs and the rantings of super radical feminists. Miami is probably the murder capital of the nation. If I relocated to Dade County, does that make me a murderer? I played football and will miss it with a passion when it is gone from my life. Does that make me a rotten male?

# Chapter 9

---

Hell Week Nights
Living Under the Influence of Women,
Power and other Illegal Substances

E ven at night, football was king. Males were all-powerful, and women were the spoils. One night, I went over to the apartment of Jarrett, linebacker Jacob Lombard, and Casey. We watched the Tom Cruise movie, *All the Right Moves* about high school football in Pennsylvania. We sucked down Lowenbrau and created our own sound track, talking and yelling about high school experiences. Mine were much fuzzier. During the one sex scene, where Casey claimed you could see Cruise's penis, Casey rewound and played the same scene over and over. After at least ten times, there was unanimous agreement that, yes, you could see part of Tom Cruise's penis.

Football, sex, aggression, and power; there just seems to be a correlation. College football and cheerleaders, college football and partying, college football and sex. Of course, lately, it has been college football and rape, college football and theft, college football and sexual assault, college football and whatever else is wrong with our society. All I know is that, for Hell Week, the world

126

is a safe place from football players. They just don't have any energy.

In our small culture of football players, sex, like sport, became a means of competition and crowning the male libido. No score was kept, but the players gave the play by play and the images were vivid and graphic. To some, females became objects of domination like the inside backer who crushed blockers to rack up the ball carrier or quarterback. "The pursuit of dominance lies at the heart of all athletic contests," Todd Crossett said in *Sports Illustrated*, "and it happens to be the dominating force behind men who batter their wives and girlfriends."

Rick Telander, in his book, *The Hundred-Yard Lie*, saw the same kind of mentality of sex and dominance in college football. "I have heard so much degrading talk of women by male athletes...that I feel certain the macho attitudes promoted by coaches contribute (perhaps unwittingly) to athletes' problems in relating to women."

Show them who is boss. Dominate and decimate, peel away the defense, divide and then conquer. Validation only came in the public display of behavior. What does it mean if it doesn't become spectacle? Does it count when it goes unacknowledged? So what if you fucked her Saturday night; if nobody is aware of your conquest, where is the gratification? "She wanted it and I gave it to her," and you make sure everybody within earshot knows what happened. Really, there should be no surprise over all of this. Audience accelerates, even provides, a forum for public consumption of "maleness."

Does sport create or foster an environment that spawns such behavior and feelings? Possibly, yet the nature of our society, the role and identity of women in black or Hispanic society, defined in music and film, and consumed by whites as well, is one of male frustration and discontent with the chipping away of what once was the male kingdom. Sally Jenkins, in *Men Will Be Boys*, referred to this perception of the male athlete as "misogynist" and laid blame to a "deadly testosterone buildup." She quoted Boomer Esiason as saying, "In certain football players, violent tendencies are going to be there, whether they play the game or not. Does football accentuate that behavior off the field? No. It's about the person, not the sport.... You'll find that 98% of the men in the NFL are gentlemen who treat women and their families with great respect. It's an unfortunate stereotype."

Jenkins went on to say that the problem wasn't the violent men in football. "Common sense dictates that football is not the culprit as much as the excessive celebration of it. Steroid abuse, binge drinking, rape banter, the pressure by coaches to be tough, mixed messages of groupies, exalted status and an exaggerated sense of entitlement from years of being let off the hook, recruited by sorority hostesses, and tossed freebies—those are the things that cause sexually violent behavior. Not blocking and tackling."

Kids today learn it at home, in school, and on the streets. To them, this is the shape of real life. Women are another stepping stone to the acquisition of power, and power is only power when it is acknowledged and accepted. Using the published confessions of Vance Johnson, accused of spousal abuse during the 1990-1991 season, Jenkins saw a similar correlation between power and violence against women, "Violence against women is about power and entitlement..."

"To me it's less about the football field," Johnson wrote in his book, "than it is about power issues. Look, I've got 76,000 people watching me every weekend. Women flock to me. I go to a restaurant and I get the best table, and everyone wants my autograph. The owner picks up the check. Then I go home and my wife treats me like just another guy. So I lash out to assert my power."

In the fall of 1994, three City College students, two of them athletes, were charged with sexual assault and rape. All three were incidents of what is commonly labeled as "acquaintance rape." All three incidents revolved around alcohol. Counselors at SBCC and University of California, Santa Barbara (UCSB) were quoted in the local paper as saying that these cases represented only the tip of the iceberg. Many rapes go unreported and leave the victim emotionally traumatized for years later.

Wrote Alisa DelTuffo, research fellow at the Institute for Child, Adolescent and Family Studies in Manhattan, "Men who need to be in control of their environment in order to feel O.K. about themselves have a problem with domestic violence and rape is a crime of violence and aggression, very rarely one of passion."

Women, it seems, are to be used, even abused, dominated and

then tossed when their usefulness has worn out. I had a chance to talk to one of the victims as she fought through the system and courts, all the while dealing with the emotional baggage such as guilt and loss of self-image. It disrupted her life and wrecked her semester. At the same time, the guy's life was permanently socially disfigured, labeled for the rest of his life as a sexual criminal, and included jail time. Nobody gets away with anything, and everybody loses.

This isn't a sport thing. It is something deeper and more Machiavellian. Sports, like football, props up the myth of the invincibility of the competitor, the "player," even promotes such behavior. But sport doesn't create this myth. As many or more players at City College roll through their academic and collegiate sport experience and are not effected by this alternate reality. They have normal, or what can pass as normal, relationships, have girlfriends, lose girlfriends, gain girlfriends and pass through this rite of passage, determined to enjoy the experience without emotional attachment.

Sport is perhaps best described as a vehicle for culture. Sport is a mirror or reflection of society. So why should it be a surprise to people and researchers that what we find in social reality outside of sport can also be found inside sport? James Baldwin wrote on male sexual identity, "The American ideal of sexuality appears to be rooted in the American ideal of masculinity. This ideal has created cowboys and Indians, good guys and bad guys, punks and studs, tough guys and softies.... It is an ideal so paralytically infantile that it is virtually forbidden, as an unpatriotic act, that an American boy evolve into the complexity of manhood."

Todd Crossett argued that just because sexually abusive and violent behavior against women is found in the larger society, that alone shouldn't be used by, what Sally Jenkins refers to as the "apologists," the NCAA and NFL, to "duck" responsibility of curbing the excess. "The standard song and dance is 'Things are bad all over and we're no worse than anybody else,'" Jenkins quoted Crossett as saying. "To me that, that's an abdication of responsibility. There is violence against women in every community, and in each one it's slightly different.... Athletes are obliged to address the problem, the same way they ought to address the problem of concussions or knee injuries, and they don't have to wait for the egghead social scientists to do it."

The year 1996 saw Michael Irvin, star receiver of the Dallas Cowboys, involved in not one, but two altercations involving drugs and sexual assault. The same year also featured two NFL expansion teams star in the NFL playoffs and, not coincidentally, both head coaches were young and strict disciplinarians, not afraid to kick players off for violating team policy and the law. Tim Green, ex NFL lineman, and now NFL analyst for *Public Broadcast Radio* and *ABC* said, "The only way you get kicked off Barry Switzer's team is if you are taken away in handcuffs."

Nebraska Head Coach Tom Osborne's decision not only to reinstate running back Lawrence Phillips, but to let him play in the 1995 Orange Bowl, after being investigated, charged and convicted of sexual assault against a former girlfriend during that season, was ludicrous. The obvious message Dr. Osborne, a Ph.D. in education and dean of college coaches, sent was loud and clear. Being good elevates you above the law. Osborne's trite absolving of his star player's behavior rested on Phillips' difficult childhood as an orphan. Society failed Phillips; therefore, his behavior must make him a victim, as well. Osborne is a spin doctor, too.

Another night during Hell Week, the boys and I watched *North Dallas Forty*. "Come on pardner, learn to play the game. If you didn't have the best pair of hands in the league, I would let them have you," Mac Davis told Nick Nolte. "You got to learn to play their game." Around them, Joe Bob is blowing cows out of the fields. "This film is awesome; rad," said Casey, as we listened to Davis espouse some trite cliches about playing the game. Thiessen lay on the couch with a pounding headache. Jarrett Thiessen was from Santa Maria. He was not big, 6'2"; maybe 215, but he loved to hit. Square jawed, short dirty-blonde hair with a wisp of fuzz on his chin, he roamed the field like a missile waiting to be launched. Which belied the fact that when he was not on the field, he was a laid-back couch potato, storing his energy for assaults on ball carriers. Jarrett played monster back and was super strong after spending all summer in the weight room. Jarret was still not that big, especially in our conference where 250-300 pound offensive linemen were not the exception, but the norm.

Santa Maria is an hour northwest of Santa Barbara on the 101

130

and is everything Santa Barbara isn't; blue collar, agricultural, teeming with migrant workers and, worse yet, inland. Jarrett brought with him the small town prejudices of those who weren't like him, such as Mexicans and blacks. Jarrett was also like Mel Brooks; everybody was fair game, from surfers and to hippies. He didn't discriminate solely on the basis of race or cultural affinity. Thiessen's main concern was that players produce on the field. "I don't care whose black or Mexican or whatever," he said. "If they come out and suck or not try hard, fuck 'em. I don't give a shit who they are." Thiessen then spat a brown stream of lumpy juice. "Fuck'em."

Thiessen loved country music and drove a fire red Ford Ranger pick-up and would be at home in Montana. His decision to come to City College was not based on SAT scores, as he scored over 750, but on proximity, his dislike of Hancock College in Santa Maria and one of our main rivals, and that a former teammate from St. Joseph's also went here.

Jarrett was one of those few individuals who could laugh at himself. For two years he was in love/lust with a women's basketball player at SBCC, but for a while she didn't know or cared if Jarrett existed. She moved back to Northern California after Thiessen's first year and he would call her up and get frustrated over the relationship. "Bitch," he would yell after slamming down the phone after a go nowhere discussion. "She probably doesn't like me because of my small penis. I can't find it at times."

Thiessen roomed with Casey, Jake Lombard, a sometimes starting backer, and two Hawaiians, Cliffie and Johnny, who slept on the couches because they were light on cash for rent. Five were jammed in an apartment big enough for 2 1/2 football players. Two televisions, a huge bank of stereo equipment, two VCRs and video games covered the main wall in the living room. I would go over and watch football games on ESPN after practice, drink beer, shoot the shit about the team, and talk to Thiessen about defense. Always, there was the ever-present Domino's Pizza. In the month of September 1995, the apartment ordered pizza 24 out of the 30 days. "Doc, I'll tell you, we order 50 pizzas, we get the next one free," Casey told me one night while we were chowing down on a pepperoni Big Foot. "How rad is that?"

Underneath the football player's façade, Jarrett was bright with a sharp football mind and was a good observer of human behavior. Toward the end of the 1995 season, Tony Coffey, the black defensive back, took to spending a lot of time at the apartment. Tony lived with his mother and sister a couple of blocks away. He would sit on the couch watching the moving images on the screen and listening for his beeper to go off. To Thiessen and the other roommates, Tony wasn't really "black." He played too hard to be labeled. He was just Coffey. Tony also had some Indian blood and his mother would, on the weekends, strap on a pair of roller skates and take a big boombox over to the pier. Wearing short shorts and a halter, she would skate in circles for the passers-by.

With the usual five or six guys sitting around on couches when I was over, the topic of conversation was limited to sports and girls; both pursued with ardent fervor. It was funny. The girls they would chase and get shut off by or maybe "score" on would be the same girls they would call on the phone and spend hours talking to or would come over, drink beer and sit and talk about the football, school and who was doing who. It was a weird kind of symbiotic relationship; girls and guys would feed on each other. None of the apartment dwellers was or had been involved in any type of substantive relationships and I never had to wonder why.

Jarrett and the others built a wall of feigned indifference concerning girls that could easily evolve into hurt and anger over the relationships. Adding to Jarrett's wall was his public comments about his facetious sexual shortcomings, his inability to get laid and the amount of time he spent "whacking off." Most of this was self-effacing bullshit and designed to put off deeper conversations that would require opening up and letting those closest know how he felt. Like the others, Jarrett's comments were artificial and a sure sign that deeper feelings were alive and kicking. Discussion concerning girls and women were brutal and frank. Most girls were bitches, sluts, whores, superficial, objects of derision, to be used and discarded before they reached out and clipped "your balls," or worse yet, reduced you to a sniveling, whimpering, love-sick, emasculated rodent.

Hormones always ran at a fever pitch and would ignite in a turbo-charged, vivid cacophony of words that covered more heartfelt feelings. With the expectations and pressures of football and the added stress of academics for many of the players who were not good students, a release valve was needed. That was why nights were spent watching one TV screen with *Monday Night Football*, or any college game during the week, and Joe Montana's *Sagagenesis* video game on the other. Beers were in everybody's hands and talk drifted around and over Dan Dierdorf's nasal whine, who everybody agreed didn't know shit.

Jarrett didn't really need to speak much to exert his leadership. His actions spoke volumes. Every game, Joe and the defensive coaching staff would grade him out as one of the highest. On Sundays, when I would go over and catch the Chicago Bears, he would sit sunken in the couch, a blanket around his spent body, and only a voice would emerge from the inert clump. Only half listening to the game and glancing every now and then at Jake play the entire NFL on the video screen, we would replay our Saturday game, play by play.

"I suck," he would usually say. "I am just not playing like I should. I am not making tackles, not playing off the fucking blocks and I just feel slow." He kept betting me that he could take me in the 40 (yard dash). At one time the bet stood at $100, but we never got the opportunity. He wasn't slow, but quickness can only be improved so far. Genes ultimately determine just how fast you can be.

"I got my first headache this season," he said triumphantly as I walked in to the apartment the night of the *North Dallas Forty* screening during Hell Week. "I got it from hitting a running back this afternoon. And it is a bad one. It's about time. I am a fucking linebacker."

"Thiessen, why not smoke a bong? It's a legal pain reliever now," Casey chided him from the floor, where he was laying looking up at the television screen. Thiessen turned and caught my eye as if warning me it was coming, giving me an out if I wanted it. I simply added, "I hear it works wonders for glaucoma patients."

"What's glaucoma, Doc," asked Cliffie from the far reaches of the living room where he settled in after practice and hadn't moved since. Clifford didn't move unless he had to. He was around 6 feet and maybe 260 pounds, rotund and dark skinned. His black hair was pulled back into a tiny ponytail. He played offensive-line and started the year before as a freshman. He was one of three Hawaiians that migrated to City College last year. The other two were a back-up quarterback who played sparingly and Johnny, a strong safety.

Johnny loved to "lay the helmet" and wasn't happy unless he was busting somebody during scrimmage. Originally from Samoa, where his father was an air traffic controller, Johnny's parents now live on Oahu. Johnny had a square jaw and, like Cliffie, jet-black hair. His teeth flashed against the olive complexion and tufts of facial hair sprouted from his chin and upper lip. Johnny wasn't big, maybe 6'1 and 200 pounds soaking wet, didn't even look that athletic and even moved less than Cliff around the apartment or at school, but when he stepped on the field, he changed from a comatose college student to a human piledriver. Johnny started last year at receiver, but after a few gut-busting runs over defensive players and savage blocks in practice and the first couple of scrimmages, Joe "borrowed" him indefinitely and moved him to safety.

Last year, the Hawaiians lived a block up the hill from campus and would wait around after practice for somebody to give them a ride home. They never really left Hawaii where the motto was "why do it," especially if requires body movement. Both Cliffie and Johnny were insatiably curious, wanting to know where I was going to or coming from when our paths crossed on campus or in the gym. They loved to ask me questions on anything that crossed their minds, as if I was Mr. Wizard or Carl Sagan.

"It's a degenerative eye disease and grass releases some of the tension headaches that result from the disease," I said. "Awesome," said Casey. Appropriately, while Nolte was toking around the pool at the big blowout party, Thiessen disappeared into his room, returning with the biggest bong I had ever seen and a plastic baggie of grass. The bong could have doubled as a pole vault pole.

"You want some, Doc?" Thiessen asked as he packed the bowl. "Nah, thanks, but no thanks." Actually, I had spent much time thinking about whether I wanted to be placed in the position of smoking with the guys during the season. Drinking was one thing, doing grass an entirely different matter. It wasn't that I was horrified at pot or grass use. I did my share while in college. I wasn't passing judgment on it, far from it. I was rationalizing that, as an instructor, it wouldn't look good if I smoked with students.

This dilemma was one of the problems of doing this kind of anthropology. There are some situations where I couldn't cross the line blurring "native" and researcher. I had to participate, but how much did I have to participate was the ethical and moral dilemma. When in Rome... Obviously, Hunter S. Thompson would not only have smoked with the guys; he would probably have supplied half the team with grass, the other half with cocaine.

Drug use on the team was no different than the rest of the student population. I knew some of the guys last season that did coke, as well, and god knows what other kind of drugs, but it is the exception, not the rule, when you find a student who doesn't at least drink or smoke pot. Thiessen lit up and sucked a huge lungful of smoke. The familiar acrid sweet aroma settled around the room. The bong went to Casey and relaxation was in high gear.

"Wait, guys," Casey said drawing our attention, "this next scene is the most awesome. It's where Nick Nolte and Mac Davis sit around the training room drinking Bud relaxing in the whirlpool, after breaking into the medicine cabinet and snarfing down a bunch of pills. And then they go into the weight room. While everybody else is lifting, they sit around drinking beer and smoking. Rad." We all watched the scene unfold, agreeing that was the way to go. "Wouldn't it be great if we had a keg of Bud in the training room, especially after practice?" Casey asked nobody in particular.

Casey claimed he was named after the great Yankee and New York Met manager Casey Stengel. No longer eligible to play, Casey helped Pat Aguilera in the cage handing out equipment. Casey had just turned 21 and was the average junior college student. The 1995 season was his fifth semester and he still had at least two more semesters left before he moved on to a four-year school to finish out. Casey was big and blonde and had played both the defensive and offensive line. He was nowhere close to being dumb, but he suffered from a self-image problem. Too many of his friends called him stupid and I had to admit that, at times, Casey lacked some common sense. Underneath the veneer of irresponsibility, Casey was bright. "Don't call me stupid," he told me. "I am not stupid."

He and I went to at least one movie matinee a week and we loved to sit around afterwards at O'Malley's or the Brickyard and talk about the films. I kept telling Casey his future was in film. I would tell him, why not combine what you like to do with your future. Casey lacked drive and kept telling me his idea of a job was like his father's, a supervisor in the Ventura Recreation Department, where he played a lot of golf and drank a lot of beer. Casey doesn't play golf, but is a major leaguer in the suds department. There were times I just wanted to shake him until his eyes rolled up into his forehead and some responsibility seeped through and registered in his expression.

The bong had made several circuits of the room, missing Cliffie over in the corner. Cliffie stoned would be a medical miracle. How close to actual death can one get and still breathe? Thiessen claimed his headache was gone. I even had a light buzz going from the secondary smoke that shrouded the room. I was bushed and needed my sleep. Last day of double days was tomorrow. I slid out on a bluish-green cloud of happy, contented people.

# *Chapter 10*

---

## Crossroads

**KIST**

*The kickoff taken by Mike Hayes at the 5. Hayes, the former Bishop Diego Cardinal is up to the 20, 25 and is pushed back a couple of yards, so for the second straight time, Santa Barbara City College will start from their own 24.*

The air had been let out of our sails by the methodical march of the Renegades. We needed to gather some momentum of our own to defuse the likely Bakersfield rout. With our offense, it was always a possibility that in one or two plays we could even the score. We lived and died on the pass; on many occasions this season, snakebitten, we had come from behind with quick strikes. We were at one of many crossroads that no doubt would appear in this game. Would we deal with adversity and charge back, or lay over and go belly up?

"Let's play our game," Chuck shouted to the offense as they trotted back onto the field. Torlando went with them, making his first appearance in the game. As Torlando calmly lined up in formation, I could see him check the play formations taped to his wristband on a plastic card. Here we were in the tenth game of the season and Torlando had yet to learn the offense. It wasn't a question of was he able; It was a question of did he want to. Since Torlando rarely finished practice or took part in drills or scrimmage, he didn't get the repetition and experience with the play list. Up until recently in the season, Torlando would always line up on the near hash mark and Chuck or Dudley would be able to tell Torlando what had been called.

"Come on, Torlando, get off the ball!" yelled Garret Ware, standing next to me on the sidelines. Garret was an ex-Vaquero receiver and now Dudley's assistant. He turned to me said, "Shit, if he just learned the fucking plays and applied himself, he would be unstoppable. Even now, most teams can't stop him." Garret helped Dudley everyday in practice, throwing routes and standing around during drills and scrimmage, giving Dudley somebody to order around.

Garret was only 22 and still pretty lean, about 6'1", maybe 180, carrying about 10 extra pounds from when he played, short hair, almost military in length and an engaging smile. He was taking classes at SBCC and UCSB and was five quarters away from a degree in sociology. He had played receiver three years ago and caught seven balls his sophomore year. "God, I miss playing, Doc," he told me during the season. "I miss the pads, the adrenaline rush, the hanging with the guys. My last year, I got hurt and didn't have a full season. I want it back now more than ever, but I can't. It was gone before I knew it," he said. Sport is a roller coaster ride that goes way too fast while you are on and then, when your ride is over, your mind is still on the rails, even though your body is slouched on a bench eating popcorn and peanuts and quaffing beer.

Garret was from Fresno and had already passed through several crossroads, such as football, his future and, of course, women. Halfway through the season an ex-girlfriend had contacted Garret from out of the past. Garret had slept with her once his senior year in high school and then she started going out with somebody else and became pregnant. Garret assumed that the child was the other guy's and lost contact, only talking to her infrequently when he went home and hearing about her through friends. Five years passed with both chasing separate lives.

A couple of months ago, after breaking up with her boyfriend,

138

she called Garret and told him she thought he was the father of her daughter and wanted him to take a paternity test. "Shoot, I mean, just a couple of weeks ago, fatherhood was not even in my mind, now I could be one," he said when he finished explaining the story to me while sitting in the sun on a stadium bench before a practice.

"You want to see a picture of her?" he asked, " I got one right here." Gingerly, he pulled it out of his wallet and I saw a small blonde smiling face. "She said that she always thought that the baby looked like me. Man, you can tell." I had doubts about what the mother was trying to do, but I know entering fatherhood, whether it be with a squalling infant or a five year old, brings it's own rush and I didn't want to spoil it for Garret. That was going to come later with financial obligations and responsibility. Too bad I didn't have a cigar.

"You know, I am leaning toward ROTC at UCSB, making the military my life for awhile, maybe the army," he said, while we watched a blonde go past us doing stadiums. "I kind of like that lifestyle." Garret would do well in a structured and focused military environment such as the football team he was a part of years ago. "Dudley has taught me about receiving and the team, " he continued, "but he just doesn't have a lot of control nor does he really help motivate his players. He just isn't that type of personality. Practices are always the same. Not much opportunity to advance if you are not one of the first team."

"So what the hell would you do different?" I asked.

"I would have more one-on-one drills and chances to run with the ball after catching it. Christ, that is a big part of being a receiver. Make it be fun for the players. Football should be fun. There are too many dead periods for a lot of the team during our practices. We have such good talent, but it is wasted in the persons of Art, Twuan and Torlando. They are so lazy! They need your attitude, the 'Doc' attitude. You go out and give 100% all the time. If anything, hopefully the young players will pick up on it, but I think it is too late for guys like Torlando. Dud is always saying, 'you guys going to let an almost 40-year-old man lead you around? Come on, someone else step up to help Doc.'"

"We don't have any consistency," I said. "I know we are going to be crushed by Santa Monica (the game that weekend) if we don't watch it. It could be pretty ugly."

"What it is, we don't have any leaders to stand up and shape these guys up," Garret replied. "To yell at them and make them toe the line. Dud sure doesn't have that kind of relationship with them." We chatted a little more about the team and then I had to leave for weights. I got up and started the climb up the 32 remaining stadium stairs. At the top I turned and looked back across the harbor and Leadbedder Beach to the islands and beyond. Another picture post card day. Garret was still sitting on the bleacher seats and looking as two more girls jogged by. Instant father caught in a college mindset. His life had reached a fork and he didn't know which way to go. But then, he is just like the other 10,000 students at SBCC. What do I want to do with my life when I grow up? Some just grow up faster. One month later Garret's blood test was positive and he joined the rank of single parents.

The next play Torlando, must have read his wrist card right and ran the correct route as he, the defensive back, and the ball all showed up at the same time 20 yards downfield. With Chuck, Dudley, Garrett and Torlando all yelling for defensive pass interference, the yellow flag came sailing through the air, igniting a little spark in our hearts.

### KIST

*Stone on first down, flushed out of the pocket, fires for Bolden. Torlando wants a flag at the 32 and he is going to get it! Big rush coming in by Jerome Simpkins the outside backer, forced Stone immediately out of the pocket and the flag came out late. Bolden leaped high in the air at the 32. Single coverage and it looks at though they are going to get Kenny Calvin with interference. A big break for Santa Barbara. This game like the 1993 game, where 5 times Santa Barbara was inside the Bakersfield 30 in the first half and only came up with 7 points.*

Garret turned to me and laughed in the joy of the moment, despite his thoughts on Torlando. "He is also fucking awesome when he wants to be!" he yelled at me, shaking my shoulder pads. On the field, Torlando took two steps toward J.T, listened for the play and then walked back to his position split wide 10 yards from us on the sidelines, the quintessential picture of the lonesome end.

Four receivers set up on the opposite side. Dependent on only J.T.'s ability to get him the ball, everything was up to him and that is the way Torlando liked it. Rely on nobody; in the long run, somebody would always screw you over. The Bakersfield back moved up close and waited for Torlando to get off the ball so he could chuck him once, slow him down so he couldn't get into his pattern. Torlando looked straight ahead, his polarized Darth Vader facemask hiding his thoughts and offering his defender no idea as to his first movement. Torlando took a quick step to the outside and then crossed back over, leaving his defender chucking air, and set sail downfield.

## KIST

*Four receivers to the near side, Bolden the single receiver far side. J.T. rolls that way flushed out of the pocket once again, being chased by Justin Jones. Gets rid of it and the pass complete at the 25-yard line! What a catch by Bolden! First down Santa Barbara. A gain of 14 yards. A spectacular catch by Torlando Bolden! First and ten, Santa Barbara from the 25-yard line.*

Even Art joined the celebrations on the sidelines, after that catch. As much as personalities determine friendships and cliques on the team, for the time of a game, when the team rolled, for the time of a game, friction dissolves, replaced by the common goal of victory. Torlando was carrying us to the Promised Land and we would let him carry us as far as he could go, with no questions asked.

J.T. was hot. His passes were finding the mark and Bakersfield was having a hard time trying to cover six Vaquero receivers. They couldn't mount an effective blitz as J.T. would roll out of the pocket, throwing on the run, his long legs leaving the blitzing Bakersfield lineman sucking air. Chuck was in his element, plays succeeding and his face was alive with the excitement of J.T.'s aerial circus.

"Let's take him on the ground," he told his headset and those around.

"Whaddid you call?" asked Dudley.

"Quarterback draw," Chuck answered over his shoulder, to Dudley, to the receivers, to the seagulls circling overhead, to the ghosts of LaPlaya.

**KIST**

*7:23 left here in the first quarter. Stone takes it himself on the quarterback draw to the 30, 25, 20,15 J.T. down at the 10 yard line. First and goal Santa Barbara! That is one way to change up the defense. A gain of 18. First time today for J.T. on the quarterback draw and completely fooled the left side of the Renegade line. A wide-open hole and J.T. exploits it.*

Two plays later, Twuan took it in from the one-yard line and suddenly we were in a dogfight, tied 7-7 with the fifth ranked team in the country.

# Chapter 11

---

## In Death, Life Goes on

The morning marine layer was breaking; scattered patches of fog were being chased away by the sun. By the 1 p.m. kickoff of our season opener with Los Angeles, three hours away, nothing but blue skies would reign over the Santa Barbara beaches. I left the locker room and the not yet awake yawning players stumbling in, and made my way across the parking lot to the walk that led up to the West Campus and the vast lawn that looked out over Leadbedder Beach and the marina. I was dressed in a City College football tee shirt and shorts and some flipflops. I would start getting my football gear on in another hour or two. As noon approached, my mind and body would begin its journey from coffee-jumped to 210 volt, electric-zapped football-jumped. But for now, I could still taste my morning hit of Vanilla Nut Java. As I began the steep climb up the 100-meter sidewalk, my mind wasn't on patterns or blocking assignments. It wasn't doing its usual fantasy of scoring touchdowns. Not even imaging, against my will, passes rolling off my fingers and nobody within miles defending me.

No, my thoughts were on the tragedy of a 21-year-old daughter being told by her father that she was going to be taken off of life support to die. As I climbed that sidewalk leading appropriately heavenward, my mind was also on the cruel twist of fate that in less than a year also takes a wife and son from a husband and loving father. There was a surreal quality about the morning that left my mind wandering outside of my body, as if there wasn't any reality to anchor it while being tossed about by evocative memories that produced shock and sadness.

I was climbing the walk to be a part of a memorial service for Vicki Paulsen, daughter of Robin Paulsen, head cross county and track and field coach for Santa Barbara City College. Last spring, I ran for Robin as a sprinter. He had spent the last weeks, since the funeral, gathering old photographs and preparing the service. Vicki had been on life support after both lungs collapsed from a swimming pool accident. She had been cognizant of life swirling around her in the hospital. Her body was on support machinery, but her mind was alive. Vicki had muscular dystrophy and, in the not-so-good times, was frequently medicated to control seizures. Vicki was also a familiar face around the track and went to a school run through Santa Barbara City College. After her day was over, she would come and patiently sit in Robin's office until his day was done and they could go home. Bobbie, Robin's wife, worked as a nurse and often Robin had Vicki in the afternoon. Some days Vickie would be vivacious. Other days, full of medication, she would be in a daze, just hanging around the edges. Vicki talked slow, but despite the drugs, a fire burned in her and she responded well to others. People took away much more than they gave after spending time with her. Not too long ago, Robin had purchased a trailer that was converted into a rolling paperback bookstore they pulled to Saturday flea markets. Vicki was in charge of collecting and selling the books and it gave her a sense of purpose.

I emerged at the top of the walk and, as the vast West Campus lawn opened up, Vicki lived again for one more day. Huge poster boards were filled with treasured shots of her childhood and teenage years. A podium was set up for Robin to deliver the eulogy. One of the more vivid images that I took from this last month of football was not of football, but of Robin. Right before the August practices were to begin, I stopped one morning to talk with Joe and found Robin typing away on Joe's computer. He swiveled in his chair to meet me. His eyes were red and sagging underneath were bags hung like balloons. His voice was soft and filled with personal agony. Robin was typing up her memorial service. Nothing could be done as she lay in an induced paralysis in a local hospital. Tubes snaked into both collapsed lungs, pumping oxygen in and making lungs and internal organs fibrous, hard and alien to the human condition.

A month before the 1995 season began she had a seizure while swimming and Robin pulled her out of the pool with a collapsed lung. She went into the hospital and the second lung collapsed and then, from there, it was mostly downhill with only a few small victories along the way. Immediately, she was put on life support. Robin and Bobbi lived at the hospital and Vicki's older brother and sister were up a lot, but they finally conceded that Vicki had taken a permanent turn for the worse and it was only a matter of time.

"What's new, Robin?" I asked.

"It will be only a couple of days, now. Her white blood cell count is off the scale. I guess we are waiting for some kind of closure so her sister and brother can get up here this weekend and say their good-byes. Then I am going to have a talk with Vicki to tell her what to expect and that we love her."

Robin and Bobbie were faced with a terrible decision that nobody should ever have to make. If they took her off life support, she would die within hours. She would have lived only a brief life compared to her life that she could have led. Compounding the agony was that Vicki was still alert. Though paralyzed she knew what was happening around her. Her brain was not damaged. So Robin was faced with the task of talking to Vicki to tell her that she would die. I found myself sitting and thinking about the situation a lot that month and wondered if there was anything else that would strike as deep into the human soul and rip the fabric of being alive.

"I am sorry," sounded weak and trite as it came out of my mouth, but I didn't know what else to say. However, inside my brain, what was happening cut deep inside and Robin and his wife became the most courageous people on earth. I couldn't imagine having to sit down and tell my son that he was going to die, when he could still see the beauty of the world around him, still hear the sounds of the music he listened to, still feel the touch of my flesh as I held him.

"I am just typing my thoughts into the computer that I am going to say at her service," he said.

In less than an hour, I was going to be lifting weights and then running sprints on the infield, experiencing the joy of feeling my legs as they flew over the ground, while Robin was still going to be here, experiencing the pain and sadness of dying. In between his fingers somehow finding the right keys to put meaning behind his thoughts, I sat for a minute or two and we talked. And then I left him to his torture, leaving death behind for now.

It seemed like hundreds of people milled around the posters set up on a promontory of the West campus. Vicki and, by proxy, Robin and Bobbie, had been involved in Special Olympics and I was sure that many of those that came to celebrate Vicki's life were also involved. I spotted Chuck on the periphery, along with Carmen, Joe and other coaches. The game just hours away, for a while, was shuffled to the back of the deck.

All last week, practice carried with it an excitement of new beginning. We were coming out of four weeks of pre-season hell and could finally take a bead on somebody other than each other for our motivation. Los Angeles Harbor College had made the drive up and, from the perch on West Campus, Harbor's chartered buses were already parked disgorging their passengers. Our offense stuttered during last week's practice. Receivers dropped too many balls and ran the wrong routes, but the defense played inspired during our daily scrimmages.

Chuck spoke at length each day that week, "Take a knee and listen," Chuck said so many times that I felt like a Catholic. On Thursday, after the completion of a lackluster practice, out came another speech. "You guys played like horseshit today." We did. Receivers dropped balls and defensive guys missed assignments. "If you guys don't pull your heads out of your asses, you are going to get beat Saturday. They are going to come out and take it to you. They are rough and physical. After our game with Harbor last year, they had a fight among themselves and the cops had to be called in. Do not respond to their bullshit. Not one of my players is going to get in a fight. You get up and take it back to the huddle and then get him the next play. Football is great because it gives you the chance to get even, but you do it between the whistles and the lines and you do it with class. The Santa Barbara way!" Chuck's anxiety over the first game was evident as he fretted over J.T.'s throwing mechanics and drilled him incessantly during practice on play calling.

As I walked among the posters and Vicki's smiling face reached out to me, football that was consuming in its intensity and draining in its need for energy was beaten back by the realities of living and dying outside the confines of a 100 by 54-yard rectangle. As much as the ceremony was to mark the passing of woman-child, there was also a mood of quiet celebration, for Vicki had brought much joy to her parents and those around her. As I talked to those I knew who were also a part of Vicki's life, I remembered last season's reality-break supplied by the sudden and unforgiving lash of fate. It struck much closer to home and knifed through the coaches and players' minds and hearts, leaving all of us stunned and shocked.

In the fall of 1994, running backs coach Mark Johnson was a happily married man with two sons and a pretty wife, Cindy. On Friday, October 13, 1994, Cindy was in transit with her father to Las Vegas for a family reunion. Mark and his two sons stayed in Santa Barbara as we played Chaffey College the next day. Her father was driving as they took California 126 from Ventura to Interstate 5. It is a winding, two-lane road to Filmore and Santa Paula through a valley of agriculture with a couple of miles that have cliff faces on both sides. It is scenic with mountains rising dramatically in the background. It also is a road of death. Outside of Filmore, as they drove through the cliff faces, a rock kicked up by a passing truck came bounding down the highway. With no time for the father to avoid the oncoming danger, the rock crashed into the passenger side, instantly killing Mark's wife and leaving her father mostly unscathed.

Some things that happen in your lifetime, you will never forget. They are etched forever in your mind and soul. The day my father died is one. I will remember coming home from work and stepping up to the apartment my wife and I shared, thinking how I was going to get over to my parent's house in time to make nine holes with my retired father. And then I opened the door and Julie, my wife, met me, crying. The next minute is always with me.

"Rob, I have some bad news for you and I can't tell you any other way," Julie said through tears. "Your father died this morning on his walk with your Mom. They think it was a heart attack."

It didn't register at first, but the news somehow fought its way through my consciousness and suddenly my world changed forever. I ran through the rooms, needing to do something physical, trying to get away from the intense pain that flooded through my heart. I ended up in the bedroom, beating our mattress and pillows and crying, with no sound coming out. "No! no!" I kept mouthing. "It can't be!" But it was.

That October 13 is another etched memory. I walked into the locker room to get ready for our brief offensive runthrough in preparation for the game the next evening. I could tell something was up. None of the coaches were around. Joe was gone and there wasn't the usual horseplay. The coach's room was closed. "What's up," I asked Benjy.

"Coach Johnson's wife was killed this afternoon in a car wreck. I guess we are supposed to stay in here." Simple words, yet his freckled face reflected the naked and stark pain of a ten year old experiencing the death of a cherished dog.

I had never met Cindy, but I knew of her and Mark's kids, who sometimes accompanied him to practice. But for some reason, it felt like a hammer had clobbered me. Like my father's death, it was sudden and unexpected and it came out of left field. I sat down and waited for a coach to come in and talk to us. I was still stunned minutes later at a little after four when Chuck came out of the office and into the locker room. By that time, the entire team was present.

I listened to Chuck's cryptic words penetrate through the youthful minds that, up to minutes ago, had been intent on an impending game. For the last two months we had been the closest thing to a family, outside of our parents and brothers and sisters. Oftentimes, we fought with each other as well as supported each other and, for many of these kids, Mark, like any other coach, was a male authority figure. We had buried our heads in football and now, like a turtle, we were poking our heads out of the shell, exposed once again to real life. And it wasn't pleasant. Chuck didn't know what to say. Does anybody really know?

Chuck broke the news to a suddenly somber and quiet team room. "This afternoon, Coach Johnson's wife was killed in car wreck. It was sudden. A rock crashed through the windshield in the car she was a passenger in on 126. There will be no practice today. Go home and get some rest and come prepared to play the game of your lives tomorrow. We have to win this one for Mark and his family." I cringed at that last statement, but later thought that acceptance of death or the passing of those close to you is to physically perform a rite or ritual to help commemorate and mark the memory. What was wrong with 80 football players doing it the only way they knew how? A player gathered us together for a team prayer and then players trickled out in ones and twos. I stayed behind and listened to players talk about what happened. I listened, somewhat incredulously, as they wondered if Mark was going to show up for the game.

"It would be like him to show up," said one. Others agreed. I wondered how many other players were out of touch with reality. A 32-year-old father of two, just widowed, showing up to coach a football game the day after his wife died. I wanted to shout, "Come on you idiots, get a grip on life and what is important." For the length of their conversation, I thought, is life for an athlete that narrow and focused and so self centered that the cruelest of happenings and twisted fates bounce off or around their minds?

Later that night, I realized that it was my own experience with death that prompted those feelings. For many of these guys, this was the first face-off with death and talking about it together was therapy. Dealing with death is like the need to ignore and/or avoid the realization of risk and mortality so much a part of the game of football. Death, like an injury that often is career ending, happens when we aren't in control of our playing destiny. To see an injured player standing on the sidelines in his street clothes during a game is to stare or subconsciously acknowledge the spin of the wheel on a cut during a route that leaves the knee exposed or the hit that leaves players like Darryl Stingly in a wheelchair the rest of his life.

In the passing of a second, as marks the slamming of a rock into a windshield, the fate of ligament and cartilage lies naked and exposed to a cornerback or the gleam of a headhunting linebacker. At this level, the price of a ticket to play is the unsigned, but implicit waiver absolving everyone except yourself of damage that lurks behind the next block or down and out. Youth allows the sense of immortality to blanket the possibility of injury. It is the perception that youth allows immunity with a thin veneer of invincibility that when chipped cracks with the speed of light and leaves the spider-web design of a pane of glass shattered by a bullet or a boulder. That next afternoon, we would climb into two buses and a trainer's van and voluntarily leap onto the smog-ridden ribbon of 101 that would take us into the most heavily traveled county in the country. But hey, if you don't take the risk, you miss out on the experience.

On my way out to the parking lot from the locker room, I walked through the stadium and remembered yesterday's practice when Mark and I were talking in the offensive backfield about our thirtysomething bodies forcing us to adjust to what we could and couldn't do. I ran into Chuck in the parking lot leaving the locker room and it was clear he was trying to retain some sense of the enormity of what happened and the job he had to do the next day. "I won't try to talk to him for a couple of days," he told me. "He doesn't need me bothering him now." All the while I couldn't get past the image of a rock bouncing along the highway of death waiting for a passing car to plunge in and steal a life.

Next day, at the team lunch of pasta, talk among players centered on the game and Mark. So sure was I that Mark would be locked in the grief of his loss that I was shocked for the second time in 24 hours when he walked in and sat down at the coaches' table. Players got up in ones and pairs and walked by to offer their condolences, to touch him or shake his hand. "I just couldn't sit at home," he told me, going out to get on the bus. "The emptiness was overwhelming and it hurt too much. I had to do something, anything to take my mind off it. And besides," he said with a rueful chuckle, naked emotion flooding his eyes, "coaching was a way to get back at her. She hated football." Dudley called him brave and Chuck labeled him courageous. To me, it was the only thing he could have done. Temporarily chase the demons away before they came home to roost in the empty house for good in the following days and months.

Chaffey beat us 51-18. We never really stood a chance that night. Mark's presence forced us to deal with reality then and now, instead of in the abstract. In one sense, he became a rallying focus that led to a muted cry for victory. In another, deeper sense, her death cast the game in a less-than-necessary die. We lost the cutting edge, maintaining the emotional peg that players base their 60 minutes of ballistic and kamikaze behavior on.

My admiration of Chuck was never so high as that night. He told me later that Mark's presence hurt us more than helped, but he couldn't tell Mark to stay home. He knew the emotional foibles of a team were such a fickle thing. Mark's presence upset the focus and concentration of the team. "We win or lose as a team," Chuck said in his pre-game speech. "We come together tonight and draw support from each other!"

At half, it was 30-6 and we were flat. Several fights broke out on our sidelines. One big one was between a receiver and Dudley over playing time and the second half was spent wishing for the final gun. Chuck watched the carnage and horror unfold, but he never lost sight of his role as a teacher that lies at the heart of his job. He kept coaching and urging us on, "Stay focused! Let's get em' back. Come together!" while watching his team die a very painful death on the Rancho Cucamonga tundra.

Mark continued to coach that year, coming only occasionally during the week, but always to the games. Not soon after the death of his wife, his youngest son was diagnosed with leukemia and Mark and those closest to him went through another period of continued mourning as they coped with his impending death. He died last summer. Mark was back the next season. He had moved into a new house with his oldest son, back to work and if not with a new lease on life, at least a deposit on his future. In the end, the game can offer lessons in life. Mark Johnson addressed a large group of mourners that came to his wife's funeral. A knot of us players stood together on a gorgeous weekday morning, including Chad Marsulak, at the time the sophomore all-league running back that churned out yardage on his own, due to a decimated offensive line. Chad was Mark's responsibility and the two became close during the early part of the season.

"You know, you can easily turn around," Mark said, his voice breaking, "and look back and what was valuable to you is gone and you have nothing but memories. I look out on you and see people like Chad, who have their whole life before them and hope that they don't make the mistake of waiting till it's too late to enjoy what they have. It is a big-time gut check now, like we tell our players, and we have to suck it up and go on. It is late in the game and fourth down. It's a Gut Check."

Robin finally approached the podium and those still walking and those standing in clumps, drew into a loosely-shaped circle around him. I had to get back to the locker room and start getting ready, so I took that opportunity to fade into the rear and start making my way back over to the gym the back way over the bridge that connected the East and West campus. For most of us players, football was like crossing that bridge. When we were playing, we were suspended above life's mortal concerns, but the bridge only went for so long; life and death awaited us on the other side.

We won the game.

# Section Three
## The Game
## Bakersfield Vs Santa Barbara
## Second Quarter

*Rick and Phil from "Down Under"*

*Our Black Messiah and his mentor, Chuck Melendez*

*Touchdown Torlando Bolden*

# Chapter 12

---

## Culture of Pain

**F**ailed drives by each squad ended the first quarter, leaving us knotted at seven. Bakersfield running back Mike Gray was pounding out yardage on the ground while J.T. was throwing and completing passes at a record pace. He had completed 12 of 13 passes and 116 yards as we changed ends of the field. Everybody was getting in on the passing extravaganza. Six receivers had at least two completions and Torlando was leading with most acrobatic. The defense was playing their hearts out, standing up to the bigger and more powerful Bakersfield offensive line. Mike Gray weighed as much as any of the starting SBCC linebacking crew.

Underneath the excitement displayed up and down our sideline, there was a hint of trepidation. Bakersfield kept sending in new personnel, while the same players trooped back and forth between field and sidelines for City College. Chuck and Joe both knew the key to winning was keeping our defense off the field as much as possible. Chuck was throwing under the Bakersfield defense, trying to play ball control. As long as we caught the passes and made sufficient yardage to keep tallying first downs, the defense would rest. We were attempting to beat Bakersfield at their game, only we had J.T. Stone instead of Mike Gray. But it was only a matter of time before Bakersfield started to play us honest, denying Ryan, Eric and Torlando the short pattern. We needed some speed to loosen the Renegades up and our rocket Arthur was still sidelined. As the second quarter started, Art was busy trying to make his case to Susan to let him play, but Susan remained adamant. "You get in there and get hurt and I won't treat you," she kept telling him. "You shouldn't be playing."

If anything, Susan was one strong individual. She had to be; she played nursemaid to over 70 players. Not much older than some of the players, Susan was big and Irish in an athletic sort of way and had been a scholarship softball player to Long Beach State before injuring her knee. She had shoulder-length brown hair and when she made a stand, she was unmovable.

As is every trainer, Susan was stuck in a no man's land. She was responsible for the health and safety of the players, but she was continually barraged by the coaches on one side and the players on the other to get the injured playing again as quickly as possible. The players, coaches and the game itself were out to undo everything she patched and mended. "Football is such a violent sport," she said once to me. "I don't see why there aren't more injuries. It's amazing you guys can take the falls you take and bounce up.

During the end of the Santa Monica game, when everybody was caught up in the excitement of the third quarter fireworks Jake Lombard, after being belted around for two quarters, took a big hit and came out under his own power. Before anybody knew it, trainers included, he was lying flat out on the ground. Susan came over and looked at him and then yelled for the Santa Monica team doctor. Afterwards, with most players and coaches concentrating on the game, Susan braced Jake's neck and stuck him on a stretcher. With three minutes to go in the game, while Santa Monica was desperately driving for the tying score, an ambulance pulled up to our bench from the track, loaded him up and took him to the hospital for observation.

It was strange. Locked in a life and death struggle with 50 seconds to go, both sidelines and the grandstand erupting into cheers and our sidelines screaming for defense, "dee-fense, dee-fense," Jake was loaded into an ambulance, red lights flashing and slowly driven off the field. The disappearing taillights were a stark reminder of the ever-present danger in our addiction for the game. While Jake lay on the ground for a quarter, nobody went over to see how he was doing, almost as if an invisible cordon of yellow caution tape encircled his inert body. Nobody likes to be reminded of the risk of the game. Nobody likes to see it with his own eyes or go up and touch a victim of the risk. Why acknowledge its presence? Why clutter your mind with doubt and rob it of its primary goal, to throw your body into the fray with little thought of the consequences? Why blunt the instinct? So Jake was the plague, a 1990s example of don't see, don't touch and the rats won't bite. Poor scared anxiety-ridden Jake. After we got back to Santa Barbara, nobody, not even the coaches, knew what happened to Jake more than the last image of Jake being loaded into the night. Fortunately, Jake was released that night from the Santa Monica hospital and his parents drove him home late that night. That Sunday, when I went over to the boys for the weekly Sunday football orgy and round table discussion on Saturday's performance, Jake was laying on the couch, very sore and ticked off that none of the coaches went over to the hospital or even inquired about how he was getting home.

I knew Susan's work intimately having undergone a variety of injuries during my two seasons, six stitches in my chin, a severely pulled groin muscle and a dislocated shoulder, along with all the minor nagging little injuries and discomfort that plague the players day in and day out. "In football, you start the season 100 percent and the first day is the last day you are 100 percent," Carmen told us at the beginning of the season, as he bitched about the number of players still in the training room at the beginning of practice. "It's a fucking violent game. To play football is to learn to play in pain!"

For Susan, who continually saw injured players beg on their hands and knees to play (I admit, I was one of those pleaders), dealing with pain was as much a product of how long one played as it was mentally overcoming the pain. "Players and their bodies have gotten used to the pain," she said. "Over the years, they have learned how to play with pain or have the desire to play the game hurt. Some of these kids have been playing football for over 10 years. Tell me there is not tolerance built up with experience."

As Susan kept saying no to Art, I was amazed at the

transformation in him from one who did as little as possible in practice due to minor strains or bruises, to one begging to play with an injury that prohibited him from lifting his arms above his shoulders. Art was being left behind in the most important game of the season, and a severed leg wasn't going to keep him out.

Ryan, Eric and I had all suffered dislocated shoulders that season. Ryan and Eric both were playing this game with shoulders wrapped so tight that I was unsure how blood circulated through their midsection. Reaching back for a fluttering J.T. pass on an up, out and up the third week of practice, I was leveled by Thiessen, taking a huge hit on my left shoulder as the ball and Thiessen showed up at the same time. I heard a crack on my pads and the next thing I remembered was looking up into Thiessen's face as he looked down into mine. I still had the ball, not even knowing how it got there, let alone stayed in my clutches. I didn't want to get up and felt nauseous. Finally I did, and wobbled back to the huddle. "That's football, Doc," Dudley said. "Shake it off and go in on the next play."

Dave came over to see if I was still in one piece and Lee followed suit. His bell had been rung two days earlier in the same way. "Shit, now I know how you felt," I told him. Lee had bounced right up, without the ball and jogged back to the huddle. I felt somewhat vindicated, even if I couldn't focus on his face. "He stuck you pretty good," he said. "They hit even harder in the games."

Susan's fingers probed around the left shoulder after that practice. "I won't be able to tell until tomorrow. You might have dislocated or even separated the shoulder." She took my left arm and raised it. "Shit, Susan, that hurts," I yelled as she brought it level to my shoulder. "Doc, watch your language. You don't want to put the cash in the can." A coffee can lay on top of the shelf that ran the entire length of the north wall. If you swore, you paid 25 cents toward the party the trainers had at the end of the semester. I am sure it was going to be a cruise to Cancun. She dropped the arm and told me what I had been hearing for what seemed like an eternity. "Ice it on and off tonight, and take some Advil. Come in early tomorrow." I lay back against the wall as she strapped on a bag of ice with an ace bandage. I had ended the day at the second string slot position with an injured wing. You don't want to lose your place. You may never get it back.

"If I had to say anything right now, I would call it a dislocated shoulder," Susan told me the next afternoon. "The swelling has really increased since last night and your muscle up there has been tweaked, to say the least. Some of the fibers have torn, creating the bleeding and the inflammation."

"So what's that mean, I can't play for awhile?"

"No, you can play, but you have to watch contact. You keep banging that shoulder, it's never going to get better. I can make a donut out of some Styrofoam for you for some additional padding, but one good pop and you are back to square one every day."

"So what, can I scrimmage?" was my next question. It seems like all last year and continuing this year, I negotiated with Susan about what I could and couldn't do following some kind of injury. I created scenarios where she would say, "Yes, that you can do." My interaction with Susan was one of give and take where meaning took on variations that changed daily. "Well, you sure can't go through the blocking drill. I would be careful scrimmaging or any kind of contact." Terrific. "You, of all people, know it's going to take time. You can't rush healing."

Susan was a salmon swimming upstream, always working against the violent currents of the game. Nobody ever healed. They just learned to bite the bullet. Like lemmings following the masses over the cliff every six years, players' participation in football was culturally ingrained. For so many of us, these two years at the junior college level marked the end of the line for our collegiate football experience. There was something driving those who stuck it out, something we derived from the pain, the long hours, the pain, the road trips, the pain and the loss of our individuality and autonomy. We bowed to an autocratic regime, a dictatorship by a council of middle-aged men who determined players' worth through their efforts of manipulating highly impressionable young minds. As players, we bought into this program willingly. In fact, we respected those coaches who broke us down any way they could so they could build us into something greater than the individual parts. Pain was the essential ingredient in creating the sum and was many things to this process. Most of all, it was a vital element in constructing a cultural identity of a football player, a "stud" as opposed to a "wimp" and one who has battled through the gremlins of mortality. A disgruntled former college football player, Don Sabo dealt with the pain of a back injury from football long after he finished playing. He wrote a scathing commentary on the role of pain and its influence on the formation of a patriarchal "society." To Sabo, to be able to ignore or play through pain defines the athlete and describes the "pain principle."

"Boys are taught that to endure pain," Sabo wrote, "is courageous, to survive pain is manly. The principle that pain is 'good' and pleasure is 'bad' is crudely evident in the 'no pain, no gain' philosophy of so many coaches and players." Rather than a building process, Sabo argued that undergoing pain instead acts to tear down individuality. "[Pain] stifles men's awareness of their bodies and limits our emotional expression. We learn to ignore personal hurts and injuries because they interfere with the 'efficiency' and 'goals' of the 'team'.... Channeling them into a bundle of rage which is directed at opponents and enemies."

Pain was used by the controlling patriarchy dominated by men "in crude and debased, slick and subtle ways...also a system of intermale dominance, in which a minority of men dominates the masses of men, to build a 'mythos of heroism' that imparts it own sense of morality of 'power-worship' on its subjects," Sabo wrote. The system derives adherence to its philosophy by generating "visions of ecstasy and masculine excellence" and sticking these visions deep into the minds of boys who support and drive the system by participation in its expression in society, such as football. Pain becomes essential as a rite of passage that is constantly crossed and recrossed during a season or a career. To Sabo, for the hierarchy to continue, stability must be maintained and pain is used as a vehicle that is necessary and, in addition, "enhances one's character and moral worth."

Coaches were the patriarchy and the message of pain was passed to their troops, subtly or not so subtly. Rick Telander called it an "almost casual cruelty." A ten-year-old expose by San Diego Charger psychiatrist Arnold Mandell detailed the great experiment of the San Diego Chargers having a team shrink attached to the team as he became just a pharmacy dispensing uppers and downers and pain killers. A more recent effort by team doctor Rob Huizinga of the Oakland Raiders told of efforts to control and ignore pain by both players and coaches alike. The Raiders purposefully fabricated injuries, and the extent of injuries, to put the player back on the field as soon as possible.

To take pain is the cultural reminder of who is and who is not a player. Conversely, to Sabo, not to take pain is to lose everything of value that was the rewards of the patriarchy; in this case, football and "camaraderie, prestige, scholarships, pro contracts and community recognition." Sabo, too, recalled a moment that later in life crystallized his pain principle. His high school coach spoke to the players before a game. "Boys," the coach began, "people who say that football is a 'contact sport' are dead wrong. Dancing is a contact sport. Football is a game of pain and violence! Now get the hell out of here and kick some ass!"

H.G. Bissenger recounts a coach's speech the night before a big game in which he told the assembled players the story of Olympic swimmer Steve Genter who underwent surgery to repair a collapsed lung. Doctors told him he would need painkillers to swim that are not legal in the Olympics. Because that is what he had worked for all his life, Genter decided to swim and forgo the medication. The coach began his speech talking about Genter feeling pain during the race. "He does a spin turn at the other end and pushes off, and comes up for air and lets out a blood-curdling scream," the coach said. "Because the pain is so intense, the sound just echoes off the walls of the swimming arena. He makes a split turn at the end of the second lap, pushes off, and he breaks his stitches, his stitches split apart and he starts bleeding. They say he lost a pint and a half of blood over the course of the next two laps. I guarantee you, I'd want him in my corner." Genter lost the gold to Mark Spitz by the length of one of his stitches.

Pain was never far from your thoughts on and off the field during a season. For those who stuck it out, there was a conscious effort to cognitively and purposefully accept the reality that you hurt if you played. Pushing your body to the limit and beyond became the desire to excel. Part, also, was the acceptance of the pain that accompanied the inflammation or ripping and tearing of muscles tendons and ligaments. "In seasons past," wrote H.G. Bissenger, "playing for Permian [high school in Odessa, Texas] had meant routinely vomiting during the grueling off-season workouts inside the hot and sweaty weight room. It had meant playing with a broken ankle that wasn't x-rayed because, if it had been known that it was broken, the player would have had to sit out the next game. It meant playing with broken hands. It had meant a shot of Novocaine during halftime to mask the pain of a deep ankle sprain or a hip pointer. It had meant popping painkillers and getting shots of Valium."

Not too far into last season, Carmen DiPaolo had yelled at the team for spending too much time in the training room. "You guys want a non-contact sport, try fucking ping pong," he said as he walked among us as we stretched before practice "You play like men in football. You play hurt!" The second season Carmen inserted volleyball for Ping-Pong.

There was little question that the game we were playing was violent. Pittsburgh Steeler linebacker Greg Lloyd was quoted as saying that football was a violent game after he was fined $12,000 for a flagrant hit on Dan Marino in September of 1995. "It's a violent damn game," said Lloyd. "It is a game players play with anger, frustration and emotion. And that is how I play the game. This isn't one of those games...[like] you can put on PBS and all the little kids can watch it and they can show it in the classroom. If you're not angry something," Lloyd said, "chances are somebody is going to be out there to take your head off."

For the past two years, like so many of my teammates, I lived in the training room, nursing pain and injury between practices, but most of us, with the notable exceptions, went out and gave a 100 percent at practice. Most of the guys at one time or another found themselves in the same predicament. For those who wanted to play bad enough, it was more the desire to play and not miss practice and chance somebody else taking your spot that everyday drove us out of the training room and onto the field. Because of the level of play and the fact that not one of us were on scholarship or indebted to the program in any way except that we wanted to play, some of the hold other college coaches held over their players did not apply to us.

I talked to Susan about pain and tolerance one day while I iced after practice and asked her about the difference in players' ability to handle pain. "Well, I have to get to know the individual's personality and how much pain he can endure and what kind of pain," she said. "When is he crying wolf and when is it going to be something major and I won't listen to him. It is amazing the difference in pain tolerance. Even within the same body, upper body, lower body."

"Can you type the personalities that come through the training room on the way they handle pain or can't handle pain?" She whirled around and looked at me to see if I was serious. I was. "No, it's individual. Look at you, are you similar to anybody else? What are you trying to say, it's genetic?" Was I searching for some master plan or perhaps genetic code that I could crack to get better faster? Was I that transparent? "It has to do with several things," Susan said. "It has to do with how their parents dealt with them. Were they babied, low pain tolerance, but if they came from a family that said if it's not broke, don't worry about it, could also be dangerous. A break could be a lot less painful than a sprain." She sounded like an athletic Dr. Spock.

Joe was on the warpath as Bakersfield was driving. In his body motions, in his language, in his gut, football was the game that separated out men from boys. We were beginning to get pushed around, Gray was unstoppable and Joe kept yelling at his troops, "Suck it up, Goddammit! No fucking pain!"

Joe also typified the pain principle. He injured his pectoral muscle while a junior at Weber State and kept playing. Years later, he still carries the knot of unhealed muscle as a testament to his perseverance or maybe to his stupidity and buying into the patriarchy. At different times during the season, we all squawked about how much it hurt and how difficult it was to play, but in the same breath, we bitched because we were losing playing time. We couldn't wait to get back and reassert our positions on the team. So we went through rehab and played in pain during practice then went back in for more rehab. "Doc," Susan told me once during the worst of an injury, "of course it is not going to get better. You keep playing with it. You have to rest it to get better. I will let you play if you can handle the pain. You are the one that will decide that."

I gave Sabo's article to Chuck and Joe and asked them to read it and get back to me on it. "It's a fucking game of violence," Joe said, after he read it, as we were drinking coffee one morning before classes. "That guy [Sabo] wasn't forced to play at the beginning or later when his back continued to hurt. He played and now he is bitchin' about it. Football isn't for everybody, just like any other sport. Nobody forced me to play when I hurt. I did! Let's face it, certain people should be players. Not everyone can play the game. Christ, even each position offers a different look at the game. I like the violence. I like the last part of the game, when you are tired and hurting and it is the sacrifice. It's a guy thing," Joe said as he gulped some more Hellraiser coffee. "Guys are, by nature, violent. Look at war. I am not a violent person. Okay, maybe I am. But the violence appeals to me. There are certain things about football that make it a sport for guys. I mean the pain isn't integral to the experience. It isn't the central focus of the game. It is execution and mental concentration. The hardest part for me is the mental concentration. Football isn't anti-intellectual and it is a game that appeals to a lot of different types of people. Look at you. You are different from Thiessen, who is different from J.T. who is different from Torlando."

Joe stopped to gather his breath. Seldom had I heard him so passionate about anything. His legs were driving like pistons as he sat. "And football was good for me when I was young. I had a different experience than this [Sabo] guy. My parents moved when I was younger and I didn't know anybody so I played football and made friends. It provided a sense of security for me and that wasn't a bad thing. When I was at Weber State I was co-captain of the team. When we went out for the coin toss, the quarterback who was also a co-captain, would be joking with the referee and I'd be thinking, 'come on, let's get the fuck out of here and on with the game.' Look at me, I am a perfect example of a football personality. I was 185 pounds and a middle linebacker. I made all CIF in high school, all-league at City College and was all conference at Weber State, the smallest linebacker in the conference. But I loved the game. I was never really injured that bad playing football, so I don't know how [Sabo] feels. I don't think it would be any different than I do now. Look at my hands, fingers and wrists. I know I am going to start feeling pain there from jamming them all the time." I looked down at mine when he said that. My fingers hadn't been their normal size for two years.

Chuck went further, "Maybe that guy had an unhappy childhood. It kind of sounded like it from the article. He is putting back his own problems on the game. After I broke my hand during the summer between high school and City College, I went through a whole season in pain just so that I could play. I mean, after the hand healed, I felt that my velocity had dropped and my delivery was affected, but I kept playing because I loved the sport. The pain was worth it."

The image of Jarrod DeGeorgia's ankle that was more blue and black than the pink of his skin, my first season, being taped by Susan before the Los Angeles Pierce game was never far from my thoughts. He couldn't walk from the bus to the locker room on that ankle, but two hours later, two braces, miles of tape and a plethora of Advil, he was taking the first snap and completing the first of 30 out of 42 passes. Because he was slower than usual with a melon for an ankle, he spent much time that night picking himself off the turf after being belted by a blitzing defense. "It wasn't a question of not playing," he said later. "I had to play. Sure it fucking hurt, but what doesn't hurt in football?"

We wore pain like it was another part of our jersey or one of the five sets of pads we put on underneath. In my previous book on sprinters, I talked about pain as if it were an old friend, one that is always there, one that you get to know intimately through a season. Why not invite it in to stay for awhile. If one begins to separate out pain from the experience of playing, pain has won and the punishment is emotionally worse than the pain itself. When you miss a practice or a game because of injury, you endure the barbs and insults of coaches and teammates, but what strikes even deeper is the mental anguish and masturbation of self-doubt. "Doc, I don't want to miss a practice," Ryan told me in the locker late in the season, after he separated his shoulder. "I have to play," he said as we both peeled off our pads, doughnut, and ace bandage that held our shoulders in place. "It is too late in the season to miss even a series in a game."

Pain was also in the panic that set in after an injury. "How soon can I come back and play?" was a question I asked Susan several times during my two years. I wanted firm answers and dates that I could hang onto and point toward. Almost always, "When you can bear the pain," was her response. "How about today?" was my stock response.

Telander wrote that injuries were not only an integral part of the game, but also a welcome part. "One of the very reasons players play the game is to have the chance to give and receive injuries…. A friendly, masculine reminder of my accomplishments as a player, and subliminally, as a man, in a dangerous sport."

Mike Oriard, an Oregon State University professor, wrote an essay on football violence in the *New York Times*. Oriard was a former Notre Dame captain and ex-NFL center for the Kansas City Chiefs and said, "It's that instant when…artistry is threatened by violence and the outcome is in doubt, that epitomizes the game's attractiveness. Injuries are not aberrations in football, or even regrettable byproducts. They are essential to the game…. It's not possible to have the desired danger without injuries to confirm the danger is real."

The risk of football becomes the epitome of what galvanizes and thrills Americans. On the eve of my final college football game, in an interview with the *Santa Barbara News-Press*, I said, "the brutishness of football is part of its appeal. The risk of hurting yourself is an exciting element in American sports. We crave that sense of danger." I considered these thoughts with three blown up knuckles on my right hand, courtesy of J.T. rockets, to match the three on my left hand, a still-swollen separated left shoulder, and two knees that pop when I stand up.

A former all-conference player from Duke wrote Telander about a story he did on Tommy Chaiken, the South Carolina player who was on steroids and ended up a nut case. It wasn't drugs that he abused in the 1960s and 1970s as a player. His addiction was to pain. "I too…had an abusive addiction, which was playing with pain," wrote the reader. "I've had four operations on my left knee, one on my right, two on my right ankle with a third scheduled for January. I walk clubfooted and struggle with inclines and rough terrain. I haven't been able to do anything resembling a jog or a run in four years."

His story is common with those who have played football for a number of years. With the benefit of arthoscopic surgeries, players are back on their feet and on the field in a matter of weeks. My brother, who did not play football, was "scoped" on his knee and was swimming in a matter of a week. The former player finished his letter to Telander with these words; "The scariest thing is…I'D DO IT ALL OVER AGAIN (emphasis Telander)! What is this mystical hold that football has over me and thousands like me?"

Gary Plummer was recently interviewed by *the Los Angeles*

*Times*'s Julie Cart for a story on pain in professional football. Plummer has had 14 operations since beginning his playing days and said pain doesn't exist until it is perceived and in the NFL pain is denied. "I know in the back of my mind," Plummer said, "I'm doing permanent damage to my body. I know that I'll feel the effects of this in the future. It's a trade-off. In June and July, you forget how much it hurts. I get excited to play again. I'll miss it when it stops."

Football is just one example in our society of abusing your body to the point of breaking it down and beyond in to disrepair. Hockey, boxing, even basketball, at an elite level and for an extended period of time, leaves the body damaged. For many Americans, recreation and sport follows the person through life. Jogging, weekend tennis, touch football, softball, bike riding benefits the body, but for many of us who are held hostage to the American ideal of mastery and competition, physical activity sends us beyond what our bodies are capable of and pain and injury result. Whether it is as an elite athlete or weekend warrior, pain becomes a badge of courage. Is this something I will sit back in 10 years and be thankful I stuck it out? The mind rationalizes in strange and testosteroned ways. But then, if I didn't want this experience of living on the edge, would I have been out there? Hindsight is only 20/20 when it comes to experience, not to ligaments, joints, and bone.

Joe's efforts to galvanize his defensive line fell on deaf ears. On the first play of the second quarter....

## KIST

*Mike Gray turns the left side and breaks one man to the 20! He is in the clear, the 10, 5, TD Bakersfield! What a way to start the quarter! Mike Gray explodes from 31 yards out, was caught at the 25-yard line, but slipped two Vaquero tacklers and turned on the afterburners and simply outran the Vaquero secondary and Bakersfield, just 7 seconds into the second quarter regains the lead 13-7. 26th TD of the year for Mike Gray. Far and away #1 in the WSC. Chad Hathaway now will attempt the extra point. Snap is down, kick is up it has plenty of leg, it is good. Bakersfield 14, Vaqueros 7. Just into the second quarter.*

# Chapter 13

## Confrontation

Had the tide finally turned? Our defense came straggling off the field after Gray's run. The score was still close; by no means were we out of it. Yet the ease of Gray and the rest of the Renegades' scoring was frightening.

"Come on offense, let's get it back," Chuck screamed as Mark Johnson huddled with the kickoff return team. Already Joe was yelling at the defense to gather around him. In a matter of seconds, Carmen's controlled fury digested and, passed on by Joe, would find its way to the sweating, sucking wind, stunned faces of the defense.

Chuck was in J.T.'s face before sending him back onto the field. "We got to keep the defense off the field," he said. "Let's hit those first down passes, make it easier on us!" Dudley was telling the receivers "We got to have it, get off the ball hard, run the routes and block, dammit." Garret was nodding in agreement; he was sweating more than the starters. "I have this sweating problem," he told me once. "I can sweat standing still, in the shade." Rivulets were streaming down his face, but he was oblivious to the flow. The game held him entranced.

168

After both teams gave up the football on successive drives, we were once again poised on the verge of catching up. A nice catch by Lee Green made up some yardage following a J.T. sack and we were facing fourth and two at the Bakersfield 44-yard line. Chuck wasn't about to let halfway decent field position slip through his fingers once again.

"Goddammit, we have to go for it!" Kratz yelled at me, standing three feet away. "Come on, Chuck, let's go for it," he turned and gave his two cents worth to the coach.

"Chuck, we gotta have it," Dudley counseled from behind Chuck's back.

Joe was thinking punt. "Let's kick it away, pin them down close to their goal line," he yelled from the defensive side of the sideline.

Joe and Chuck had different football philosophies. Chuck was riverboat gambler while Joe played the percentages. Both were continually trying to get the other to see their side in the most hectic portions of games. Raw and naked emotion driven by the pace of the game would cascade up and down the sidelines during each and every quarter. We were facing Santa Monica, whom we never had beaten in the 10 years, the third game of the season, at Santa Monica. We were playing well and had them up 14 with eight minutes to go in the game. We needed to grind out some first downs and run some clock off. With our offense we didn't run clock, except when we completed passes or ran one of our limited running plays.

Earlier in the game, wrapped up in the heat of competition, Chuck had yelled at Joe about Santa Monica's success in running on the defense, "Fuck! Joe, Santa Monica is running over that big offensive lineman and pounding everybody, why the fuck aren't we blitzing more?" Joe just turned his back to the commentary, walking away from the advice, muttering that Chuck didn't know his ass from a hole in the ground, while Chuck didn't even wait to see if Joe had heard, turned away and muttered something about Joe not knowing where his head was at.

With just minutes left and the game on the line, Santa Monica scored, bringing them to within seven. Five minutes remained and we desperately needed a first down or two to kill any chance the

Corsairs had to score. Chuck opened the series up with a short hitch pattern which came up incomplete. Joe was livid, his face contorted in the agony of disbelief. "Eat some fucking clock, run the ball, kill some time!" he screamed at Chuck. "Don't take so many chances!" he bellowed at the top of his considerable lungs.

Chuck screamed back, "Get used to it!"

The emotion resembled a sound wave as it traveled through each of us, from coach to coach. It was an orgasm of intensity that brought you to the brink of another dimension of reality where life began and ended with the movement of a leather ball and the clash of pads and the violence of 22 young men intent on mayhem.

The next play, Twuan gained no yardage. Santa Monica burned one of their time outs, stopping the clock and with Torlando's assurances that he could beat his man deep, J.T. changed the third down call of a 10-yard out to a fly pattern and overthrew a streaking Torlando. Three and out and we punted to a pumped up Santa Monica team, buoyed by our inability to move the ball.

The next five minutes was painful as the clock moved in slow motion. The defense was exhausted. Santa Monica mixed up their plays and 4:30 later after our punt, as time expired on the clock, punched it over the goal line. Down two, they converted on a quarterback sweep and as Santa Monica swarmed on the field with a tie, but a moral victory, we stood shell-shocked, unable to move. A tie was like kissing your sister, I thought, watching Santa Monica students and players dance and celebrate.

Joe was so angry and frustrated that he couldn't get his thoughts out. He stood on the 40-yard line, ripped off his sunglasses as the conversion succeeded and with a primal "Fuck!" hurled them in the late evening chill as far as he could throw. I watched them turn end over end as they sailed over my head, the cord attached that kept them hanging around his neck, trailing like a tail of a comet. Without watching them land, Joe stalked off the field, his face a picture of churning emotions. He was still unable to talk with any calm, 30 minutes after the game, repeating "fuck" over and over again in the parking lot where our busses were parked. As our struggles had gone that night, the glasses finally hit at the five-yard line short of the goal line. Pat sent Casey down to pick them up. As he passed me he said, "Did you see Coach Joe throw his glasses? Man, that dude was mad. Rad, man, rad!"

Chuck had already made up his mind. He took three strides onto the field and yelled the play to J.T. "Make it work, make it work!" he yelled. Bakersfield dug in and everybody around me knew this was one of those pivotal plays that determine outcomes and it was only the second quarter. J.T., in the "gun," stood expectantly, waiting for the snap.

"Gotta have it," Dudley muttered as J.T. snared the long snap and.....

**KIST**

*Vaqueros trying to keep the drive alive. Rush comes. Stone looks for Hill at the 15. Has him at the ten, 5 TD, Santa Barbara City College! Do you believe it?! If you are a Vaquero fan you do! Twuan Hill burns Jesse McNaughton, strong safety in single coverage. A 44-yard TD pass with 12:10 to go before halftime and Santa Barbara is back in business.*

On that play, Chuck was a genius.

# Chapter 14

_____

## The Drive to Excel

The minutes marched by, both teams exchanging punts and then, again, we were driving. J.T.'s passes threaded their way through the Bakersfield secondary. With about six minutes to go in the half, J.T. was close to 200 yards passing on 13 completions. He came into the season finale needing 304 yards to break 3000 yards for the season and the question by the second quarter was not if, but when, he was going to reach that milestone.

Nobody would deny J.T.'s season was less than magical, yet J.T.'s performance was at times inconsistent throughout our 10-game schedule. He was easily rattled and his lack of self-confidence was his worst enemy. Frustration with overthrown passes, interceptions, and misreads followed him from game to game. In a nutshell, J.T. was a freshman. But when you only get two years in junior college eligibility, there is no room for freshmen mistakes. Every down counts, every game brings the player closer to the potential end of his football career. In J.T.'s case, he was a sure ticket to move on.

For others, like Ryan Capretta or Eric Mahanke, the opportunity to play after Santa Barbara City College lived on the number of catches and receiving yardage they racked up in their two years. Most importantly, opportunity rested on the film of Ryan or Eric in action. Being great in high school was a godsend if Ryan had chosen to go after a scholarship at a four-year school. By choosing City College, Ryan and Eric threw the dice and gambled that their careers at pass-happy AirChuck U would vault both into the stratosphere of Division 1 schools.

Ryan had already nabbed three passes in the first 22 minutes of play, Eric a couple, and now, on this drive, there was a chance to grab the lead and put doubt in the Bakersfield juggernaut. J.T. was going to be looking for either of the surehanded receivers. After Mike Hayes returned the Bakersfield punt to the 30-yard line, six minutes remained before the half. We needed a sustained drive and score to eat clock, tire out the defense and go into the locker room up on the cocky Renegades.

"This is the time for Capretta," Kratz told me as the offense took the field. "Just get him behind the defense on a drag across the middle and we got six points."

"That's right," said Stuart Boyer keeping Kratz and me company. "Cappy's the man."

Chuck, looking to cross the 'Gades up, attempted to run and Twuan was hit deep in the backfield before he had a chance to hit the gas and lost five yards. A hold on the same play put us back on the 18 yardline and all of sudden we were going in reverse, losing ground and in danger of being pinned up against our own goal line.

"J.T.'s gotta find Ryan," Kratz said to nobody in particular. "Fuck, Torlando's playing his no-show game, Eric's great on the short passes, but Capretta's the man to go to in the clutch." On second and long, J.T. scrambled and evaded the continuous Bakersfield blitz and shot a rocket up field.

## KIST

*Second down again a long situation for Santa Barbara's Stone. In the shotgun at the ten, Stone fires complete up to the 30-yard line. That's Capretta once again, a gain of 12 and will bring up third down and about 4 for SB. An outstanding first half and that is what Santa Barbara needed, a big game from him today and he has responded. Fourth catch for Capretta here in the first half.*

173

J.T. looking for Ryan on third and four overthrew him on a seven-yard hitch. Deep in our own territory, without mounting a serious effort to march ahead, we were forced to give the ball back to Bakersfield, leaving the door swinging open for them like the saloon doors in the old West.

A junior college's two main missions are to educate those not ready for or able to succeed at four-year schools and to provide vocational-like course opportunities for the community. At $39 a course, Santa Barbara City College was probably the best bargain outside of quarter beers at the Beach Shack, a local watering hole for the under-25 crowd in downtown Santa Barbara. Two bucks guaranteed that you didn't walk out of the bar on your own power. Every Fall, Peter MacDougall, the college president met with an auditorium full of potential male and female student-athletes and encouraged them to make the most out of their athletic and educational tenure as a Vaquero. I sat and listened for three years to his speech and knew that his words were dancing on the periphery of the athletes' consciousness.

Sitting in the locker room, it was nothing to listen in on conversations where the topics of arrests and probation were not uncommon. In fact, one offensive lineman on the 1995 squad had a large gold number 55 hanging, a la Deion Sanders, around his neck. One day in the weight room I asked him what the number represented. I expected it to be his uniform number in high school or YFL. "It is the number of the Mexican Mafia from my home town in Mexico," he replied in all sincerity while he banged another set of curls. He turned out to be hotheaded and very temperamental. One practice, after he screamed at T.K. and told him to fuck off in many different ways, all of them extremely expressive, he was suspended for the day. I pictured a thoroughly hardened #55 at San Quentin in three years. Prior to the 1995 season, the two most visible examples of failed youth given second chances were Ricky Demarist and Keith Royal, both receivers, one Hispanic, one black.

Demarist was probably the most gifted. He was a magician dressed in pad, a shade under six feet and 165 pounds. His feet and hands were limbs of illusion as he danced around and over defenders. Like a few of the players, he was also an unmarried father and a chronic delinquent. His only saving grace was his youth and people who believed in second, third and fourth chances. Chuck Melendez was constantly put on the spot by Demarist's probation officer as a "deputy" to help reign in Demarist's penchant for trouble.

Needless to say, his high school years at Bishop Diego were also filled with trouble, but sports provided some degree of discipline. "I wasted some time by not applying myself at school," he would tell a reporter during the 1994 season. "Football has always been a way for me to discipline myself and occupy my life." Demarist stumbled big after graduating in 1991 when he was arrested for drunken driving and served some jail time. Norris Fletcher, his high school coach, said, "He's a smart kid, it's just his attitude. I think he appreciates everything we've done (Fletcher and his wife) even if he doesn't say anything about it." Out of high school, Demarist had several schools show more than a passing interest. "He could have gone to East Texas State, Eastern New Mexico or Utah State," said Fletcher. Said Demarist, "I wanted to go somewhere out of high school, but I chose to stay here. It was kind of a mistake." Kind of.

Like so many local "studs," Demarist never left the sanctuary of home waters and never realized that leaving was the best thing for him. Instead the local studs chose to stay in an artificial environment, complete with the influences that lead them into the rubble that became their youth and possibly will be the rest of their life. Nobody knew Demarist. He was a closed fist and rarely socialized with other players, except DeGeorgia and Simon Banks. He never reached out or tried to help others, well aware of the wonder, oblivious to the awe most of us felt about his ability.

The die was cast from the beginning of the year when Demarist missed three straight days of practice during August. Dudley was left sucking around for news of his absence from players in the locker room. Demarist knew he could get away with murder and still start and get his catches. On his return to practice, after the "vacation," Dudley could only explain Demarist's absence to the rest of us as "stress with his kid, personal problems and his probation officer." Chuck sat down with Demarist after his return and got into it with him over his being late to practice, sitting on his ass when he does show, and missing whole practices. Naturally, this did nothing to endear Demarist to the head coach.

Chuck looked back now on that stormy year with Demarist and realized how many mistakes he made, not being tough on him when he missed practices, not holding him accountable for his actions, and treating him as special. "I wouldn't do the same thing again with him," he would tell me over and over again. "He used me and I let him." Vivid in my mind also are the frequent occasions Demarist would come off the field screaming at Jarrod to get him the ball as if there was a conspiracy to limit his catches and his exposure.

Demarist was a manipulator and used his relationship with Chuck as a means to legitimize his sophomore year. Demarist was also one of the most gifted receivers I have seen. Said his high school coach, "Ricky is a natural. The ball just disappears in his hands. He'd catch a 10-yard hook and make an 80-yard play out of it. Our game plan was easy when he was here. I'd just write down one thing: Throw the ball to Ricky." Demarist was a natural. "I just try to get it (the ball) and go," he said. "When you are in that drive, trying to win the game, you just think about what you have to do. It's instinctive."

Demarist left City College with several school receiving records, breaking the previous mark of total number of catches in a season at 66. At the same time, Demarist was also the laziest athlete I have ever seen. His practice ethic was nonexistent, but somehow, when it came to the games, he was always there in the thick of the battle. Chuck constantly bitched about Demarist's penchant for freelancing on offense, never running the precise routes, and making things up as he went. When all was said and done, in the heat of the fray, I remembered the plays Demarist would pull off and just marvel. One in particular was vividly imprinted in my mind. After catching a simple option, he just danced, juked and sped his way the length of the field. Always eluding the defender, as if by magic, escaping and with our hearts in our mouths on the sideline, doing it over and over again in that one play. Watching the film on the following Monday was a treat.

It is difficult, but not impossible, in the world of sports, to scavenge stories of athletes who overcome childhood and adolescent troubles and go on to succeed. For Norris Fletcher and Chuck, it was a prayer that Demarist would be one of those stories. Fletcher even went as far as to say he might be able to get Ricky a tryout in the Arena Football League through an ex-player of his. "He would be perfect for that league, but he needs to get his life together first," said Fletcher. Demarist was receptive to this idea, wanting to transfer to Cal-State Northridge the following year. "Right now, I want to stay in school and go to Northridge. If I continue to have a good season and get another 3.0 GPA, I am sure I can go there." He didn't. He dropped classes and was forced to go Division 2 when he didn't get his two-year degree from City College. He ended up with a scholarship to Morningside College in Sioux City, Iowa.

At the time, I thought about this marriage of player to school and ended up thinking that what Demarist needed was to get out of Santa Barbara where he could start over with a clean slate. His year would be like a year spent at reform school. He left in August of 1995 for the nation's midsection and a step in the right direction. I remembered thinking that, in the humid Iowa heat, Demarist was going to learn quickly that other places were not like the cradle of Santa Barbara. He was back in less than a month. He told friends the coaches were the cause. In other words, Ricky may have had to toe the line and work for once. Demarist was surely a comet, flashing his way across the sky. When he was visible, Demarist left a tail larger than life, burning brightly, only to suffer an ignominious end as the fire faded just as quickly, just as surely.

Keith Royal was a big, strong, fast receiver and was different in many ways from Ricky Demarist. Keith Royal was also 25, a recovering alcoholic and served a year for robbery. He played at Lompoc High School, 45 miles up the coast and a little inland from Santa Barbara. Keith also had a child, a girlfriend who moved to Las Vegas, and borrowed her very nice BMW with oversized wheels.

The biggest reason Keith differed from Demarist was his willingness to work at getting back his football skills. He spent the spring and summer of 1994 getting his feel for the game back. Keith was very personable and seemed to be slotted for considerable playing time once the season began. He was six feet and close to 200 pounds and, compared to the smaller Demarist, Simon Banks and even Josiah Williams, he would bring some mass to down field blocking.

He ended up short a unit to be eligible for the 1994 season and

Chuck found a weekend Shakespeare course through Idaho State University. Keith drove to Pocatello, then to Cedar City that weekend and immersed himself in 500-year-old prose. "I liked it a lot," he told me. "It was kind of fun and it was put on in this outdoor theater." This was almost as funny as Demarist having to drive up to San Francisco to take in a one-unit weekend Disney film festival at San Francisco State. Of course, Demarist's probation officer reamed Chuck after that, as Rick did not inform him he was leaving town.

Keith worked hard during Hell Week and was slotted for considerable playing time. Unfortunately, he took a shot during one practice and bruised his sternum. Later it was found out that one of his cervical vertebrate was damaged and Keith was advised to stop playing and, over the off-season, have an operation to fix it. He came to the games and to some practices, but quietly faded out of the picture.

The 1995 squad continued that tradition of harboring, and even sheltering, troubled youth. Second, third, even fourth chances have become an integral part of junior college football in California; not just in life, but in performance, ability and academics. Many times these disparate chances were wrapped up in the same individual and all too often these were the players most likely to go on if they survived the winnowing process of paying their dues.

# Chapter 15

---

## A Perfect Soldier

Again, the defense was called upon to halt the impending march of the Renegades. Their progress was inexorable as much as it was a fight of brawn and wills. Jarrett Thiessen, Chris Hill, Tony Coffey, John Sonoma and Mike Hayes stood hands on hips, breathing hard, waiting for Bakersfield to initiate the next surge of power and strength. They represented a line of determination, but with a sinking understanding that this game, the battle, and eventually the war, would be lost. They were the perfect soldiers. They were the warriors who stood and fought the unwinnable battle, never sacrificing the discipline, order and obedience instilled in them. It wasn't a matter of freedom. They fought as if the end would never come, even though grunts of pain and exertion up and down the line of scrimmage heralded such a fate.

Through the season, every practice, game in and game out, those four players were the perfect soldiers. It seemed every game another would step up and lead his charges. Chris Hill intercepted three passes in the Santa Monica game and was voted conference defensive player of the week. John Sonoma intercepted one pass, recovered a fumble, had two sacks and a rash of unassisted and assisted tackles in another game and also was voted conference defensive player of the week. Jarrett and Mike were unofficial generals on and off the field. It was now their will and determination that was going to have to rally their troops to find in their souls, hearts, or as Casey referred to it, their "balls" to stop the 'Gades.

The second play of the drive, Gray took the pitch out and powered his way past the line of perfect soldiers. Blockers leveled Thiessen and John Sonoma and Gray had only Mike Hayes to beat for the score. Mike giving up five inches and 45 pounds ran him down and pulled Gray to the turf 21 yards later. Wobbling a bit, Mike got up slowly, clumps of turf hung from his facemask. A train wreck would have done less damage. Bakersfield was methodically carving huge holes in the line.

"They are just too fucking good, they are big, and they react so quickly," Ryan said, as we stood together and watched our tired defense slowly make their way down field. Every play, Bakersfield functioned as one wheel with eleven different spokes, rolling forward, stopping only temporarily as if a stone was encountered to block the way. Then easily dismissed by the next roll of the wheel, the momentum would continue. As every play ended, from sideline to sideline, red jersied players would try to regroup. They would pick themselves off the turf after being taken out of the play by the Bakersfield onslaught.

The next play, a reverse to the second running back, netted thirteen yards before being stopped by Tony Coffey. In reality, Tony stopped the play by being run over. It was another train wreck. In three plays, Bakersfield had driven close to 40 yards, all on the ground, all a matter of coordination, teamwork and execution. "Come on, defense, suck it up!" Chuck shouted to his team as he watched them being shredded by over two tons of San Joaquin Valley muscle. Joe was standing on our 20-yard line, his arms a whir of motion, signaling in plays, as his concentration was split between the field and Carmen's canned voice on the headset. Everybody in the stadium knew where the ball was going next and by which route, straight ahead and on the ground and 2500 people and players watched Gray receive the handoff and run over three players...

## ROBERT R. SANDS

## KIST

*Gray, 15, 10, 5 down to the 3-yard line, like a raging bull. First and goal, Bakersfield. Mike Gray using his muscle on the inside plays and his speed on the outside plays. That time took it right up the middle. Bakersfield winning the battle in the trenches and in the secondary.*

Football bears the closest resemblance of all sports to war, a metaphor for a battle of many things: bodies, hearts, souls, intellect. Yet its closest resemblance lay not in the violent clashing of muscle and brawn, but the higher struggle for victory over an opponent that involved a keen sense of strategy and a coach's absolute control over his soldiers. It is not too difficult to see the connection between sport and war in our society, especially since the American ideal was founded on a violent revolution. The freedom that we so cherish has been protected through a series of wars and battles. Football can trace its beginnings back to battles between villages in ancient England using inflated cow bladders as the ball and the whole countryside as the field. Crops and those structures standing in the way of the game's progress were decimated and the "game" ended when the bladder was kicked across an agreed-upon goal line.

In the 1800s, this obsession of good clean Saturday afternoon fun had become adopted by the school systems in England, promoting manliness in an atmosphere of intelligencia. The general concept was the same, pitched battles, but the game was adopted to fit the availability of land or, in many cases, lack of land. In the British mentality, hard bodies complemented a sound mind or how else were they going to be able to colonize the world? Both soccer and rugby grew out of this national obsession. Each form evolved out of personal quirks and chance occurrences during games. Rugby was born when the soccer ball was picked up and ran with by an impatient player.

It was only a matter of time before the cousins across the Atlantic picked up on the football mania and created their own obsession. First it was soccer, and then a traveling rugby team from Montreal's McGill University came down to visit Massachusetts and Cambridge University. The Canadians brought with them an oval-shaped ball and Air America was born. In the waning years of the nineteenth century, American elitism took its place alongside English superiority and football was promoted as an activity that produced strong male bodies in a time when industrialization and urbanization were selecting for other less-masculine ideals. In addition, Teddy Roosevelt satiated the thirst for manifest destiny by invading the postage stamp that was Cuba and tossing out the Spanish; there were no more wars to satisfy the need for national (read male) domination.

It is obvious that the American way of life celebrates the protection of our ideals through war; Veterans' Day, Memorial Day, Flag Day all speak to this founding inclination. If there were no wars to prove a man's mettle, there needed to be substitutes and football came closest in its violence, strategy, and bloodletting. Frequent injury and even death marred early games in the States, but after a threat by President Roosevelt to outlaw the sport, the game cleaned itself up and began trumpeting its benefits, such as moral fiber and physical prowess.

Scholars such as Mike Oriard and Michael Messner lay partial responsibility for the rapid popularization of football on the beleaguered male ego. During the rise of American football, masculinity was withering on the American vine of social and gender equality. There were no wars, save for the one between the sexes, and football was a way of excluding the fairer sex and reclaiming the virility of the warrior and the honor and courage that endeared soldiers to society. Games became instant legends and parables for continuing the heroic tradition of the Greeks.

Early twentieth-century America was also a cruel juxtaposition of wealth and poverty and to writer John Seabrook, football was a game for the lowly and the immigrant. "It was a take-or-be-taken society," wrote Seabrook, "and football was a way of making a game out of that; a mean game for a mean world." The fight went from the foreign battlefields of war to the domestic and social Darwinian battle for survival. "The bruising union battles around the turn of the century were physically revisited on the field, there was an undercurrent of brutality that is very much a part of the game," said Seabrook.

This phenomenon of transplanting war for sport is not unique to American or English football. It seems to occur in those cultures that ran out of victims or become victims that fell prey to the other scourges of the nineteenth and twentieth centuries, British colonialism and missionaries. In the Melanesian Trobriand Islands, pre-colonial culture rested on raiding neighboring communities for, of all things, women and pigs. Men became warriors and died revered in oral traditions. The British first colonized the islands and then later, missionaries evangelized the islands. War, killing and polygamy (a reason for war) were outlawed. Trobriand males were reduced to denizens of wimptitude. There were no more rituals of painting bodies and weapons for war, any magical ceremonies for gaining the upper hand on the enemy, no resultant legends of courage passed around campfires, and no exciting history. How exciting is growing a yam?

The British gave them soccer, but there were no correlates for kicking a bladder or running in circles around a field in Trobriand myths and legends. What did catch their fancy, however, was British cricket. The Trobriand Islanders looked beyond the slow pace of the game that would put the players and fans alike to sleep. Instead they fell in love with the duel between pitcher and batsmen, the velocity of the ball propelled by a motion so closely allied with their own spear throwing prowess, and the contact of the ball as it jumped off the bat.

The islanders transformed cricket into their own vanquished culture of war. Villages played afternoon matches during the harvest season. The number of players was unlimited, all males, once warriors, took part. The players painted their bodies and bats in the design of war and players and umpires performed magic before and during the matches. Chants and cheers greeted scores and outs and celebratory dances performed by all players were done in formation. Matches became battles, players became warriors, tradition and pride once again, fueled by the deeds of the players, became the stuff that legends used to be made of. The village chief rewarded valor on the tropical pitch with gifts of tobacco, as he once rewarded bravery and a warrior's skill in battle. Today, cricket has become, as war was before, an integral part of the Trobriand soul.

Is it any wonder that the game of football in American society has become so integral a part of our culture? Is it any wonder that football has become laced with metaphors of war? Is it any wonder that those behaviors so necessarily instilled in soldiers have become cherished in football? We have game balls and championship rings that are given and worn like medals of valor, parades given by "villages" to welcome back the victors of Superbowls, rewards and bonuses meted out to the heroes and injuries suffered in the heat of the game are lionized and then ignored by the players, a further testament to their bravery and courage. In the ultimate melding of turf and battlefield, we have, every year, the Army versus Navy football extravaganza played in Philadelphia Cadets and sailors in full uniform cheer their fellow players, and warriors, onto victory. On this afternoon in November, the distinction between war and football blurs and the symbols for each become shared, and celebrated.

Successful football demands complete abdication of the individual to the good of the team. The game offers a struggle for control of a small piece of land, representing a much larger struggle for control and mastery over the opponent. There are generals and soldiers, field generals and grunts. There are replacements entering the fray for support, to replace the fallen and injured.

Perhaps Vince Lombardi's coaching methods and strategy best compared football to war. Colonel Earl "Red" Blaik, Lombardi's coaching mentor at West Point, instilled in him the need to see football as an extension of battle strategy. As Michael O'Brien points out in his exhaustive treatment of Lombardi, the future coaching great received his early tutelage at West Point, the institution that prepared young men to be soldiers. Football was "violent chess," Blaik liked to argue, but even more football was, "…. In its steep physical, mental, and moral challenges, in its sacrifices, selflessness, and courage, football, beyond any game invented by man, closest to war." It wasn't too difficult to pass this maxim off as integral to the success of a team at a service academy. Lombardi was teethed on this outlook and rose in the coaching ranks to head coach of the Green Bay Packers. Lombardi was a shrewd judge of character, knowing full well that a football team wasn't an army and a football coach wasn't a general. The analogy to war only went so far. There was violence, cooperation and obedience so eleven men could work together to get one ball across a line.

Lombardi was so successful at what he did because the players hadn't grown as big as the sport. Winning was the only thing. Personal glory and satisfaction took a back seat to victory. Later on in his career, the wind of social change was blowing; intermittently at first, but more steadily as the Viet Nam "conflict" escalated from a breeze into a typhoon. According to Jon Seabrook, in the 60s and 70s, football "was everything rock and roll was not; it was discipline rather than hedonism, showing team spirit instead of doing your own thing, a jock/stoner dichotomy memorably expressed in the movie *Dazed and Confused.*"

David Maraniss recently wrote in *Esquire* that Lombardi left the game at the right time. Lombardi retired in 1970 and died shortly thereafter from cancer. Namath, and those who followed, rivaled the importance of the team. In the twilight of Lombardi's coaching career, this quintessential authority, as all authority in the 1960s, was under fire. On the playing field, the battle went deeper than coach versus player. The game was surrounded by a monumental social upheaval where everything in the fabric of American society was being ripped asunder. The freedom that was demanded outside of the stadium was slow to be realized by the players. The turf was one of the last bastions of real order that supported the concept of team. At least inside the field, Lombardi could still expect the team to triumph in the face of personal glory.

With players like Paul Horning and Broadway Joe Namath, wrote Maraniss, Lombardi knew individual freedom was becoming idealized against order. Even in the end, Lombardi was showing signs of adapting his perfect soldiers to the new social order. Had he lived and continued coaching, Lombardi would have adapted because flexibility and choice, both on and off the field, were built into his system. Lombardi never wanted robots; he knew the game presented far too complex strategies to be mastered by robots. What Lombardi wanted from his Green Bay dynasty were thinking players who could respond intelligently to the many different variations they would encounter on the field. His plays were simple and limited in number, but the players knew those plays backwards and forwards and could tease out any number of variations that could happen, if confronted with an array of situations. Lombardi spent hours going over the famed Packer sweep so that the players could respond to whatever defense might be encountered along the way. To Lombardi, that was the real freedom: a choice to choose between the right and wrong play. Freedom was quarterback Bart Starr calling his own plays.

Freedom was the knowledge that no matter who lined up across from you or what defense was in front of you, it was familiar. The obedience, cooperation and teamwork framed Lombardi's ultimate expression of freedom; freedom to win at all costs. Perfect soldiers were intelligent and adaptive, more than programmed. They won because they responded. Perfect soldiers always won, because the rest of the world was imperfect.

Rick Telander wrote that Vince Lombardi corrupted football more than any other coach in the history of the game did. "He bullied his players in a way that quite literally dehumanized them, he opened the door for all kinds of abuses in the name of winning," wrote Telander. The Lombardi mystique can play both sides of the fence. Jerry Kramer, best known not only for his block that paved the way for Bart Starr's touchdown plunge that won the 1965 Ice Bowl, but also his best selling book, *Instant Replay*, swore by the man and his style. Lombardi's brother Joe gave a recent interview to the *Journal of Coach and Athletic Director* and said, "He had that extra something about him, a strength and a certainty about the rightness of things. He was the law in our house. Whenever I got out of line, he was the one who would judge and apply the discipline....[Vince] was a perfectionist, a total football person, organizational man, control 'freak' discipline was everything." In addition to his football acumen, Lombardi was a man of letters. "He had a genuine thirst for knowledge," said Joe Lombardi of his brother. "He could sit down and read a book at one sitting, and retain everything he read."

Lombardi is still is an icon, but his message has been demoted to a cultural sound byte that plays well in a Nike commercial. Life has passed Lombardi's spirit by. Wrote Seabrook, "The values of brute force no longer resonate as deeply with America as they once did.... creativity and entrepreneurship have more currency in our lives than physical labor, and personal initiative means more to us than following orders."

Just like every other player and coach that came out of the 1960s and 70s, Joe and Carmen were conscious disciples of Lombardi. They saw the structure, order and obedience of Lombardi's ways and they strived to duplicate that environment. Football wasn't one of life's blackboards where players could chalk

186

their own destiny. As for the DiPaolos, players were "faceless performers for the team" and football was more about character than personality. To Joe and Carmen, the game was war and pride and self-motivation were the essential ingredients for success. The game was indeed a test of manhood because, to triumph in such a violent sport demanded the ability to perform with dislocated shoulders and pulled muscles, gimpy ankles and mild concussions.

The DiPaolos didn't have the luxury of coaching phenomenal athletes that were capable of adapting to any number of situations. They had the reality of coaching marginal athletes in ability and/or intelligence. They had to appeal to a more basic and primal quality to challenge their players: that of manhood. No scholarships to dangle over their heads, no money to induce performance, no bottomless well of personnel made it imperative to gain a hold on the bodies and minds of the players. To make it binding, Joe and Carmen had to capture the players' fraternal souls.

Joe never let his players off a tether. He wasn't sure they could function without his umbilical cord. And he knew that the other teams were in similar straights. Sure, every now and then, an exceptional defensive player would come along in the conference and would carry a team, but that was the exception, not the rule. You coached them to follow orders, listen and then perform. Chances were the other teams were doing the same thing and it was the team that went out and followed the play the way it was diagramed that would triumph.

To Joe, perfect soldiers were not independent thinkers. They were followers. "You play the way we taught you and you win. It's as simple as that," Carmen would say. Even if you didn't equate football with war, players had to believe that in the end each game was a battle and, most of the times, victory went to the most organized and disciplined team. Those who didn't give 100 percent while their teammates did, were not perfect soldiers.

This day, Joe was seeing his troops as the humiliated and defeated. They were getting beat by soldiers who were more perfect. More than beat, they were getting pummeled and pushed all over the field. And it wasn't just the big running back Gray running over his players, it was the entire Bakersfield offense removing defenders like a fly swatter brushing pesky little flies out of its path. Gray just steamrolled the heart of Joe's defense, Sonoma and Thiessen, as he gained another 10 yards. He would have gone all the way, except mass finally stopped him short of the goal line. Even Gray couldn't run through eleven bodies stacked up. Bakersfield was Sherman's army, rolling along, all gears synchronized, as if nothing could stop them, nothing except the Atlantic. The Confederates knew where Sherman was going, but Atlanta burned just the same.

"Get tough, defense. Plug the middle!" we shouted out. "Stand that fucker Gray up," Kratz screamed. Thiessen was yelling at the defense as they milled around him. Nobody said much back. Oxygen was hard to come by. A yard away stood pay dirt. That yard looked like inches. Bakersfield lined up perfect soldiers all. Gray rammed into the line once more and Thiessen, Sonoma, and our collective hearts rushed in to meet the advance, standing up the Bakersfield line and swarming around Gray. But Gray didn't have the ball and Joe's perfect soldiers died a little more.

### KIST

*Sparks rolls to the right side and fires, TD Bakersfield! A four yard TD pass from Nathan Sparks to tight end Josh Acosta. Nathan Sparks' first pass of the ball game and completed, a four-yard touchdown. Bakersfield regains the lead!*

War is fought in battles and skirmishes; you lose, you regroup, you win, and you press on. Halftime was five minutes away and offered a safe haven to lick our wounds and regroup. But until then, we were getting the ball and the time to march down the field and score. A kickoff and four plays later, Bakersfield had the ball back at midfield. One dropped pass by Torlando and a quarterback sack and the Renegades were back in business. In just five plays, as the half ran out, Bakersfield was in the end zone once again to go up 28-14. We limped, staggered and walked across the battlefield. "It's going to take a fucking miracle for us to come back," Kratz said to me as we climbed the hill into the sanctuary of the team room.

# Chapter 16

---

## Even though I Walk through the Valley
## of the Shadow of Death

**D**reading the next onslaught of the mighty Bakersfield offense, we sat silent and beaten, hunkered down in the haven of the lockers, where just 90 minutes before we had marched resolutely out of to meet the modern-day Philistines. A resigned calm settled over us; not one that was peaceful, but a calm much like the eye of a hurricane offering sanctuary before the return of the winds. We knew what was coming with the 'winds," but had neither the numbers nor the strength to outlast it. Ripped apart and mortally bleeding, some players laid on the blood-red carpet. Others didn't make it that far and leaned up against the lockers, tired legs stretched out, helmets lying in state next to them.

The ease of Gray's runs was frightening and even though we had scored and moved the ball at will against the Bakersfield defense, resignation was written in our eyes. Starters were sweating, their uniforms caked in dried mud and dirt and their faces matted with the effort of 30 minutes of play. Twuan sat, head hanging and tired. He had played like a demon, but now, resting his body, he was not the madman that went off on the team before we went out for our pre-game drills. While we finished dressing

189

and sat preparing for the game, he told us why we had to beat Bakersfield. "God dammit, we are better than this," he screamed. "It's time that we showed it to these motherfuckers. We have to get ready to suck it up and stick it to these fuckers. We have to go out and play, even if we hurt, and win. We have to go to a bowl game. We are capable of winning. You have to believe it!" He rambled on and on and Kratz and I sat unbelieving in the back of the room. "This is the Twuan that just two games ago quit the team," Kratz said to me quietly as the ill-fated Messiah for the day continued. "He hasn't been a team player all season long. Why the fuck should we listen to him now? Christ, this is just too funny." Although Twuan had caught some passes, his running had been bottled up by the huge Bakersfield line.

Dudley quietly circulated through the room, talking to individual players concerning their play and what they could do to improve. Chuck sat huddled with J.T. dissecting the Bakersfield defensive sets. Chuck sensed that a fiery half-time speech was pointless. He knew we had played our guts out the first half. Ryan, Eric and Benjy sat, drained, in their usual corner. Ryan and Eric's shoulders were still painful, especially after getting knocked around like pinballs in the Bakersfield secondary. David joined us and talked quietly about the game. "Gray is just huge and too fast," I said. "He must have over 150 yards already. We can't stop him. We throw and they run."

"Yeah, I don't think we are going to be able to stop him," David said. "We are just going to have to score faster than they do to have a chance and hope for some turnovers."

Joe and Carmen were out in the outer locker room yelling at their players, but it was a muted yell. They, too, knew the players were playing their hearts out. We sat and waited for some inspiration to come from someone, but it was tardy, to say the least. Chuck was shell-shocked. J.T. was unbelievably hot, but we still trailed by two scores. We had to match them score for score the rest of the game and make up the two TDs. Chuck didn't know what to tell 60 players who played their guts out, but were getting tossed around like rag dolls. He had in the past delivered gut-wrenching halftime tirades, but this game was different. We were executing as well as we could. It wasn't the time for fire and brimstone.

Last season, as we sprawled in the Chaffey College

gymnasium, thoroughly embarrassed at halftime and reeling from the shock of the death of Mark's wife, Chuck put on one of his better halftime shows. "LISTEN UP!" he yelled as he jumped up on a wooden box. "It is now a big-time gut check! You didn't come out with any emotion and they just came out and knocked the shit out of you!" It was cold outside, but Chuck was sweating bullets as he tried his hardest to beat back the demons of a gridiron death and challenged us to play beyond mortality. "We are blaming people, we are blaming officials, each other and we are falling apart at the seams and that is bullshit. What we gotta do is come out in the second half and play with emotion and we didn't play with any fucking emotion, guys. We have to play with emotion! Otherwise you are going to get your asses knocked off and that's what's happening. It's bullshit, we are not ready and its bullshit that we are pointing fingers. What we have to do is respond. It's character building again. If you guys want it deep inside your heart then come out and beat these guys."

Ready to slay dragons, we charged out of the gym, but as much as Chuck's words and intensity lingered in our hearts, our minds and bodies fell prey to emotional overload. We played even flatter than we had in the first half and we left the cold night wishing that life had a fast forward button to skip past the bitterness. Now we were looking for something like that to pull us out of the shadow of our season's final death and lead us to victory. As I sat there and took in the locker room scene, I agreed with Kratz; a miracle signaling divine intervention was our only chance.

I loved the game of football. It filled my days and ate up my nights. By the end of the second season, my passion for the game had taken on a spiritual dimension. Since the start of my research into sport and culture, I felt that sport had many similarities to religion and my experience with football reinforced this belief. My life was split into a sacred and profane. I experienced the ordinary while I bumped along on a daily road of the mundane, taught classes, took classes, graded, planned lectures and relaxed, but once I stepped out onto the field, I stepped into a sacred and altered state of reality. My focus changed, my personality was subsumed by something greater than myself, my teammates, and even the coaches. For three hours every afternoon and during the games, my existence was wired into my body. Our legs gobbled up yardage, our lungs burned from chasing down errant passes, fingers, most of them swollen, grasped leather, eyes read coverages and minds mediated instinct with desire.

Everyday practice was haunted with ritual and ceremony. Practice was structured around the daily repetition of drills, scrimmages and motivational talks from coaches and ended after scrimmaging with position-specific conditioning drills, sprints, bleachers, push-ups and sit-ups. Like the repetition of ritual so integrated into any type of religious experience, such as Hail Mary's, the spoken Lord's Prayer, the weekly sacraments; the mundane was lifted above the ordinary by creating unique situations and then repeating them day to day. On game day, activity became more hallowed, more contemplative, and more important. There was the team prayer, the coin toss, the National Anthem sung by a scratchy recording of Whitney Houston over the stadium loudspeakers, the ritualized forms of encouragement and celebrations, the ending handshake between victor and defeated in the middle of the "battlefield," the final prayer and the patterned responses given to the reporters by stars and coaches alike; all separated the game experience from the profane.

To anthropologists, religion is ritual backed by myth which lifts humans above mortal everyday existence, connecting them with a force more powerful than themselves that deposits them into an altered state. "Athletes," said writer, now attorney, Howard Slusher, "come to see that there is something beyond mere mortality, beyond the understandable, which extends man beyond the powers of rational mind and physical body." Charles Prebish, editor of *Religion and Sport,* viewed sport as a "formal, sacred religious tradition" based on the "transforming power of contact with ultimate reality." This process occurs through transformation of space and time. Space is transformed from profane to sacred in stadiums, gyms, and fields. These become the "center" of the sport world.

Time is also transcended in religion. The clock may run signifying the passage of sacred time in a contest, but ordinary time is suspended. Sporting contests produce sacred time that is measured by the pace of action. One need only watch the last two minutes of a basketball or football game to understand this

192

suspension of ordinary time. In sports like baseball and golf, ordinary time is not instrumental in deciding outcomes. The action is carried by a period marked only by a beginning and an end, where action proceeds at a pace tied not to a measure, but to the funneling of ritual activity through the sport.

For many participants and non-participants, sport is more than just a facet of life. It takes on a much "higher," even metaphysical dimension. Human performance and the trappings that surround the culture of athletic experience invoke reaches literally into the soul to produce the necessary emotion and competitive spirit to excel on the playing field. The philosopher Michael Novak, author of the classic piece on sport and religion, *The Joy of Sports*, perhaps best described this belief that sport is sacred. To Novak, sport could be construed as religion, in the sense that they are organized institutions, disciplines, and liturgies and in the sense that they teach religious qualities of heart and soul. Sport is not the Judeo-Christian ideal, but sport is, as anthropologists believe religion to be, a system of beliefs, sacred in the experience it invokes and a basis to construct a lifetime around. "In particular," Novak wrote, "sport recreates symbols of cosmic struggle in which human survival and courage are not assumed." The warriors of the gridiron replayed and reinterpreted the symbolic struggle of good and evil. That is why coaches implore their charges to play from the "heart," the need to "dig down deep" or to undergo a "gut check" and find the motivation in one's soul. In other words, to discover your character.

The ancient Olympics were athletic festivals held and participated in to honor the many gods and to legitimize, and even honor, mortal membership in the state. Individual athletic feats were dedicated to the gods, but so very similar to most religions were the "pomp, circumstance and ritual" that enveloped the performances. "Since then," said Novak, "sport has always been endowed with a matrix of ritual, opening and closing days of the Olympics, opening day of baseball, the Superbowl; Christ, pageantry, and hyperbole reigns." In a more secular age, "the rituals of sport really work: they feed a deep human hunger, place humans in touch with certain daily perceived features of human life within this cosmos, and provide an experience of at least a pagan sense of godliness."

For the 55-65 players that ended the 1994 and 1995 seasons as Vaquero football players, their performance and participation expressed on the field acted as a mosque would, centering and focusing the player on quenching a thirst for sacred experience. There was something about the game that went beyond the boundaries of a field that made me return day after day despite the pain or perhaps for the pain. Something generated by the interaction of the sport and personnel produced a feeling of otherworldliness that soothed a part of me not massaged by everyday life. It daily awakened in me a dormancy of testosterone, endorphin, adrenaline, and competitive fire that spoke volumes without needing words.

My two-plus years of field notes were filled with entries of personal enjoyment and delight of performance. "I can't wait to get to practice tomorrow. The thrill of ending practice on a completion of a 93 Fade (a bomb) is almost indescribable!" I wrote one evening. "My hands cradled the leather as if it were an egg and I tucked it under my arms and was gone. My feet felt as they were wings, being pushed by the late afternoon breeze."

"When I am in practice," I penned another day, "lectures, grading, studies drop from the ledges of my mind, like autumn leaves falling from their seasonal perch. All I see, think and experience is the whack of pads, the neat spiral of J.T.'s ball, the plant and pivot of my right foot in a pass pattern. My mind grapples with the intricacies of playing the game right, as if my whole being, my aching shoulder, legs, tight hamstrings, creaky left knee, gnarled and swollen fingers, and my always burning desire to do better, is wired into the offered by J.T.'s right arm. I become, like everybody else on the field, part of an ever-moving micro-cosmos that fits neatly inside a 100 yard by 54 yard rectangle. Ironic that the flight of such cosmos comes down to simple geometry."

Another aspect that ties sport to religion is that the sacredness of sport lies in its temples and the stadiums, where reality is left behind when entering the turnstile, plunking down the tithe and gingerly walking on hallowed ground. The concrete edifice seems to warn, "Beware, all ye who enter. Suspend your existential worries and caress the mortal soul with the immortal commandments of competition." Fans pile in droves to fill the cathedrals of sport. In unison, they also suspend the profane to exhort their team on to victory. Caught up in the cacophony of sound, thousands of throats scream as one with just one purpose, to elevate the mere mortals that perform on the sacred turf to god-like status.

Taking in a Kansas City Chief football game at Arrowhead Stadium or watching in person the annual Ohio State-Michigan football game, one can quickly grasp the intensity and "sacred" nature of the experience. It is just not the sheer amount of sound produced that lends to this "otherworldliness" of the experience, it is the feeling of undergoing a common experience, as in the case of Buckeye Stadium, in Columbus, Ohio, through congregation with 100,000 other souls.

Paul Weiss, author of *Sport: A Philosophic Inquiry*, suggested that while performing the athlete creates a distinct "...domain with its own beginning, ending, process and laws. What he is and what he does is for the moment thereby severed from the rest of the world." It is a world that is separate from the profane. "Like a religious man," wrote Weiss, "who turns from the world to open himself up to his God, the athlete places himself before whatever eternal and impersonal judge there is."

Sport aligns participants and audience with past heroes and lays the foundation for future icons. The athlete's role looms larger than life, becoming the savior figure for those watching, and will become lore for those who will read or learn about the athlete's exploits in the future. Even if the game or sport changes in structure, athletes are connected in time and space. Athletic performance becomes an ageless psalm, read and reread to generations that follow. Over time, these performances become like myth and speak to places not known and evoke imagery of accounts that take on almost supernatural qualities.

A pilgrimage to football's Hall of Fame leads you to a church in the round housing the past "saints" of the gridiron where the miracles and feats are enlarged and reproduced beyond life. Over time, these performances become myths and speak to places most of us have not known and evoke imagery of accounts that take on almost supernatural qualities. The past is glorified, objectified and mere men who wear funny little helmets and awkward clumps of body padding somehow are deified.

Dr. Lloyd Saatjian, pastor of the First United Methodist Church in Santa Barbara, told me an interesting story relating to the power of myth. "Have you ever been to the Football Hall of Fame that resides in Canton, Ohio?" he asked me. When I shook my head no, he continued. "You ought to go someday. It is something to see," he said. "There are three statues, busts of three men. One is Vince Lombardi, the other is Y.A. Tittle and the third is Paul Brown." In my mind I heard the concluding words of the Lord's Prayer, "...in the name of the father, son and Holy Ghost."

"It was interesting. The heads of Vince Lombardi and Y.A. Tittle were worn down to a fine finish as if they had been rubbed down to the bare metal," he said. "I asked one of the guards why and he told me that people come to stand in front of these statues and rub their heads; maybe for luck or to pay their respects."

In his piece on the Four Horsemen, journalist Grantland Rice conjured up images of biblical proportions when writing about Notre Dame football in 1924. Central to these mythical, almost mystical, images, are the athletes. A few step outside mortality and produce patterns of excellence so high that humans live up to them only rarely. When one encounters these elevated souls, there is feeling of a quality that separates them from others.

Athletes who perform for many or just a few are not just entertainers, filling a role in an athletic drama. There is something else to their personae that lives beyond or deep within each of us. It is something so powerful that stories, myths and legends about athletes can shape a person's outlook on life, as well as to live in glory for generations after. So evocative that the simple telling locks us in reverence and awe and our faces light up and words dance a passionate mambo in description.

People claim intimate associations with elite athletes and superstars. These athletes become like brothers or best friends and are referred to on first-name basis; "I want to be like Mike." Even with this artificial familiarity, there is identification with these athletes that borders on priestly. Like gods and spirits, which become property of all to be shared and prayed to for salvation and forgiveness and to be modeled after and emulated, athletes assume a frightening power. The feats and lives of athletes of the highest caliber explode in society in an expression of immortality. "Once they become superstars, they do not quite belong to themselves," said Novak. "Great passion are invested in them. They are no longer treated as ordinary humans or even mere celebrities. Their exploits and failures have a great power to exult or depress."

Athletes like John Unitas, Joe Namath, Walter Payton, Joe Montana, yes, even O.J. Simpson breathe and live in response to the years that slip by. One grows old with these remembered images and personalities. Somehow the images and memories stay fresh and vivid, even growing in believability, not yellowed and crackled like the newsprint or the newsreel first recorded on. Spanning decades, the athlete remains pure in performance. Novak opens his book waxing eloquently about George Blanda and the miracle 1970 season. Blanda repeatedly led his Oakland Raider teammates on weekly journeys back from the jaws of defeat. A legend was born and somehow that legend will never die, even though George will someday lose the battle of life.

Added Weiss, "Like every other body, the athlete's decay and eventually passes away. But there is a sense in which he nevertheless continues to be. Since he has abdicated from all other positions to make himself a man who is an effective, excellent body, he has defined himself to be an incarnation of those persistent laws, which cover the operation of that body. He is one with those laws, their very embodiment, and is so far forever. As an individual he passes away, of course, but his individuality is irrelevant to the more basic fact that he has made himself into a place where those laws for the moment are."

It is not just George Blanda or Mickey Mantle who in time-honored tradition, salve and attend to our spiritual need for athletic miracles. Closer to home, it is also the performance of local heroes that live in the hearts of those who witnessed or, were a part of history in the making, on a brisk October evening on a wet field or in a hot, stuffy Indiana gym while the Arctic gales of late January fiercely blew. Legends of a 90-yard TD run in the waning seconds of a district game or a clutch 40-foot desperation jump heave as time expired to send the high school team into sectionals, shine just as bright and refuse to die. No matter the numbers that remember, be it in the millions or the hundreds, it is the collective act of telling and retelling of the legend once more that locks it forever into a life separate from the passing mortality of the participants.

Thirty years later, the quarterback who scrambled for that 90-yard run is only a shadow of his former self. Life has worn him down. He has five kids, sells insurance and waits for his two weeks of fishing in the summer. Mention the run and his eyes light up, revealing a burning fire that illuminates under an aging body. Those that saw it will revel in the same feeling. Perhaps, each will pass the legend down to children and possibly on the eve of the yearly big game, it will live once again in the pages of the local newspaper. For Blanda, as Novak wrote, "His own body and ordinary self became as it were, inwardly suffused with a power not his own.... For those who saw the actual deeds, their beauty spoke for themselves; their excellence pleased; something true shone out."

From ritual to prophets, sport reaches heavenward, while plumbing the depths of the soul. This athletic nirvana is reached only through the marriage of mind and body or, perhaps better said, through the body and soul to the exclusion of the mind. For many, athletics is anti-intellectual, just as many feel religion stunts intellectual thought and growth. In the most liberal sense of the phrase, sport actually transforms and produces an altered state in the athlete.

Michael Murphy, author of *The Future of the Body*, goes as far as to say, "athletes...often experience paranormal events and ecstatic moments bordering on the mystical." During the last two seasons, I came to think of the playing field as a situation apart from normal life. It helped produce an experience where participation, even success, was dependent on one's body and mind coming together in a marriage, not of convenience, but with a goal beyond the development of either one. The goal was to transcend the ordinary and perform at a level above the profane. And in many cases, this involved undergoing pain, rising above psychological states of doubt about performance, and transforming everyday personality into what is commonly called in football, "game day face." This was where a player becomes a vessel for a consciousness that is geared to suspending life for three hours and reaching peak performance.

As Murphy writes, "Flesh and consciousness tend to co-evolve during the practice of strenuous disciplines. The mind," he continued, "frequently opens in sport suffusing bone and muscle with its latent energies, whether or not the athlete can describe what is happening to him." In eastern religions, through meditation and other psychological experiences, such as sleep deprivation and hunger, the mind enters an altered state. Hallucinations are common to these experiences as the mind distorts what is reality during the profane.

It is in sport where the body becomes a necessary component of the transcendental experience and nirvana is inherently wrapped up in performance. Murphy goes as far as to call sport a "Western Yoga, an earthly form of transformative practice. Through a contagion we are hardly aware of, athletes in top form awaken a secret sense that we harbor capacities for extraordinary life." In a moment of adrenaline-addled frenzy or the quiet, gritty "gotta have it" determination of crunch time, the body is capable of producing performance that ranges far beyond the imagination of the athlete. Tennis players call it "playing in the zone," where your body has become an internal metronome and it tick-tocks in consistency. The player's mind is suffused with an unbelievable sense of confidence and everything hit has eyes and raises chalk. Or a golfer with a swing that produces unerringly accurate shots. Or the basketball player who has the "stroke," and shots find nothing but net. Or the quarterback who completes 10 or 15 passes in a row. This is athletic nirvana, rarely reached periods where the mind and body put it all together.

Torlando Bolden and Twuan Hill ripped off long touchdown runs during the 1995 season. We watched them on video at Monday's film session or tuned into the four-time weekly Vaquero highlight show on the local cable channel. Over and over, in slow motion, their individual moves bordered on miraculous. In one, Twuan spins and jukes his way through thirty yards of defensive players and not once runs more than five yards in a straight line. Listening to them talk about it during film, they didn't know how they made a certain move or went one direction instead of another or, how they got the strength to break tackles or carry two or three guys for extra yardage.

In the sense of the struggle between good and evil, the outcome of sport takes on a metaphysical dimension. Outside of the rare occasions of a tie, the athletic ritual-like struggle comes down to a simple determination of win or lose. The euphoric feeling of a victory and the depression felt with a loss leaves one reliving, over and over again, the symbolic struggle of life and death. In the immediate aftermath of an athletic contest, when one is still in the grips of the "athletic state," a loss becomes the closest thing to a symbolic death. In just those few seconds, while the muscles of the body are close to exhaustion, close to physical death, the mind teeters on the brink of mortality. In a way, it is worse than death, for death has an end, a finality to it. In another way, it just feels like dying. But for both feelings, it is not the end.

In religion, there is a similar symbolic metamorphosis between life and death. Rituals such as communion produce within the individual a sense of death. To take part is to be ultimately given life. As in sport, defeat oftentimes leads to a rebirth in the next game or contest; death leads to resurrection and a fuller life. The great equalizing line instilled in children from the time of T-ball or youth soccer, "It is only a game," attempts to hide the power of sport to, as Novak writes, "exhilarate or depress far greater than being mere pastimes." It is an attempt to curb the deleterious effects of the extreme pendulum swing of emotion that results from sport. Show me an athlete, no matter the age or sex, who says that sport is only a game and I will show you an athlete in name only.

God had a hand in changing the 1995 Vaqueros in the days following the end of our season. A few found a higher inspiration. Twuan, Chris, and Mike came to Santa Barbara breathing a gospel life. Living on their own for two years, away from parents, friends and church, created fun-loving vessels. Twuan became a "lover," boasting of his girlfriends. Chris and his cousin were noted partiers. They loved to express their spirituality in prayer and devotion on the field and in the locker room, but their lives were a mixture of penance and pleasure. Following the last game of the second season, they all trooped home to Florida for Christmas vacation, fully intent on coming back and finishing their degree so they could go to Division 1 schools. In fact, both Chris and Twuan were being courted by the likes of Fresno State, LSU, and Kentucky.

They came back for two weeks and were gone from Santa Barbara after the first week of the spring semester. They left, not as they had played on the field or lived their life here, electric, fast, no holds barred, oblivious to the wake of emotions they stirred up in others, but with a whimper, changed by the face of their God. Over Christmas, Chris spent three days in the grips of a religious fever; on his knees, speaking in tongues, being chased by demons. It was like something had reached inside his skull and ripped out the pleasure centers. To him, it was scary and prophetic; change your life or not go to heaven. Twuan watched Chris go through this profound change and followed his cousin down the path of salvation. Three hundred and fifty-pound Mike had always been quiet, but now, in the midst of rebirth, he fit right in. They came back changed 180 degrees. Quiet, respectful, the earthy rough edges of their personalities were filed down to a dull finish. No more jokes, no more sex, no drinking, no partying. For two weeks, they confounded and amazed their friends and teammates. And then they were gone.

Chuck called in his army and we all bunched up in the team room. As we sat anticipating his words, he stood there, his head hanging down, eyes on the floor and his arms wrapped behind his back. Finally, he lifted his head and found the drive to push words from his mouth. "We are not bad off. There is no need to hang your head! We are playing even with the fifth ranked team in the nation. Keep doing what you are doing. We are not out of the game by any means! Defense, we stop them a couple of times and offense will put it in. I am proud of you guys. You play your best and that is all we can ask for. Leave it all on the field today, gentlemen. Now let's get a prayer."

On the way through the locker room, I talked to Jarrett about the game. He was battle-weary with grass stains, dried mud caked on like a paste, mud on his face, chunks of turf caught in his face bar and a red stain that was his or others inner juices that blended in with the scarlet red of his jersey. A definite All-Madden pick. "Christ, they are so big and fast," he said, his voice subdued and dipped in pessimism. "Especially that fucker Gray."

"He is a semi with a Porsche engine," I agreed.

"He is a ton to bring down," he said. "I don't know how we are going to stop them this half. You offensive guys have to keep them off the field so we can grab some rest. We are going to have to play out of our minds to stay in this one."

It was bleak, but not desperation time yet. As we walked with resolute determination out of the dark of the locker room and into the bright light of the waning day facing the Goliath that waited to finish us off, the famous Psalm 23 verse seemed to be a more appropriate religious image. "Even though I walk through the valley of the shadow of death, I will fear no evil for you are with me, your rod and staff, that comfort me." The stadium gave way to the "valley" of the field and we conjured up emotion to once again meet in the end zone and gather strength and energy from each other. We definitely could have used an extra rod and staff.

**KIST**

*Santa Barbara moved the ball well this first half. Rushing yards, Bakersfield, 25 carries for 219 yards. Individually, Mike Gray 17 carries 180 yards, TD runs of 31 and 1. Santa Barbara had 8 carries for 11 yards. Bakersfield only passed for 4 yards, but that was for a TD. And Santa Barbara passed for 208 yards. Total yardage, Bakersfield 223, Santa Barbara 219. Only a 4 yard difference, Bakersfield 1-3 passing, J.T. Stone, 21-27 with one interception. J.T. needs 304 yards passing, as you said 21-27, 208 yards, so he now needs 96 for 3000 on the year.*

# Section Four
## The Game
## Bakersfield versus Santa Barbara
## Third Quarter

*A Ghost of LaPlaya, Receiver's Coach Steve Dudley*

*The man in the middle, Head Coach Chuck Melendez*

# Chapter 17

## Skin Deep

G rim faced, J.T. spiraled warm up tosses back and forth to us as the defense started the second half on the field bracing for the next onslaught of the Renegades. Not many words were spoken and all that was audible was the slap of the leather as it settled into hands. "All right, defense, tighten up. Let's get it back for the offense!" Chuck yelled as he began his pacing on the offense sideline.

We paused in our warm-ups and watched the Bakersfield kick returner use a couple of blocks to return the ball over the Renegade 40-yard line. This drive was important. Stop them and score and we are down by a TD and back in the hunt for the biggest upset in recent Vaquero memory. Our sidelines belched out encouragement as the defense dug in. Chuck and Dudley were yelling encouragement, but absent was T.K.'s voice that carried the loudest and the furthest. T.K. was missing from the sidelines. He was hunting duck in northern California on a trip he had planned before he accepted the coaching job in August, but somehow that didn't bother his players. T.K. had lived and died with them all season and had delivered a stirring speech to the team the day before he left. What we were missing was his intensity and the ability to knife through the game's politics and appeal to the naked emotion of the player.

But T.K. wasn't there as the Bakersfield quarterback, Sparks, faked to Gray into the line, the first play of the second half, faked the entire defensive line, faked Joe and Carmen, faked the entire sideline and tossed only Bakersfield's third pass of the entire game.

### KIST

*Nathan Sparks rolling to his left and Sparks fires to Acosta at the 45 to the Santa Barbara 40 and dropped at the 35-yard line by Chris Hill and Anthony Coffey. Not before a gain of 21 and a Renegade first down. Bakersfield comes out of the locker room airborne and big gain on first down.*

T.K. Walters wasn't there to scream about character building as the momentum we took from the locker room deflated like air from a ruptured blimp. T.K. Walters wasn't there to physically and verbally assault our desire and manhood on the sideline and try to breathe life back into this game. He also wasn't there when, just two minutes into the third quarter, on four plays, two passing and two running, Bakersfield stormed in from the two-yard line to go up 31-14. T.K. was, instead, hours away blasting ducks from the afternoon sky.

The game was in danger of being a blowout. It seemed like years ago that the score was tied and, in the last four series before the half, J.T. had been stymied by Bakersfield's thundering rush. At one time or another, everybody but Bakersfield's trainer had come flying in after J.T., giving him little time to set up or, worse yet, made him run for his life. Reality was setting in and a sense of desperation was invading the sideline.

Art was back in the game. He had cornered the team doctor in the locker room during half time. "I want to play and Susan won't let me," he told him. "Okay," the good doctor said, "how high can you lift your arm?" Art brought it up, with difficulty, to shoulder height. The doctor said, "Okay, you can handle the pain, you can play." Susan wasn't buying it and as Bakersfield kicked off, I watched as she told Art if he went in and came out banged up, she wasn't treating him. "Art, you have a dislocated shoulder," she was trying to tell him without emotion. "You could do some serious damage if you get hit on it. I don't think you should be out here at all." Twuan and Chris, along with Art, ganged up on her and started yelling on the sidelines. Susan held her ground in the face of this withering barrage of "bitch" and other uncomplimentary labels.

With Art in, we finally had some outside speed to loosen up the Bakersfield secondary. We were very capable of exploding; a bomb here, and a couple of missed tackles there and, in a matter of minutes, we could climb right back in the hunt. The first play of our first series of the second half, Art joined Torlando and Lee Green on the line of scrimmage, and with J.T. and Twuan in the backfield, five out of the six offensive skill players were black. I didn't really think much of it until I looked around and saw Eric, David and Ryan standing with us on the sidelines. And even then, that thought slipped quickly from my mind as they spread out to their positions and readied for J.T.'s signals.

One afternoon, two weeks before the end of the season, with Torlando and Art gone and Lee late to practice, I ended up running on the first string with the rest of the receivers, Benjy, Ryan and Eric. We came out to take a breather and Eric commented that this was a far different team than at the beginning of the season when he was the only "white" starter. Pat walked by and called us the albino brothers. Four white receivers, a black quarterback and black receiver's coach. Everybody agreed, an uncommon sight in college and professional football.

When does uniqueness give way to feelings of racism? The receivers were a microcosm for the rest of the team; out of 14 receivers, six were black. Six "niggers" and eight "honkies." There was more than just color that separated lifestyle, background, upbringing and stereotypical perceptions from different personalities. Casey, like Thiessen and others, brought up in rural areas, could never get away from his childhood prejudices. "More points should be given for a white guy who scores a TD," said Casey, during one of our Sunday football watching orgies. When Eric scored against Moorpark, Casey came up to me on the sideline and said, "How rad is that, a white guy who scores!"

It is the same on the flip side of the coin as the black players questioned white players' "natural abilities" like speed and moves.

"I'll tell you, Doc, the brothers just got the moves and the juice," Chris said. "It's nobody fault, God just made it that way." In the game of football where there is a unique combination of precision, cooperation, speed, guile, and spontaneous creativity married to structure, there is room for everybody. Lying just below the surface, occasionally surfacing, there are stereotypes that are pervasive and everybody, no matter the race, buys into them.

It was almost Christmas 1994, a year before the Bakersfield game, and Bo, a receiver from my first season, and I met at 12 noon to run routes. Bo was the epitome of the blue-collar jock. He had some ability, but he made up what he lacked on sheer guts and enthusiasm. He had short-cropped hair, not bad speed, and was over 6 feet. But then that would basically describe most of the receivers that year. Bo was also white.

For ten minutes we alternated between throwing five routes and running five routes. We were just getting into it when, out of the blue, a couple of guys walked onto the track. One split up into the nether reaches of the stadium and the other, tall and lanky, ambled over to where we were tossing the pigskin. "Do you mind if I throw some to you," he asked. I was not very receptive. We were into the flow and I didn't want to waste time. "We are running routes, you know," I answered in hopes he would leave us alone. "Don't worry," he came back, "I used to be a quarterback. "Oh, all right,' I said. "Bo, let's run every other one." Bo's arm wasn't that hot anyway. Maybe we would luck out and he would have a semi-decent arm.

It quickly became apparent that he did used to toss the ball. His throws were frozen ropes and carried yards down field. He asked us if we played here, about the team and ourselves. Finding out about my situation, he exclaimed, "a teacher and a player, and at 37. You are my hero!" Then he gunned another missile in my direction. I told him I was from Iowa and Illinois and received a Ph.D. from University of Illinois. "I went there," he said. "I graduated in 1983."

"I missed you by three years. I didn't get there till '86," I said, becoming interested. I ran a couple more routes and then it was Bo's turn and I took a breather. "Did you play at Illinois?" I quizzed him. "Yeah, for a couple of years." Along with my brothers, I knew Illinois football backwards and forwards and my interest was really piqued.

"What is your name?"

"Eason, Tony Eason," he said matter of factly. Oh, shit, I gulped to myself. Touchdown Tony Eason, only one of the premier and prolific passers in Illinois history. "Didn't you play for the Patriots...?"

"...And the Jets, too," he filled in. Tony Eason now lives outside of San Diego and plays golf at 8 handicap. He offered Bo and I tip after tip on running routes and catching the ball. He could still air the leather after not throwing for "a couple of years." "This is the best fun I have had for awhile," he told us, after hitting me 60 yards down field on a streak.

In between patterns, I sucked him dry for information about his playing days. Of course, Bo didn't remember him; not surprising. "I miss the last two minutes of a game," Tony said. Everything clicked then. I missed the locker room with the guys and I miss the money." We spent time going back through the years at Illinois and the players I remember that still roll off my tongue and he played with. He didn't look much like a pro quarterback, but when he released the ball that afternoon it wasn't too difficult placing him in the midst of a slowly crumbling pocket. Many times, Bo and I dropped perfect passes and he would smile and clap his hands and say, "get them the next time." It wasn't hard to feel good about what we did right.

Bo left after an hour or so and I ran a couple more post corners and then we stood in the middle of the end zone and talked race and sport. "You know," he said to me after I broached the subject of blacks in sport, "I never really knew about racism until I left the NFL. Inside, we were all just players. Personally, I think blacks are better athletes," he said matter-of-factly.

"What about cultural influence?" I asked. "What about the fact that all you ever see are blacks with speed. Shit, even the linemen run 4.7 40s."

"I'll bet you that if you lined up a million black sprinters and a million white ones, you would find out that blacks are just faster," he said.

"Maybe, but we don't know for sure," I shot back.

So we went back and forth, throwing out our best ammunition.

"If you muscle sectioned blacks you would find they have, on the average, more fast twitch muscle," he said at one point.

"Yeah, remember what happened to Jimmy the Greek," I said.

"Maybe he was too close to reality," he answered. "Look, I am not a racist by any stretch of the imagination. I just saw what I saw and when I was playing. I saw blacks running 4.3 40s and whites running 4.5 40s."

"What about the white burners like Golden Richards, Doug Donnelly and Roger Carr. What about them?" I gave it back.

"What about Roy Green," he asked. "I can name them forever, can you? For every one you come up with, I can spot you ten."

It is not difficult to see where football and its present racial makeup would form perceptions of behavioral determinism, where blacks are considered better natural athletes; whites, more cerebral. Carl Lewis explained dominance by blacks in sprinting to a better sprinting body with a longer legs and levers. On the other hand, Brooks Johnson, one-time Stanford and U.S. Olympic coach, said there isn't any advantage to blacks and there was "a white Carl Lewis out there, we just haven't found him."

Physical anthropologist, Robert Malina has written extensively on genes, race and sport and said that there are anatomical and muscle differences between blacks and whites, but not enough to be deterministic in performance. When it comes to elite performances in sprinting, a hundredth of a second can separate first from fourth place and that small difference could make a difference.

"I did my doctoral research on black sprinters," I told Eason, "and Willie Williams, the sprint coach at University of Illinois ran against some of the greatest white sprinters in history during the 1940s and 1950s that were just as fast: Bobby Morrow, Dave Sime, Lindy Remigino. These names don't probably register with you, but back then they were hot shit. Now, blacks are so prevalent in sprints as in other sports because what else are they going to do without the education or financing available to many whites?" What about other sports like football where athleticism plays a large part in excellence, but is not the only determinant of performance? Many other factors enter into the equation and this opens the door for assigning behavioral traits to certain populations of athletes, i.e. playing smart versus dumb, hard worker versus gifted, instinctive versus quick learner. And, for the most part, these dichotomies fall along racial lines.

I said, "Harry Edwards (sport sociologist) says there are fewer job possibilities in the highly visible professional jobs like doctor and lawyer for blacks, and black kids see the instant riches of the professional athletes and entertainers and it is too good not to go for."

"That is all fine and dandy," Tony said, " but what about now when opportunity for blacks is opening up? Shouldn't we get a balancing of race in sport?"

"Possibly, but this isn't going to change overnight. It is more of a generational thing," I said. Back and forth we went, under the clear blue skies and rolling surf just feet away. It was fun to talk to someone who wasn't a college football player, but looked at things from the locker room of professionalism. Neither of us convinced the other, but Touchdown Tony was speaking from a stronger position of the insider. He had more than anecdotes to back up his thoughts.

I didn't want to leave. There are rare times in research when you hit a "gusher" of information and you want to milk it for all its worth. But my legs were tired and sore and I was starving. "You know, I have never thought of it your way," he said as I was getting my gear picked up. "You have years of research to back your side up. So you think it is sociological why blacks are faster?" How can I answer that I thought? Do I really believe that it is all cultural? Maybe I resisted thinking like that because, deep down, I didn't want to think that I couldn't get any faster because I was white. "I am sure that is part of the reason," I said as I chose the fence to sit on. We shook hands after wishing each other luck and I glanced back as I walked off the field. Touchdown Tony Eason was in the middle of the end zone, hitting an imaginary 7 iron.

J.T. backpedaled as he searched for an open receiver, but Bakersfield gave him little time and buried him under a mountain of muscle. He was looking for Torlando, but two defenders shadowed him and J.T. ate the ball. Dudley sent Dave back in for Lee and, as Lee came running off the field, I knew, at that very moment, not one of us was entertaining the thought that the racial composition of the receiving corps had changed.

The savage rush came once again, smelling blood, hunting J.T.

down like a wounded deer. This time he got the pass off to Dave before being upended, but Dave only made it back to the line of scrimmage and was swarmed under. By now, Bakersfield had little doubt what we were going to do every play. They just lined up five down lineman, threw in a couple of secondary players, and rushed in, their ears pinned back under their helmets. It didn't really matter what color the receivers were, J.T. couldn't get them the ball.

The 1994 and 1995 Vaquero football team was an even mix of Black, Hispanic and Anglo players and the locker room was always a scene of intersecting lifestyles expressed in music, humor, off-field leisure time, but lifestyles fell to the wayside when football was the topic. I remember getting dressed early one day and listening to Jerome and some of the black Culver City players explain to Twuan, Art and Chris Hill about gangs in Los Angeles. "Man, I tell you, you can't be too safe in another gang's hood," Jerome said. "Those mother fuckers gonna fuck you up, you wear the wrong colors or don't give the right sign. You don't go into the Crips' hood if you are a Blood. Keep the windows rolled up and don't stop for nothing. Those niggers are bad!"

Art couldn't believe it. "Man, you gotta be shitting me. It's that bad?"

"No, motherfucker, it's that good," Jerome replied.

"It's not like that back in Florida, where we come from," Chris said. "We got the drugs and people get killed over that shit, but we don't have the organized gangs."

Then there were the times when insults flew and the blacks would diss each other and the white players would stand around and wish they could be so quick.

"I'm telling you, yo momma is so fat, when she bungee jumped she went all the way to hell."

"Don't be talking about my momma!"

"Your sister's teeth are so yeller, when she opened her mouth, cars slowed down."

"Don't be talking about my sister!"

No matter where you lived, growing up prepared you for the dozens, but how many whites attended Compton High School or some of the other black high schools in LA? Along with Art, and outside of Torlando, there was a large group of LA blacks who called themselves the "Brotherhood." They would throw parties and hang together, trying to carry over some of their LA identity into white-bred, Anglo-Saxon Isla Vista.

"I went to a Brotherhood party last week," Casey said, before the Compton game, "and I was the only white guy there. It was strange, so I left because one of the non-brotherhood blacks was trying to get into a fight with me."

"Some of the Florida guys would hang out with the brotherhood when there was a party, but there were a lot of times when they didn't," Pat Aguilera said. "But a big determining feature was where the players lived," he continued. "Those that lived out in Isla Vista hung together, while those who lived downtown would do the same. Many times, where you lived kind of determined you hung out with."

Still, there were only a few players, both black and white, who would hang with different groups. Tony Coffey, the black sophomore defensive back, spent time over at white power central, Casey and Thiessen's apartment, and the relationship between the players always fascinated me. In fact, Tony was his own man and fit in well with any group of athletes and was a facilitator to boot; quiet, always a smile, deferential, when it was required, inspiring through his play and his maturity. He would make a great politician.

"Coffey ain't a nigger, not like some of those other LA guys," Thiessen told me. "Tony is an allright dude. He has his head on straight!" Which meant, Coffey doesn't wear his blackness on his sleeve like the others.

"Nigger" was a word that was loaded with emotions like anger and humor. It was defining label of identity that was dependent on context and who called whom a nigger. "The word poured out in Odessa (Texas) as easily as the torrents of rain that ran down the streets after an occasional storm," wrote H.G. Bissenger, "as common as part of the vernacular as "ol' boy" or "bless his 'itty biddy heart" or "awl bidness.... Like household cleanser, the term had a dozen different uses in Odessa. People said it in casual conversation. They also said it publicly, as just another descriptive adjective. Some people looked tall, some looked short, and some looked nigger." That was the Deep South, land of the good 'ol boy

213

and rednecks.

On our own team, the meaning of nigger was different depending on who was using it. Nick Tolbert, a black defensive back from Culver City, called Jerome a "nigger" or labeled his homeys "niggers," or else described a piece of social interaction, "man, I tell you, the nigger was moving" and it was non-threatening. "He was gone for a TD and there was nothing I could do about it."

Casey said an opposing player, "plays like a nigger." Darryl Bryant, black inside backer tells Twuan, "The damn nigger from Ventura ran away from me and there was nothing I could do about it." Jake, white inside backer from Santa Maria, said, "Our niggers have to play better."

Affectionate teasing from blacks or simmering hatred and mistrust from whites, the word was schizophrenic. Nigger was bandied about with so much frequency during practice that, in the middle of the season, Chuck finally told everybody that was one word he didn't want to hear no matter who it came from. In the locker room after that pronouncement at practice, some of the black players said to each other that they were going to use it no matter what. It was their word. It was their way of talking and some Mexican was not going to stop them. After that, overt usage of nigger lessened, and instead went underground.


Race and sport are two very interrelated products of the twentieth century. In the scheme of the things, blacks in the money-making pro sports or the elitist country club sports have only been a phenomenon since Jackie Robinson pioneered black involvement in 1948 with the Brooklyn Dodgers. That is not to say that athletes like Jesse Owens and the smattering of black college football and basketball players that came before the talented Robinson didn't lay the foundation for those who followed. In the last four decades, black participation in sport has resembled a flood of biblical proportions, inundating and changing drastically the landscape of American sport and society. Outside of the heavy proportion of Hispanic baseball players, the majority of college and professional basketball and football players, boxers, sprinters and even middle distance runners are black.

It is impossible to conjure up images of athletes and sport where blacks are not the major "players." American sport that was once so whitewashed is now vibrant with hues of browns and blacks. Michael Novak wrote of basketball as an electric and exhilarating jazz. Football has become an aerial ballet, fueled by an octane turbocharger and sprinting is a rush of velocity, unheard of even ten years ago. At the 1996 Olympics, Michael Johnson crushed by tenths of a second the 200m record that was the oldest standing track. In an event where hundredths separate out winners and last place finishers, that time vaulted Johnson into the stratosphere of sprinting lore.

Speed has become the signature of American sport. In my book about black sprinters and cultural identity, *Instant Acceleration: Living in the Fast Lane,* I wrote that speed was a cultural icon of past and contemporary black and urban society and was infused, even wired, into life on the streets. It had its origins in the migration of black ex-slaves to the northern urban industrial centers. Modern American society continues this terminal velocity as if we were barreling down a Colorado slope, pushing the envelope to go faster still, our skis flirting with flight. Speed pervades and even though in auto racing speed kills, our culture is rife with instant acceleration. Sport has become a modern-day barometer of what we are, and speed is the common denominator. Speed has gone urban and speed has gone south. A recent *Christian Science Monitor* article on Florida football reported that, in 1995, 132 Florida high schoolers broke the 11-second barrier in the 100 meters.

In my lifetime, there has been a dramatic changing of the guard in sport. Sport is now firmly in the hands of the black superstars. Every once in a while, there are the few white athletes that are offered up to placate the white businesses and masses that support the infrastructure of professional sport; a Larry Bird, Steve Young, Mark McGwire. Sport, before any other American experience, was the playground of integration. Sport now drives the train of American commercialism and the social engineers are the black athletes. A far hue and cry from the pure and unadulterated hatred spewed at the early black pioneers that dared step on and defiled the racially pure and sacred field of white dreams.

To those on the outside of sport, in front of their TV sets on

Saturday and Sunday afternoons watching football or basketball or even track and field, it looks so clear and black and white. There are more blacks playing than whites, and the blacks that do play seem to be, on the whole, better natural athletes. There was much sociological research done in the 1970s concerning not only why there were so many blacks in sport, but also what position blacks played. In football, blacks were never quarterbacks, centers or middle linebackers because, as the reasoning went, these positions demanded intelligence and "we know damn well, blacks don't have the cerebral capacity for that," Brooks Johnson sarcastically said. Blacks, instead, played those "natural ability positions" away from the center of the field, such as receivers, cornerbacks and running backs.

Scathing commentary on white reaction to blacks in football emerged in the 1960s and 1970s with Jack Olsen's *The Black Athlete* (a four-part series in *Sports Illustrated* later turned into a book). Martin Kane's 1970 piece "Black is Best" in the same magazine also looked at the nature of race and the athlete, but concluded there were differences in ability between the races which led to the contrast of style and performance. Lately, there have been more studies done. For example, *Runner's World*, "White Men Can't Run (August 1992)" and Sports *Illustrated* "Is it in the Genes (Dec 7, 1997)," with most concluding that there are some physical differences between black and white athletes. With help from the civil rights movement and larger than life personalities like Harry Edwards, racial inequality in numbers of black athletes and coaches and front office personnel created a revolution in American professional and collegiate sport concerning the nature of the relationships between black and white athletes.

But as I tell my introductory class in cultural anthropology, sport, like any other institution, reflects or mirrors the larger society. What we find in society will be seen in sport. It just so happens that sport in our society is a highly-visible slice of life and magnifies the nature of human interaction. What is visible to those outside of sport are the numbers and performances and the statistics generated by the sport; what we can see and quantify. However, inside the circle of athletes and coaches, it is much more than numbers; it is a collision of lifestyle and culture. During practice and games, race, like Tony Eason said, matters very little. In my

216

study on black and white sprinters, how we chose to identify ourselves was based on being a sprinter, not on facets like race or ethnicity.

Even coaches can't seem to get away from stereotyping athletes. Judy Oppenheimer wrote of her son's coach's attitude towards blacks. The coach "...liked the fact there were a lot of black players. He just believed black kids made better athletes. They ran faster, hit harder. They stomped over other players; they were more arrogant, tougher, meaner. 'They've got some instinctive aggressiveness to them a lot of white kids don't have,' [the coach] said. 'Maybe it's from growing up in a more hostile environment. You'll find a few white guys who are mean cats, and that's what you want. But you line up a hundred black and a hundred white, there's gonna be a lot more mean black kids than white kids.'"

Third down, facing a fifth consecutive series without a score, we needed to at least dent the Bakersfield defense, make them bend and work a little. A rested defense is an unstoppable defense. J.T. went to the well, avoided the rush finally and found Art ten yards up the field for a completion. Unfortunately we needed thirteen for a first down and Chuck, even though everybody was yelling at him to go for it, decided not to give Bakersfield excellent field position and opted to have them pinned down at their goal line. So we punted.

As I sat in the locker room before going out onto the field for the last time in my brief football career, I saw color; blacks, browns, and sun burned reds. How could you not? Color is a very real part of what we physically see when we look at other people and it is no different in the locker room or on the field. Color is one of the variations that provides the human condition with a genetic flexibility to adapt to potential changing environments that used to confront our species at every turn in the evolutionary path. Color is one of those features which defines our humanity.

It isn't the color that defines racism and stereotyping, it is the twisted mind that you can't see buried inside with ignorance and cruelty, that provides a misguided commentary on behavior. After spending so much time with players, color fades and becomes only

217

a backdrop for the real portrait of sweat, hard work, pain, humor, desires, futures and hope that emerges from each and every player. It wasn't color that gave our team portrait life; it was background, the ability among other things that made us different and unique and at the same time so similar. Jarrett and Chris treated each other with respect and a certain kind of love on and off the field, even though they both had their personal thoughts on race. It was football that brought them together and football that gave them the chance to know each other. They probably will never see each other again, let alone correspond, but both will take their two years together and file it away in each of their fickle brains and relive it every now and then.

In many ways, Tony Eason was right. The locker room breaks down walls or barriers of race and culture by providing the time necessary to understand that which is different. What may look like racism is just conflicting personalities without race thrown in. I liked some blacks and chose my off-field interactions with others carefully, just as I did with whites and Mexican-American players.

John Hoberman, a Germanic Studies professor at University of Texas, recently published (1997) a book entitled *Darwin's Athletes: How Sport Has Damaged Black America and Preserved the Myth of Race* in which he argues, for 300 pages, that black hyper involvement in sport, especially college and professional sport, has created a fixation on black sport involvement and achievement in American society. The mega-success of the small number of elite athletes (in many sports, blacks make up a majority of these athletes) has created and continues to foster a dependency on athletics in black American culture. The only highly-visible road out of urban hell is sports.

In addition, corporate America and the media paint black athletes with such vibrant strokes that it is hard for any racial or ethnic group in America, as well as most western nations, not to equate blacks with the genetically-anointed superstars of the playing fields. To Hoberman, the dramatic change from the days of segregated professional sport to the highly visible televised images of the many black athletes in college and professional sports today does not lend itself to racial harmony. On the contrary, "the athleticising of black identity" has helped to "preserve," not eliminate, the centuries-old perceptions of non-white inferiority by casting blacks as athletes first, humans second.

Hoberman's thesis has much merit to it. Yet, inside sport, in the locker room, out on the field, in the huddle, far enough away from corporate America, where the press can only observe from afar, players depend on players. What Hoberman argued is that there is an obsession with the perception of black superiority by blacks and non-blacks alike. He said everybody buys into the insidious stereotyping of blacks as genetic supermen and the even more insidious, less visible, perception by whites that genes may have gotten blacks to the medal stands and world championships.

Rationalizations for athletic superiority by athletes is not out of the ordinary. They are humans just as well, some searching for reasonable answers to questions, others rationalizing prejudices and ignorance. In the heat of the action, when a giant wave of human flesh and muscle is blasting toward J.T., his first thought is not going to be "where are the brothers so I can pass to them." His first action is to look for all those with red jerseys on and let it fly. It is color that matters in the end, but not that which we wear on our skin.

# Chapter 18

## Booksmart and Life Experience

Twice after that punt, we stopped Bakersfield. Three times, we got the ball back; twice we punted, once J.T. was intercepted. The defense was making a stand, but the offense had taken a back seat. Under a continued intense rush, J.T. was overthrowing and underthrowing and, when the passes were complete, the Bakersfield secondary would close like a curtain and keep us from advancing. On defense, our secondary was being run ragged, making tackles and chasing Mike Gray.

Chuck was frustrated; his offense was being stymied when they needed to be scoring. Torlando and Art dropped sure passes, but Chuck still believed we could at least give Bakersfield a run for their bowl game. If we were to get back in, it wasn't Dave or Eric who was going to get us those quick scores. It was Art or Torlando, and somebody needed to wake them up. If Chuck had time to think about the confluence of the season and this game, he would have thought it ironic that we could play so well and then play so inconsistently, all in the same season, the same game, the same quarter.

The season had been scripted almost like last year; same amount of wins and losses, same amount of bullshit with the players; cast changes, personalities stay. J.T. didn't learn fast enough, even though he put big numbers up. The offensive line was depleted and J.T. scrambled more and more. J.T. also began running scared when he didn't have to, leaving before the pocket actually dissolved. One good pop and J.T. would have been gone. Today, he was being battered and that pop could come at any moment. This was a sure way to end up with Benjy Trembly at quarterback and finish up 0 and the rest of the season. Benjy was steady at receiver; a quarterback he was not.

Twuan, Torlando and Art had been difficult to work with, to say the least. Getting them to practice and making them work like he wanted them to was up to a higher power. Many times, Chuck felt he was working with adolescents. And it didn't help that the coaching staff went ahead and treated them as if they were kids. He just didn't understand where the commitment was, not like when he was playing. Trying to understand the minds of 18-year-olds was a pain in the ass, Chuck said. Good thing his job didn't really depend on his wins.

He frequently thought his life centered on this stupid game. Watching enough film to become a critic, worrying about J.T. and trying to figure out where Torlando, Art and Twuan's minds were at, if they were anywhere, running the weight class, scouting when he had a chance; the day wasn't long enough. If that wasn't bad enough, he doodled new plays on scraps of paper and napkins when he wasn't doing anything else. The only relaxation he really had was Saturday nights at O'Malleys when they were playing home. He was already looking forward to his season-ending fishing trip that lay at the end of the rainbow.

The defense had to hold again, to give us another shot at the ball and narrowing the margin. On the field, Chris, Mike, Jarrett and company were dog-ass tired. All game long, they had been chasing Gray and the second back, Lane, all over the field. Rarely were they stopped at the line. Often, they were through the backers and then it was up to the legs of Mike, Chris and Tony to make touchdown-saving tackles. Mike would rather face a midterm, an essay one at that, than face Gray for another quarter and a half. But

221

school was not even close to his thoughts now. It was only Gray. "Come on, defense!" echoed our sideline, "Stop them here." Joe was as tired as his players. Willing them to play above their abilities was a hard job. His gray Vaquero polo shirt was drenched in sweat and standing as close as you dared, it was possible to feel the waves of frustration that rolled off him.

The tension that underlay the marriage of sport and education is fraught with conflict of ultimate goals and an unquestionable future and it starts well before the players get to college level. For so long, football has been considered anti-intellectual. Its very nature, as Telander and others have argued, goes against the grain of the spontaneity and creativity needed for mental growth. Bissenger waxes long about the Permian High School's role in educating their football athletes. He followed several athletes on their daily journey through the halls of education and found their academic pursuits minimal, if that. Assigned work was either done by somebody else or never turned in. Teachers made allowances for the players' lack of progress, and attention in class was fleeting. Sounds like many high school students today. Bissenger is quick to chronicle a couple of players who were as academic as they were athletic; one even ended up at Harvard. In the end, he lays the fault of football players' woeful academic record at the doorstop of the community; if these players were not exalted as heroes and teenage gods, if their status was not so rarefied, they, too, would be held to the same academic requirements of other students.

Gary Shaw, in his expose of Texas College football, *Meat on the Hoof,* experienced the contradictory nature of football and academics. Incoming freshmen to the University of Texas football team were assigned to a "brain coach" who made sure the mechanics of the system worked with the ultimate goal, not being the grounding of the player in a liberal arts higher education, but the continued eligibility of the player. Courses were selected not for the content, but the success rate of the class for passing through football players. "Obviously for Hewlett [the brain coach], the only important factor was winning the grades. And he could tell us how to get there," wrote Shaw.

Initially, Shaw was concerned about his education; but with the extreme regimentation of the football program, he was mentally bludgeoned into seeking the path of least resistance; it was the nature of the beast. Everything was done with efficiency, so the soul could be devoted to the Texas football tradition. From the middle of his freshman year, Shaw looked for the simplest route. "From this point until I graduated, I usually concerned myself with finding the shortest routes to the end results.... So far as we were concerned, our education was just another external measure. And so most of us, including myself, became interested in finding the easy courses rather than the stimulating ones." Cheating, cribbing notes, having girlfriends or female acquaintances write papers or take tests became commonplace, if not tacitly approved, ignored. A professor, used by the football coaches to pass a student, rebelled soon after finding out about the deception. He told Shaw, "I have since found it necessary to completely divorce myself from any connection with the football program at Texas. I have realized that my aim of aiding in the education of students is in direct conflict with the football program's aims of bypassing an education. The football program at Texas has absolutely nothing to do with a university's proper function, and I am saddened by the fact that university professors are among those this program smoothly uses to its own ends."

Even more recently, are the multitudes of "scandals" that emanate from athletic programs like the University of New Mexico basketball players that received grades from a religiously affiliated junior college. Jan Kemp, an academic counselor to the athletic program at Georgia, was fired after blowing the whistle on wide-scale grade improprieties concerning football players. Just recently, during the 1999 NCAA basketball championships, it was found that basketball players at the University of Minnesota had papers written for them by other students. For a year, as part of my work-study job during the first year of my graduate program at Washington State University, I was an assistant to the academic coordinator that primarily handled the football team. It was our mission, not to see the student-athlete be successful in getting all that he could from his class, but to make sure the student-athlete passed through the rings so he could continue to be a part of the team. We looked for short cuts, pleaded for extensions from professors and basically short-circuited the primary aim of preparing the student to suck the most that he could from the course.

Graduation rates of student-athletes are abysmal in major four-year schools. Coaches and athletic directors are quick to point out that there is not much difference between graduation rates and GPAs between student-athletes and the general student population. With all the tutoring and counseling available to student-athletes and the advantage of registering before the general student body, the comparison breaks down.

That is not to say that all football players or, athletes in general, turn out anti-intellectual or don't graduate. There is always the exception; Pat Haden, former USC and Los Angeles Ram quarterback was a Rhodes scholar. Emmitt Smith just received publicity on finishing his Bachelors at Florida State, six years after he left.

Defensive Line Coach Don Hopwood was a home-grown exception to the norm. After leaving UCLA well short of a degree, Don tried to come back and finish, but found it all but impossible. "I tried to do it during the time when I was working on San Juan Island in Washington," he said, "I couldn't go to school at the same time, so I would come down in the summers and go to UCSB. I got my grades up. It came to a choice of going to UCSB and I couldn't even get into school for a year and then it would have taken a year and half to finish. So I called UCLA and they said you could start next weekend in December and be done by August. I just commuted and went down there and they said they would help me and I was put in the *Final Score* program."

*Final Score* is a program offered not just by UCLA, but by many NCAA Division schools. *Final Score* has been in existence since 1984 at the Los Angeles campus and according to Frank Stevens, director, and college teammate of Don Hopwood, "has graduated over 150 athletes." The program is offered to all sports, male and females, but due to the large number of players involved each year in football, 110 with 85 being on scholarship, many of the student-athletes involved are former football players. NCAA Division 1 and 1AA athletes are given five years of eligibility to finish four years of a sport. In many cases, this is the average number of years for the general student population to graduate at UCLA according to Stevens. It is not surprising that many student-athletes take longer than that to get their degree.

"I mean, we ask so much of the student-athletes," said Joanna Bennett, assistant to Stevens. "Practices, weight training, games, travel. We have to give it back in some way. Players leave early to go pro, or finish their eligibility and have try-outs and some make it professionally and they never get their degree," she said, "and if things don't work out, they find themselves without much to work with."

"These players are starting to realize," said Stevens, "that there is nothing out there after they're done. There is nowhere to turn without that degree and they are coming back to finish what they set out to do. After reviewing each case, we determine if they need financial aid. Some are in a bind and we provide grants-in aid, student support, tuition and fees and a stipend of books. Some who have made it in the pros or who have full-time jobs don't need the financial assistance, but like those who are on financial aid, we provide to all the program's students, academic counselors, full use of the campus computer center and other types of services."

Like so many college students today, athletes like Don were also subject to the first time college syndrome. Many wasted their first years, dropping out or flunking out of classes, not finishing semesters, and just being flakes. After their careers ended, they grew up, or grew tired of being in a position with a glass ceiling, or found themselves stuck in a dead-end job and they followed the growing number of returning adult students back to campus.

"We have had some student-athletes who were marginal when they were here, first," said Joanna, "and now, the second time around, they are changed. They take it more seriously. Many of those in the program end up advising those just coming in, helping their transition back into school and help them cope with the big age difference between them and the normal college students. We have had former student-athletes who were attending school in the late 1970s recently come back to UCLA."

The mission of the junior college in higher education is to provide not only educational, but vocational training to local residents, provide easier access at a much more manageable cost to the college experience and make it possible for those deficient or at-risk students to succeed. There were no scholarships for the players at City College. There was no external motivation to pass your classes, no threatening your scholarship or partial ride, no public humiliation or public outcry. It was simple; you needed to pass 24 units from season to season and after your freshman year had to maintain a 2.0 average. If either or both weren't accomplished, you were ineligible for further participation. Failing either, or both, did not mean you were suspended or kicked out of school. For many players, however, there went the reason for being in school.

Junior college in Santa Barbara, and in California in general, puzzled and amazed me. To finish a two-year program, many more students than expected took three, four or five years. To fuel this slow rate, students could drop courses without receiving a failing grade until a month before the end of the semester which, by some interesting coincidence, was usually the week after the last regular season football game. Players would hang onto their 12 units, of which at least four or five were P.E. units. Included in these 12 units were three units for football and one to two units for weight lifting classes. Players were then taking maybe two or three, if that, academic courses per semester. After the last game, the player would drop those classes in danger of flunking. Usually, they had stopped going after the first month of class or were showing up occasionally so the instructor wouldn't drop them and put them below 12 units, meaning instant ineligibility. This would only buy time for the athlete as he would need to make up those units in the spring or summer semester so he could be eligible for next season (The year after I finished playing, the date to withdraw from a class was moved up, thereby eliminating the chance to drop past the end of the football season.).

For many of these players, academic deficiencies were a major reason for attending and this reasoning was like pouring lighter fluid on a fire. They had difficulty handling twelve not to mention the added burden of more course work in the spring and then the accelerated nature of summer school. One method of helping the incoming player with getting his feet wet was to gray-shirt him, which meant having the player sign up for under twelve units his first semester. He was not a full-time student then and couldn't play, but this practice saved him from losing a year off his eligibility clock at the D-1 school. His freshmen year wouldn't start till he was a full-time student.

However, for all the players who ended up academic casualties, there were just as many who were successful and matriculated to four-year schools even if they didn't go on to play. Jarrod DeGeorgia left City College unable to go D-1 because of his grades, but finished his playing days at Wayne State College. Twuan and Chris went onto four-year colleges. Chad Marsulak and Simon Banks stars of the 1994 seasons attended Cal-State Northridge and Ball State University. Jarrett Thiessen and John Sonoma finished at Sacramento State. Oleg and Ruzik, ex-army Ukrainians who starred at City College in 1994 and 95, graduated from Portland State. In fact, while at City College, Ruzik was conference academic player of the year, maintaining a 3.7 GPA. Not bad for a Russian army officer from the Ukraine. There were just as many or more that went on to to four-year schools and chose not to play. Neil Dreste, a linebacker from 1995, ended up at Cal State Chico and now is just a normal college student. "I lost the desire to play," he told me at the end of the summer of 1996. "I will miss it for sure, especially in August and September, but I won't miss the politics and bullshit!"

In defense of the academic deficiencies of the players, the general student population at City College also featured a number of students who were marginal or high-risk students upon enrollment. In my classes, I would start with 60-70 students and, by the end of the first midterm, the class size would have decreased by 1/5 to 1/4 and by the last month of class would have a little over half of the original class size. In a class I taught at Ventura College in 1994, one girl was taking physical anthropology for the third time, trying to pass it and get rid of the "F" she received the first time.

Santa Barbara City College was the number one junior college in the state in a number of categories. A good number of students would transfer directly into University of California, Santa Barbara after finishing their general education requirements. With the cost of tuition at City College hovering at $13 per unit, around $250 total for a full-time student, the student could afford to eat $39 if the class wasn't working out. As well, many of the students were either working full-time or working several part-time jobs just to survive in Santa Barbara in addition to school. And it was the same way with many of the players. Oleg worked full time at night at a liquor store; others were like Rick and bounced weekday nights and weekend nights at local bars. If one collared a job, one did not let it go easily. Benjy worked 30-40 hours a week at a Carpinteria Chevron and Lee worked at Jiffy Lube, and the list goes on. If the players didn't have the motivation to adhere to a "Spartan existence" as Shaw related about Texas football, then their careers were very short-lived. For the players who were married and/or had children, life was frantic. It wasn't any wonder that the success rate of players on and off the field was circumspect.

Torlando was a good example of this. He graduated from Santa Barbara High School, yet was vastly under-prepared do to college work. His test scores were abysmal and his one try at a four-year school ended before the Fall semester began. He definitely was a candidate for remedial coursework at City College to help him make up for the woeful preparation he took out of high school. He refused to admit to himself, let alone others, that he had a concentration problem or lacked the skills necessary to comprehend information taken from lecture and reading. He attended classes only sporadically during the 1995 football season, passed only the physical education classes and was ineligible for the next football season.

City College basketball coach, Morris Hodges and I had several discussions on what it would take to not only get Torlando eligible, but to prepare him for more college. The first step was to find somebody interested enough to help him along, spend time with him, explain things in such a way that Torlando would see that the help was not out to make him look dumb. The second, and just as important, was to keep him involved in athletics as a means to provide additional motivation and use his participation as a way to monitor his class work; if he didn't go to class or underachieved in a course, dock him on the field. In a sense, academics and athletics would work together to get him back into school. Unfortunately, neither one of us had a chance to implement this strategy as Torlando took leave from campus during the summer of 1996 and became a ghost.

The difficulties of black athletes on university campuses are many and the coach is oftentimes unable to help reconcile some of these problems, such as academics, absence of a strong male figure in the background, extreme culture shock and cultural isolation, especially if going to school in rural university campuses. A black athlete from Chicago is hardly socially equipped to handle four years of Missoula, Montana or even the rigid, structured environment of the Mormon in Provo, Utah. An exception to this was the tale of Ronny Jenkins, the 1995 Hueneme High School running back who, in one game, gained 637 yards rushing against Rio Mesa High School smashing the then national record of 615 yards. Recruited heavily by Brigham Young University, he signed with the Cougars in late spring of 1996. He said in an interview that his choice was based on the structured routine and somewhat isolated community of Provo. Not a Mormon, he said he understood what was expected of him and he and his mother felt that it would be the best thing for him. BYU was the only team that recruited him heavily, talking to him every Monday during the season and off-season. As a freshman on the 1996 BYU team, he played often, averaging 70 yards rushing, 100 yards passing and 2 TDs a game in a passing-crazed program. Jenkins was suspended for periods of time both his sophomore and junior years for conduct unbecoming a good Mormon. He has since decided to transfer to another school for his fourth year of eligibility.

"Problems [of black athletes]...coaches are poorly equipped to deal with.... Coaches are looking to manipulate and win, while blacks are looking for an identity," wrote Rick Telander. "[The black athlete is] buffeted by the demands of their sport, an academic curriculum they may be ill-prepared for, and the alienating, even hostile, atmosphere of the white-dominated campuses."

Wrapped up in the plight of the black athlete, or any athlete for that matter, who comes from a single parent household, is the lack of a consistent male authority figure. The autocratic nature of football thrusts a coach into that position. The needs of the player and coach are considerably different leading to false or barren promises or attention given to the athlete by the coach. Absolute power corrupts absolutely; the power of the coach to grant playing time (and the attention perceived from that playing time) to the player becomes overriding. Football is not a fuzzy cocoon of parental love and affection. It is, instead, one of violence, extreme tests of physical skill and ability, high pain tolerance, and taking risks to please the coach/father figure. Out of the chaos that is urban America, out of the morass of "machismo" and failure of potential role model males in the inner city, it is nigh on impossible for black male youth to construct a positive self-identity. "The crying need," wrote syndicated columnist William Raspberry, "is to find ways of playing to the strengths of black males without 'wimpfying' them. Our failure to do so may be one reason so many black boys disdain as 'white or sissified' attributes associated with academic and professional success."

Still, with the same results, an entirely different situation can be seen with a number of Mexican-American players at City College. Not lacking the male figure, the Mexican family is strong, at least in the sense of having both male and female parents usually present. Traditionally, the male in this arrangement is king and reinforces his position through a sense of machismo and manhood. Not surprising, football prizes these same features of manhood and physical challenges.

Chuck took J.T. under his wing the minute J.T. stepped on the campus in August of 1995. J.T.'s parents had just undergone a divorce. Chuck spent hours tutoring him on the offense, reading defenses and providing help in his classes. He occasionally picked him up in the morning and took him home at night after practice. He yelled at him for mistakes on the field, chided him for his shortcomings in the classroom and, outside of J.T.'s earshot, talked about him as a father would a somewhat errant, but well-meaning son. Chuck was single and did not have children so, in a way, J.T. filled that niche for Chuck. On the other hand, Torlando was from a fatherless family with older brothers, most who had stepped over the line of the law and been called on it. Torlando had a large extended family with aunts, uncles and cousins, but none were ultimately able to provide the guidance or direction Torlando needed. In a way, Torlando was too far gone for Chuck to make a visible dent in his life. To Torlando, Chuck wasn't the father figure or even male authority figure. Chuck was just another figure in a position of power that Torlando needed to achieve results and successes. Talking to one of his aunts during the spring and summer of 1996, she said it was impossible to tell Torlando anything; he wouldn't listen. In the early spring of 1996, Torlando was picked up in Isla Vista for possessing a firearm. For the second time, this arrest violated his probation brought on by the 1993 assault. In June 1996, he was sentenced to serve 50 days in city jail for that probation violation but, somehow, through plea bargaining, ended up serving no time.

On junior college campuses, athletes on the whole are a high-risk academic group. First, junior college athletic teams are filled with two types of student-athletes; marginal student and good athlete, or marginal student and marginal athlete. Exceptional athletes toil at this level for one reason–they did not have the grades and or test scores to be eligible for playing at a university or four-year college the first year or to receive a scholarship. These athletes, like J.T. or Torlando, stay close to home, pay cheap junior college tuition, gain experience and maturity on the field and hopefully address their academic deficiencies and then, upon receiving their AA degree transfer to a four-year school and be eligible to play right off the bat. Without an AA degree, the student-athlete is forced to go D-2 or lower if not a qualifier out of high school. In terms of quality athletes, the junior colleges in California have become lucrative markets to Division 1 schools because the 64 junior colleges offer a vast market of talent, seasoned and "ready to wear."

There are the marginal athletes who have no chance of going on to big programs and maybe they get a degree and maybe they don't. Some of those who go on choose smaller schools, D-3 or NAIA, and play and then again, some just transfer to four-year schools and sit in their dorm rooms or apartments and remember their playing days while watching college football on Saturday afternoons.

Marginal athletes and marginal students rarely finish their degree after exhausting their eligibility. Most were in school to play and, after the Saturday afternoons of limited action, leave school unfulfilled in their quest to distinguish themselves on the turf and units shy of graduation. Some, like Josiah and Jerome, end up in the big house. Others like Benjy, who wanted to be a fireman, chase professions that don't require a college education.

Finally, unique to the junior college experience, there are those few adult returning students who played high school ball and never went on to play after graduation and now are just coming back to get a college education and still haven't forgotten their glory years on the gridiron. There are not many of these players. Guys in the mid to late 20s, a rarity to find one in his 30s, strap on the pads after years, to watch the years melt away and attempt to feel young once again. One linebacker from the 1994 team was 25, had served some time, was unmarried, living with the mother of his two kids and

231

was taking classes in horticulture and landscape architecture to help him professionally. He balanced playing and courses with a full-time job. "Why am I playing? I'll tell you, Doc. I was good in high school," he said, "and then I ended up in trouble, spent some time trying to figure out what I wanted, and then came back. Why shouldn't I play?"

And then there are the rare footnote or two who never played or lasted until the first game, old-timers forgetting or letting the years dull their senses to what football entailed, trying to dig way back into their past to drink from the fountain of youth. Larry was a 36-year-old vet, stocky, a little chunky with a flop of reddish-brown hair. He traveled around for a decade after the service and ended up in Santa Barbara and decided "to get some education." He signed up for the summer football class just to get in shape and decided to stick it out in the fall. After the first week of summer ball, Larry suffered through creaky muscles, bitterly complaining about the conditioning. Playing tennis three times a week and running occasionally hadn't prepared Larry for the rigors of the turf. He made it through the first scrimmage, with both legs heavily wrapped in ace bandages, but bowed out soon after for the good of his mind and body. "It wasn't worth it," he said, as I ran into him on campus that next spring. "I had all these math classes and I decided I wasn't going to play, anyway. Why break my body down?"

Royal Gladden was a 38-year-old black man with streaks of gray running throughout his hair. He was going to school for the first time, waiting for an insurance suit to get settled so he could come upon some money. His legs always wrapped, he stuck out the 1994 season. Frequently, he was unable to even dress for practice, never playing in games, but always a part of the team.

Justin lived on a boat in the harbor, dove for abalone during the season and hung around the periphery of campus, taking a class or two. He was a 34-year-old large man over 6'3" with red hair bleached almost blonde by the sun. He came out for spring ball in 1995 and spent considerable time in the weight room. But you could tell he was a flake; different and living perilously close to the edge of homelessness. He loved the campus life of nubile sun princesses and the culture of youth and he was out on the make constantly, not hesitant at all to start up a conversation with any girl that happened by. He actually looked halfway decent in practice, but never followed through on getting the classes for the fall. T.K. told me that he felt used by Justin having spent considerable time working with him that spring. "The abalone season was down and I didn't make much, so school is out this next year. I got to spend most of my time trying to make ends meet," he told me when I ran into him in the weight room during the season. I always believed that he had no plans to come out and was content on hanging around and being a part of the social life that swirled around the bluffs overlooking Leadbedder Beach.

Tom Green, 6'4", 250 pounds, was a black-haired Irish 23-year-old criminal justice major with a B.A. from University of California, Santa Barbara. Tom missed the years of high school ball in Lompoc, 45 minutes northwest from Santa Barbara and ended up taking a seven unit vocational class in police studies. Tom hadn't played a down since high school, but he talked to Chuck and took two weightlifting classes and three units of physical education to fill up his 12 units. He played a major contribution as a defensive and offensive lineman in 1994. I remember Tom making a sack in the fourth quarter during a crucial juncture of a game. He leaped off the fallen quarterback and ran around in a frenzy, shooting off the "six gun" pistols magically transformed from his gloved hands. "Goddamn, I love this game," he said afterwards, while drinking a beer at a party we both were at. "I will never forget that moment for as long as I live."

Tom "red-shirted" the 1995 season and managed a local restaurant and bounced at O'Malleys to make money. At 25, for no other reason than to play football, in between his two bartending jobs, he returned in 1996 to finish up his eligibility. He played sparingly though the first three games, but the fourth game managed to get in for four or five series. Tom was like so many other twentysomethings in Santa Barbara. They worked to make a living, enough to stay in paradise. Sounding so much like his coach, Colin Flynn, "Why should I hurry to leave here?" he said in the summer of 1996. "It's gorgeous, the girls match the scenery and it's great working in O'Malleys. Why should I grow up too fast?"

Many times I would walk across campus through the secure world of white-bred higher education, surrounded by the familiar countenances of my world and run into players on my way to class or to teach. I would immediately feel a sense of brotherhood and for the time of hand slapping, some roughhousing or even the more superficial levels of inquiring about our respective injuries or pains, felt more comfortable with the players than the comfortable world of my profession and background. I am not saying that it was a warm and fuzzy feeling that transpired between players. In fact, occasionally this blending was rough, earthy, raw and cut to the quick, very much like the game itself. Nestled in between the periods of harsh bonding, where insults acted to express friendship, there were moments of quiet affection. "I never really got a chance to know Twuan until I spatted his cleats before one game this season," Mike Hayes said. "For almost two years we were on the same team and I didn't really talk to him, but during that five minute period in the locker room, I got to know a little bit about him, Florida and his life outside of football." There were a lot of these "moments," when standing beside a player during a break at practice or in the locker room, in the shower, football would take a back seat and the player would become more than one-dimensional.

Evan was a 6'2" 245 pound 25-year-old offensive tackle with short blond hair that played high school football at Chadwick, a private school in Los Angeles. He had moon cheeks and a dimple in the middle of his chin. His face reflected the transition between innocence of youth and the uncertainty and trials of adulthood. He traveled some after graduating, attended college and dropped out. Evan was intelligent and worldly in a sea of teenagers. He started back at UCSB in 1994, after dropping out the first time, right out of high school. In between, he worked as a social activist for migrant workers. "During that time," he said, "there was me and 25 Mexicans living in a house." He spent time on the East Coast because his girlfriend went to Wellesley, but came back and got hit with the bug to play football and followed David Weismeiller to City College and Chuck Melendez. "I found that I did better academically in school when I was playing football," he said.

Dressing in the locker room after practice, before ducking into the training room, I started talking to Evan. "Big night planned?" I asked him. Up to this point, I barely knew his name. "Nah, I have to work tonight delivering pizzas until late," he said. I asked him if he lived with David, as he would leave with David after every practice. "No, not really, I sleep in my pickup truck that I park behind the pizza place where I work," he said matter-of-factly. "Right now, I can't afford the rent." I expressed disbelief and wondered how that worked. "It works okay. I have a camper on the truck and I take showers here. I spend time over at Dave's and grab naps in the locker room before practice."

I occasionally remembered coming into a darkened team locker room early and a big body would be stretched out in the back with a head resting on wadded up towels. "I have a sleeping bag and plenty of blankets to keep me warm and after working I am so tired I fall right to sleep. I was living in a place last semester, but that didn't work out and instead of plopping down rent, I decided to save some money and do it this way." What some people will do to exist and follow their dreams. After that, I found out Evan had taken some anthropology and we spent time talking about related topics not evenly closely related to football. Many times I would think of Evan's living accommodations and wonder about the thin line that separates many junior college students from the homeless panhandling on Lower State Street at all hours of the day.

Evan eventually moved back into an apartment at the end of the season and actually came back for his second season in 1996 but, after hurting himself, he got a job in Los Angeles and came up to watch the games on Saturday. I saw him one Saturday morning walking up from the field and we talked briefly. He had gained some weight, but looked good. "I want to come back and play one more year, but I am making good money now and if I did come back, I would have time only for classes. I miss it, but maybe my time is over and I have to move on." He said that wistfully. In his voice was a mixture of "I wish I could and I know I can't." In a way, he was saying his good-byes to a season that was and the season that could have been. He had gone from a truck bed to a full time job making more than enough money to live on and he had his whole life ahead of him and, for a moment, he would have traded it for ten more football games and just enough to get by on. Such is the addiction and lure of football. Is it any wonder pro players play until they can't walk anymore, till their joints resemble leggos and they can't get through a day without painkillers and/or alcohol or both. After careers fulfilled or cruelly cut short due to injury, athletes are still young in mind, but not in body.

Gray started the drive with a five-yard run off-tackle, one of his shortest of the day. After that play, Gray and Lane took turns for four plays pounding through the defensive line, each time the runner was finally tackled by either John or Chris Hill, a shoestring away from breaking it for a score. With just over three minutes to go in the third quarter, Mike Gray burst in from the twelve-yard line and Bakersfield went up 42-14.

# Chapter 19

---

## Our Reflection in a Facemask

Not a chance in hell," Kratz replied, as I asked him if there was a chance for us to get back in the ball game. "We are so far down, we could have four more quarters and it wouldn't do us any good." Even for Chuck, it was hard to generate the emotion needed to pass it on to his players. Each Bakersfield touchdown hammered another nail into our coffin and Chuck was bearing the brunt of each blow. There was still another quarter to go and Bakersfield wasn't showing any signs of easing off. Thoughts of winning had long been replaced by hopes of staying in and making the score look presentable. Now, the real worry for the sophomores was having our last game end in a humiliating blowout on our home field.

Desperate to make something, anything, happen, Mike took the kickoff deep in our territory and tried a reverse to a second string running back who was promptly dropped at the five-yard line. We could not have been in a deeper hole had we tried, down four touchdowns and our backs up against our own goal line. As I looked up and down the sidelines, players had their heads and helmets hanging, attentions drifted as many forced their thoughts away from the horror that was taking place 10 yards from them.

I tell my introductory students in anthropology, sport can be a mirror or reflection of society or a culture. The behavior you see in sport is taken from the larger culture that surrounds it. Sport can be defined as formalized or institutionalized, involving strategy, chance or skill, with a set of rules, between individuals or teams or even within oneself and there is usually some reward or recognition, be it monetary, status or material gain, accrued from the contest and, lastly, there is a clear-cut winner and loser. In essence, to the victor, go the spoils. Football contains many behaviors that can be traced back to society at large. Recently, Sam Walker of the *Christian Science Monitor* wrote, "Today's college [football] game, like American society itself, is faster, flashier, and more technical than ever."

There is "competition," "winners and losers," "contracts" that percolate through football and even though college football players don't get paid, there will always be an Oklahoma or Miami. There is violence inherent in the game. But then, again, too much violence is penalized. Most violence that is glorified in our society ultimately is framed in the context of right and wrong. In football, violence is patterned and regimented. It is done with a greater goal in mind, victory and a test of manhood and guts. There seems to be some correlation between football and sex. Football represents millions of dollars in revenue. Players make huge contracts, and males love to watch football. Money seems to be an aphrodisiac on two levels; the attraction of players as revenue and notoriety, and the lure of millions of males to the TV sets on Saturday and Sunday afternoons and many nights during the week. Instead of looking at it from an athletic standpoint, we invert the equation and look at it from a power standpoint.

Even at Santa Barbara, there were some football groupies, though nothing like the out-of-control behavior found at large universities. There were post-game parties where players and others congregated and drank and smoked till they were out for the count, but then it was no different than any other college or frat party. (I attended several team parties and even learned what a beer bong was). Players were not the gods of campus and so few turned out for our games that we were probably the best-kept secret in town. There were always the girls that would come and work out, either climbing the stadiums or running laps and would always show up right when we came down onto the stadium floor. It was not many and they soon became quickly enveloped in the evening recreational joggers and walkers that descended on the track after five.

We weren't the smooth, publicity-savvy athletes you find at bigger schools. These players were coarse and insecure, even shy around people other than players. In short, they were like any other 18 and 19-year-old males.

In our culture, sport and society have married and it becomes difficult to untangle the interwoven threads of metaphor that bind the two together. Politics becomes a sport; businesses live or die on success that can only be translated using sporting terms, such as we need to "score," "its a slam dunk," "go all the way," "let's hit the home run." Coaches like Pat Riley, Jimmy Valvano, Lou Holtz, Joe Paterno, Paul "Bear" Bryant live larger than the sport which created their personae. They end up cultural icons speaking from a well of knowledge that originated from manipulating boys on a field of grass and dirt or on a gymnasium floor. It shouldn't be that much of a surprise to us because the players, once they step off the field, become like anybody else; students, fathers, druggies, Einsteins, what have you.

The fascinating part of using sport to study culture is comparing cultures that compete in the same sport. Within the constant of football or baseball, we should be able to pick out different behaviors that can be traced back to the society at large and these should vary from culture to culture, sport to sport. I remember avidly watching the 1994 World Cup and was fascinated by the match between the teams and their fans, especially the Brazilians. The team played like the fans yelled and screamed. Many of the players had just one name and they were so flamboyant and electric in their style of play. If you watched in detail, you could notice the methodical precision of some of the European teams, most notably the Germans and English; not much speed, but a crunching style of play.

Football in Texas is king. Reading H.G. Bissenger's *Friday Night Lights* and Gary Shaw's *Meat on the Hoof* illustrates this perfectly. Considering such a revered activity, one should expect to find much in that culture that relates to that activity. Rituals and myths act to reinforce and maintain the sacred position of football in small rural hamlets and giant urban centers. Football has invaded the schools, towns, the minds of those close and just peripheral to the activity. Everything about Texas is big, the state, the oil revenues, until recently, the size of cattle ranches and ranchers, and the historical personalities like Davey Crockett and Sam Austin. That sense of large is found in the size of the players, the number of players, the way whole towns, whole regions, even the state take after football. High school football championships are played before 50,000 fans. On nights that a high school plays away, the towns are deserted as caravans of hundreds of cars fill the local highways on their way to support the local boys. And as Texas can still be thought as a state of manhood, football is an all male club; women need not apply, but that doesn't mean they can't cheer their men, sons, boyfriends or help their husbands follow the game.

The game is played in Texas with an emphasis on strength and speed; strength from the big boys, and speed from the blacks. The cult movie classic, *Dazed and Confused*, set and filmed in Austin, Texas was a look at high school rites of passage. The movie depicted the stranglehold football had on the students, the school and the town. Toward the end of the film, two girls lectured the star quarterback on their privileged position in life; as football players, they had everything and were given all the breaks. *Friday Night Lights* chronicles the same thing, only 15 years later. Nothing seemed to have changed. Football is still king. Almost a decade after *Friday Night Lights*, that cultural reflection is cast in the movie *Varsity Blues*.

Florida imprints its own style on football. Without reservation, Sam Walker labeled the Floridian stranglehold on college football as a dynasty. "The best teams nowadays have three things in common: speed, a pro-style passing game, and a Florida zip code," Walker wrote. "For the moment, Florida has stolen the game of college football from the cold factory towns of the North and, in all likelihood, changed it forever."

In 1986, while finishing up my thesis in anthropology at Iowa State University, I was interviewed by the *Des Moines Register* on the role of race in the domination by black athletes in college sports. I told the writer that the "domination (I preferred over representation) by black athletes was environmentally based, including factors like geography, tradition, urban versus rural background, and socioeconomic class. "It is a matter of culture, environment and opportunity or lack of it and not much else," I said. Specific to Iowa athletes, there was also the factor of which sports get emphasis and receive the greatest publicity. "In some of the rural areas," I said, "you have some athletes who have to play two or three sports a year. As a result, there is less concentration on a particular sport." In Iowa, where the winters are long and brutal, and many small rural schools field eight-man football teams, the sports that gather the most attention are played inside, such as basketball and wrestling. When all you have are two or three hundred students in the whole high school, it is much easier and less expensive to field the winter sports than football or baseball.

Jim Orcutt, a Florida State sociologist, zeros in on the same explanation for the Florida dynasty. "A lot of parts of the country are football crazy, but they haven't developed this kind of dynasty," he told Walker. "It comes from the environment down here. It's a more wide-open kind of football with an emphasis on speed. It's a lot like the culture of Florida." Like Texas, Florida has a rich, deep talent pool to draw on, especially the predominantly black urban areas around Miami, Tampa Bay, Daytona, etc. As well, remembering what Chris Hill said, in rural areas in Florida and throughout the south, there are pockets of black communities that funnel athletes to join the urban high school athletes.

Florida speed sits on top of the athletic pond with roots that run as deep as water lilies, waiting to be scooped off the surface. Not only are the kids fast, they play and run against kids that are just as fast. Like the endless summers of Southern California, accounting for a majority of junior college football players who go on to play at four-year schools (Florida's junior colleges don't offer football as a sport), the climate in Florida is conducive for year-round sport. University of Miami's football coach, Butch Davis said, "I think the climate has a lot to do with it. A lot of kids get a tremendous amount of outside activity growing up here. There's just a prolific amount of good athletes."

With the good, comes the bad. The Florida schools also are the most notorious for on and off the field bad behavior. The recent NCAA rule on post-play celebration was instituted in direct

241

response to Miami's taunting and fighting that occurred during games. Both Miami and Florida State have been investigated by the NCAA for violating regulations and Miami has become the Oklahoma of the 90s; players being involved in criminal behavior leading to arrests and criminal charges.

Throughout my playing days, I had been knocking around in my head the impact of the way of life on the game and it's importance on the economic and social base of the community. High school football is larger than life in regions that are poor, such as rural Texas, rural Pennsylvania, West Virginia, most of the southeast, Alabama, Georgia, and Louisiana. Besides expressing a rural versus urban dichotomy and a socioeconomic continuum, football powerfully shapes gender roles and the development of rituals and behavior that usher in manhood.

J.T. completed a 7-yard hitch to Eric over the hands of the relentless Bakersfield rush. Few words of encouragement trickled from our bench, but the completion gave J.T. some maneuvering room. On second and short, J.T., with Torlando on the bench, finally was able to avoid the rush, rolling to his right and spotting Art steps ahead of his two defenders.

### KIST
*Stone looking for Williams down the left sideline and has him at midfield on the fly pattern!!! It is a footrace, 40, 30, 20 and Williams dropped at the 10-yard line. First down Santa Barbara! Touchdown saving tackle by Cedric Ashley. J.T. Stone on the bomb and Arthur Williams running the fly pattern. Beat double coverage and only Ashley's speed prevented that one from being a 90-yard TD. It goes for 79 and Santa Barbara setting up shop at the 11-yard line. 1:54 left to play in the third quarter. That should put Stone over the 3000 yard mark for the season and what a pass to do it on.*

### Culture Bound
Compton, California is notorious for poverty, high crime, urban unrest and blight. The game following our upset win over 17th-ranked Moorpark College, we journeyed to winless Compton College looking for a sure win and a chance to spread out playing

time. The game itself, at least in preparation, took a back seat to the fact that we were traveling only two hours south of us, but in terms of experiencing another lifestyle, we were traveling into another dimension. Not too long ago, the mayor was charged with embezzling, there was a shooting at a McDonalds killing several and its streets are oftentimes battlegrounds for gang wars. The unofficial slogan for this game had been coined, "Drive by the Tartars." The city of Compton, like the team, is all black. But, unlike the poor rural areas in Texas and Florida, organized sport was a very low priority on the totem pole of life. Going down there was a cultural, as well as an athletic, experience. In the back of my mind fermented a rural Midwestern phobia for anything black-oriented; a fear of violence and death associated with urban LA neighborhoods. I knew it wasn't just Compton. Walking the West Side of Santa Barbara or strolling down off-State streets like Chapala or Bath in the evening could be just as dangerous.

In anthropology, there is a concept labeled "culture-bound" which simply means the construction of theories about the world and reality based on the assumptions and values of one's own culture or upbringing. It was too clear that so many of us on this football team were "culture bound," filled with the influence of our background and upbringing. For the young players, mediating this influence was the exposure to other cultural variations through television, or what I like to call, the MTV and FOX effect. Programs such as *Melrose Place* and *Beverly Hills 90120* become surreal interactions of teenagers complete with a preponderance of social behavior in a one-hour episode that one couldn't possibly endure or hope to see in a lifetime.

The Compton experience represented "culture shock" for many of us, but many players were already in "shock" from their teammates. In sport, you are literally thrown together and forced to depend on others; in many cases, on those who hold vastly different perceptions of what cultural reality is. To the fans, all that can be seen is the physical nature of 60 minutes of football once a week. How hard it is for a player from Santa Maria to play side be side with another player, for instance, from Culver City? You are not going to have deep philosophical discussions on the nature of race relations while both blocking down on an off-tackle run.

"I can't believe we lost to Compton. We lost to fuckin' Compton," said Thiessen. Saturday evening, after getting back from Compton, Casey, Jake Lombard, recovered somewhat from his neck injury, John, Cliffie and I sat munching fries and guzzling beer at Woody's, three blocks from the boys' apartment. Eight hours before, we took the Compton field, that resembled LaPlaya Stadium's turf, confident that we would destroy Compton like every other team had before us. Three hours later, we left the field, not just beat, but outplayed, manhandled and embarrassed. "Yeah, beat by fuckin' Compton," said Casey. "We suck." We were working on our second huge tray of fries and second huge pitcher of beer. We ended up at Woody's after piling off the bus at 6:30 p.m. and making a stop at the apartment.

The game started at 1 p.m. for two good reasons. One Compton's field had no lights and second, even if they did, nobody in their right mind, including Compton, would play at night in Compton. As it was, there was no admission charge to the game, because it was too dangerous to have money lying around.

"Something wasn't right from the beginning," I said. "I felt like I had landed in a twilight zone."

"Yeah, I know what you mean," Jake added. "It didn't even feel like it was a real game. And then the game started and we were blown off the ball and then it was too late."

"You gotta give credit to Compton," said Jarrett. "They played good. They were hitting and once they scored on us early, it just built them up. It was also their fucking homecoming game. They had something else to play for." Soaking up the beer with greasier fries, we drank some more and then left, taking Casey's old Suzuki Samurai three blocks to the apartment. Not before John, in one of his more eloquent speeches, had the final word. "We suck."

It was hot and humid when our two buses reached Compton's field at 11 a.m. after driving through miles of an urban concrete jungle. Snipers, gang wars, drive-bys were in our conversations in the locker room all week. The blacks from Los Angeles, like fish out of water, joked about life in central LA. "Doc, I hope you don't get shot. You sure stand out with that white hair of yours," one of the Culver City defensive backs told me.

The school sits on a flat piece of urban decay, so much different than our own breathtaking view of the Pacific. Most were faced with this cognitive dissonance as we stepped down off the buses; this wasn't real. Eric and I dubbed the scene that confronted us, "the Compton Triangle," will we leave alive? The boundaries of the field, enclosed by an eight-foot high chain link fence, defined a secure sense of comfortableness. If anything, the turf, the yard markers, the goal posts, and even the sprinkler heads that actually stuck out above the grass level at some areas of the field separated out the unreal from the real. Outside the fence lay a world of urban violence far different from what many of us only read about in the *LA Times* Metro section and hear on the LA TV stations.

We forgot that the Compton players knew no different and a football game seemed like a walk in the park to them. I was tight and so, after stowing my gear, as is my weekly ritual, with J.T. and some others, I walked out to the field. I spent the last two nights sleepless, tossing and turning, thinking about routes and assignments. Several Compton players met us on the field and led vocally by a defensive back playfully lectured us on propriety and territoriality.

"This is my field," he chanted. "Don't come near me. I own this field." He looked at J.T. and asked him if he was the quarterback. Without waiting for an answer, he continued. "Don't be throwing nothing in my area. That shit won't fly"

"I am going to take him apart," J.T. muttered after the brash back sauntered off. Many of us on the field commented on the back's bravado, messing with our minds, which already were out of synch. We were not only playing a game against an opponent, but in the back of our minds, we were playing against a lifestyle that was alien to many of us. Eric told me on the bus ride back that it was nothing like he had ever felt before on the field, an eerie feeling of nothing going right; the feeling of being on two separate fields.

On the sidelines, the ticking clock and sense of panic created animosity; the offensive player screamed at the defense, the defense wondered about the offense and the coaches yelled at the officials. Mark Johnson was hit with an unsportsmanlike conduct in the fourth quarter that characterized the futility of the contest. We didn't handle adversity well. Up, 14-10, 17-14 and even 21-17, we buckled and gave up and, on the other side of the field, Compton got stronger by the minute. For so many of us, our eventual loss was because we "fucked up." Yet for the more objective, Compton did not only step it up, they took it to us. J.T. threw four interceptions, two deserved and two due to Lee. One of those interceptions was tipped and the second one was at the goal line on our last ditch drive with under a minute to go and a chance to come within three and an onside kick recovery. Lee's route was a curl, but he failed to come back for the ball and the vocal Compton defensive back stepped in front and picked it off to seal our fate.

Delivered under the shade outside the locker room Chuck's halftime speech was a series of cliches: come together, suck it up, play with heart, a big-time gut check and come together as a team. He spoke, he yelled a bit, and then he left. Dudley stepped into the void and told the receivers to be positive and play your game. But it was T.K. who delivered the clincher. T.K., who was the cheerleading coach, the bundle of raw emotion and energy who I feared would suffer a cardiac arrest every game, and to most of the players, the coach who was inspirational stood up and lashed out at us. "Fuck, you should be creaming these guys!" he screamed at the top of his lungs. "They aren't that fucking good. Now get off your asses, quit bitchin' and moaning, acting like a bunch of pussies and go out and play your fucking game!"

Two passes, one incomplete and one complete against Bakersfield's secondary, produced a total of six yards and we faced a third and goal at the Bakersfield five. Chuck and Dudley were surrounded by a suddenly alive group of football players. This was a start, a wake-up call and we needed to dial it in. Chuck was almost at midfield. "What did you call, Chuck?" Dudley called to Chuck who was still a good ten yards on the field. "Quarterback Draw," he exclaimed as he backed his way off the field. J.T. settled back into the shotgun and took the wobbly long snap backpedaled a step and then shot up the center of the field. He was hit a yard before the goal line and fumbled....

**KIST**

*And now J.T. trying to take it himself on the five-yard line a quarterback draw, fumbles the ball, it is loose in the end zone...*

Our hearts dropped into our stomachs as we saw the ball pop out of J.T.'s grasp. We followed the ball and the pile that grew around it and waited for the official's sign...

## KIST

*And it is recovered by the Vaqueros, TD Santa Barbara City College!! We will see who comes out of the pile, getting the accolades, looks to be big number 73 for Santa Barbara, D.J. Molina who makes the recovery and the first man to pat him on the head is J.T. Stone. ...Bakersfield 42 Santa Barbara 21.*

With fifty-two seconds left in the third quarter, a tentative first step back to respectability.

# Section Five
## The Game
## Bakersfield vs Santa Barbara
## Fourth Quarter

*I practiced to make perfect...when the time came*

*This was a picture of my "family," for six long months; the receivers. Standing, from left, Jerome White, Benjy Trembly, Eric Mahanke, Coach Steve Dudley, Coach Garrett Ware, Derone Hatcher, David Weismiller. Kneeling left to right, Ryan Capretta, Warren Green, Jeff Lough, Arthur Williams, Torlando Bolden, Twuan Hill. Sitting, left to right, Lee Green, Rob Sands, Troy Tremblay, Stephan Kratzer. Missing, Stuart Boyer.*

# Chapter 20

_____

## Playin' Time

**B**akersfield advanced the ball quickly at the close of the third quarter, but the momentum of the score was still with us as the fourth quarter opened. The game was waning, matching the quickening afternoon and the falling sun. Time was running out and we needed three quick scores. It wasn't impossible. Our offense was high octane, but you never knew if the explosion led to acceleration or implosion. Our fortunes were changing. Molina's fumble recovery-touchdown as the third quarter closed had to be a good omen. The defense was going to hold. Maybe Gray would get tired, even hurt. Sparks hadn't done much through the air. Chuck and Dudley were yelling like maniacs, trying to pump us up. The offense was yelling at the defense. "Come on, hold them, kill those fuckers! Stop their shit!"

One more Bakersfield score and it was all but over. In the back of my mind, I knew I was getting in this quarter. This was my swan song and I was going to be ready. There was so much symbolism running rampant that afternoon. My life had become one intense otherworld experience, centered in a rectangular space, bounded by white lines, enclosed within a human fence that ran on both sidelines, set within a giant concrete temple and witnessed and validated by over 2000 worshipers in red. The past collided with the present; there was no future for the next 15 minutes. I found myself part of the animated chorus that screamed support and encouragement to the 11 disciples on the turf.

"Playing time" were magical words to those relegated to seeing more action from off the field rather than on it, seeing the tackles rather than feeling them, watching the passes, not receiving them. All season long, so many of us had toiled in relative obscurity, getting in for a series or two every game, some less than that. But save for Drone and Jeff, most of the non-starters had stuck the season out. Now we stood on the sideline, yelling for the defense to put a stop on Bakersfield, get the ball back and score again, knowing full well that the closer we got to Bakersfield, the less chance any of us were going to see the field. Of all the players who had started with hopes and showed ability to get playin' time, I felt the worst for Phil.

Phil had already left the country. He left limping, his knee finally giving out, reducing him to getting around on crutches. After displacing his kneecap in the first fall scrimmage, Phil had played sporadically, coming back too soon off the injury and injuring it again in the middle of the season. The seventh game of the season against archival Hancock College, Phil decided that he was going to play no matter what. "I didn't come all this way to bugger my knee," he said in the training room prior to the game as he was getting his knee wrapped. The kneecap was back in place, but it would only take a knock and off it would come again. Phil was frustrated and Australian and those two features set his mind to play.

Phil played in the first half of the game, even grabbing a pass. Not long after that play, on a block, he slammed his knee into an opposing player's helmet and in the grinding collision, Phil's career as a running back at City College ended. Big Phil, not one to lay and writhe in pain on the wet evening turf, pulled himself to his feet and hobbled off the field. Reaching the sideline, he ripped off his helmet and threw it into the ground, all the while screaming, over and over again, "fuck!" at the top of his considerable lungs.

In the glare of the field lights, his bald head glistened with sweat and the traveling white of his jersey was stained black with the Righetti High School stadium dirt. In those seconds, while he ranted and raved, he was just about out of control and teetered on the edge of losing it. "Goddamn it to hell!" were the first coherent sentence out of his mouth, as he limped over and pulled himself on the training table, behind our bench. I walked over with some trepidation and listened to the frustration that spilled out of his mouth like a hot angry river of lava, flowing out of the burning hell that was his heart's volcano. "My fucking season is over! What a fucking waste!" Later, after the game was over, Phil was more under control and sat with an ice bag wrapped around his knee. "I am going to go back to Australia next week," he told me. "There is no reason to stay here. Susan told me the kneecap popped off again and it won't be better for a number of weeks, let alone before the season ends." His face was darker than usual, so I let him be, awash in the depression of the moment and the pain of a distended kneecap.

Phil left Santa Barbara that next week. His knee would take some time to heal and, since he was only here for a year, there was no sense in him finishing out the semester. I sat and talked to him in the training room the Monday after that game and he was pretty buoyant considering his injury. "I am glad I came," he said, the muscle stimulator machine shooting volts into his leg. "Football here is so much better than home. I would never had the opportunity to discover for myself what I was capable of had I stayed in Queensland. I know I can play at this level. A break here, a break there, I would have been in there. I think Kon and I should have played more, or at least be given the opportunity. I had some nice runs during scrimmages and at Cal Lutheran, but I never really got a chance to get untracked. I know I fumbled more than Chuck wanted, but still, I thought I deserved some time."

Bakersfield started the fourth quarter, first and ten from our thirteen yard line. With electricity finally surging up and down our sideline, the defense somehow reached deep inside and found the strength to repel the Renegades. An off tackle run by Lane was stuffed at the line of scrimmage. Bakersfield chose to go to the air on second down and Sparks was thrown for a ten-yard loss by the revived Vaquero front line. With Jarrett and Chris screaming at the rest of the team on the field, the defense dug in and, for one of the few times all day, linebacker Darryl Bryant didn't worry about the run and came barreling in on Sparks. He rushed his throw and Jarrett was there to knock the ball away from the intended receiver.

"Way to go, defense! Way to hold them! Good fucking job, defense!" rained down on the tired gladiators that trotted off the field from our sidelines. We had won our first skirmish since late in the first half and not even the field goal that put Bakersfield up 45-21 dampened our resolve to cut even further into the lead. There was still well over thirteen minutes to play, plenty of time for J.T. to work miracles.

For the entire season, the non-starters vacillated back and forth on promises of more play from the coaches, but each game chances came in a trickle or, for some, in a drop. Frustration welled up and surfaced in conversations at practice, on the sidelines during the games or in extended-play conversations on bus rides. These acrid dialogues vented these feelings and allowed players to blow steam and continue to practice. On any team sport, competition between players for playing time was, at times, more intense than that experienced on Saturday afternoon against our opponents. This was the nature of the beast and one that could easily rip apart the fabric of team cohesion. For the coaches and players, there were different agendas. For the coach, the goal was to win. For the players, winning was mixed in with the desire to win and play. Chuck needed non-starters for a number of reasons, bodies to scrimmage with during practice, fill out drills and a repository for potential players when injuries occurred. He needed to keep the scrubs interest in the team or else he could have been easily left at the end of the season, with no replacements for a decimated team. In addition, Chuck knew full well that games are sometimes won on the shoulder and legs of unsung heroes thrust into the pressure cooker of a close game due to injury or, in our case, mutiny. Dudley continually reminded the scrubs of the game winning play of a scrub receiver deep in the fourth quarter three or four years ago. We really didn't know if it happened or not, but that wasn't really the point of the "legend."

"Man, this guy was there in the right place at the right time," Dudley said. "A starter went down, I looked for the second stringers and they weren't anywhere around, so I sent this guy in that had little game experience and he caught the winning pass." The moral of the myth was always be prepared.

Chuck depended on the concept of team and the players' desire to be a part of a sport, at any level, to maintain interest through the season. For the most part, we, as scrubs, bought into the illusion of the concept of team, believing in the end that team success really did depend on our presence. As the season progressed, and it became clear that Torlando, Art and Twuan were afforded a great deal of leeway when it came to participation in practice, our frustration became difficult to control. We would fill in their positions at practice, but then see little opportunity develop out of this performance during games. Practice was the only time that we could showcase our talents to the coaches and to go 100 percent and then to see that effort wasted on granting playing time to others created a cynicism that tied us together in a battle of good versus evil. In the end, however, nobody was forcing us to continue to play, or paying us so that we were obligated to be there in practice and during games. For Stuart, Troy, Kratz and myself, this was the last opportunity to be a part of an organized football experience. This was the last time to be so near the pulse of action, a heartbeat or ripped tendon away from playing time.

Drone and Kon were fed up with their scarce amount of action during the season and chose the Ventura game, two games before the end of the season, to quit. One afternoon, the week before the brothers quit, Kon and another defensive back were talking about playin' time in the deserted locker room after practice. The back told Kon, "Torlando and Art, even Twuan don't put up in practice because there is no need to. Man, it's like, I can get a bitch to give me a blow job whenever I want it, just go over and I get head, why should I go to the effort for a relationship when I don't need it?" All through his explanation, the back was talking to Kon, but he was aware I was listening in. After he was through, he turned and looked at me. "Get it, Doc?" I nodded. "Yeah I get it and even though I probably would have put it a different way, the sentiment is understood."

Kon was nodding his head through the analogy and couldn't wait to get his two cents in. "I tell you, the coaches play favorites and for all the time I put into this fucking team this year, I don't get playing time!" Kon had a pick stuck in his bushy afro and his jeans rode low off his hips, exposing half of his red print boxers. His shirt was off and his tattoos seemed menacing, reacting to what he was saying. He slammed his locker shut and continued. "Shit, I am second-year player, a sophomore and I think I deserve a chance to play. I run shit, Twuan plays half-ass during fucking practice. Man, sometimes he don't even come and I get no fucking chance to really show what I can do. So for the next three games, I am not going to put out. I will come to practice, do the fucking dance they want me to do, but right now I could care less."

After it was apparent he wasn't getting in during the Ventura game, Drone sat wrapped in a blanket perched on his helmet at the far end of our sideline, darkly muttering to himself and his brother, Kon. In the post game locker room both went off screaming "Fuck, fucking coaches, fuck!" Joe walked through and caught their performance and told them to "shut the fuck up." They kept at it and, as Joe told me later, "They kept screaming and I told them they were off the team and then Kon starts to yell, 'I am a man, I am a man, you can't do that to me right in my face.' I just looked at him and told him that he was done with this team and to get the fuck out of here and walked away as he was still screaming," Joe said. "Man, they are weird!"

I saw Drone walking on campus that following Monday. He was about to start across the bridge of "life" separating east from west campus and I stopped him to find out about the locker room scene with Joe. "I am fed up with this shit," he said. "So is my brother. Dudley and Melendez dicked us around all year and we ended up with shit."

"Man, don't quit with only three games left," I said. "Finish up the season; don't burn your bridges. What if you want to play next year?"

"It's the principle of the thing," Drone said. "Why should we stay out and get no time or even respect, for that matter? We are out of there."

Drone and Kon suffered from their attitude as much as the coaches' perception of their abilities. They were hard-working players, both at practice and when they got into games, but they were also rebels in how they looked at who played and who didn't. Not content like the rest of us, who didn't play regularly, to wait for the time that may never have come, they pressed the issue. Their attitude was belligerent, their demands to play thrown in the coaches' faces. Drone saw it in black and white, "I played hard in practice, I was always there, I should play." Oh, if it was that easy.

Dave Weismeiller talked about it at practice that same day. "I thought Drone and I were the same kind of person. He was better than I was, faster than I was. He had hands and he could move when he got the ball. He didn't really get a chance. He had two, three balls thrown to him, caught two and dropped one. After he dropped that one, that was it. Dudley didn't just like him or whatever. It is just like Troy. I think Troy is good, personally. He was good at the Cal Lutheran scrimmage. I don't know if he is not paying attention, or what. But Drone is the saddest case of all. I hope he is out there next year. I told him you shouldn't quit with two games left in the season. I could see him quitting halfway through the season, but not with two games left. I used to talk to him when I was upset, too, and we would make each other feel better. I think he could have had a chance to start right now, if he and Dudley had hit it off better."

Symbolic of what had happened, Drone and I parted company, him heading across the bridge and me down to the locker room. I told him to stay in touch. He grinned that infectious grin of his, braces shining in the sun, said, "Take care Doc, catch them if they come your way," and walked across the bridge towards the rest of his life.

Midway through the Fall, I sat down with Mike Hayes to get his thoughts on how the season was going. Mike was an irony. He was incredibly astute when it came to talking about football, not just the plays or the 0s and Xs, but the psychology of the game and the constantly shifting interpersonal relationships that make up the team, but when it came to the classroom, Mike couldn't turn his brain on or keep his attention focused and it wasn't for lack of trying. Mike was just not a classroom guy. Inside the classroom, the professor started talking and his mind immediately pounded to get out of there and then it was worse than being blocked out of a play by an offensive lineman. Mike saw himself with a lot of things going, football, seeing his daughter, and many times he ran out of energy or motivation to keep going to his classes.

"I have this theory," I told him once, "that at the end of this year I am going to look back and say, I wish I had the chance, even though I am 38. I mean I am in there playing like everybody else is, and the fact that I am 20 years older doesn't mean anything. I wish I had a chance to do something. You need to grab this chance and milk it for all that it is worth."

Of all people, Mike was the most likely to get through his football and college career, intact, because of his work ethic. When it came to granting "time" on the field, more times than not, the players had a better idea of who could play. Mike was well aware of the receivers' strengths and weaknesses. Lee, Troy, me, even David were not going to run over people. Troy was big and strong, but lacked the natural ability to make it payoff on the field. When Mike hit Twuan, it was like slamming into a rock, but when he hit Troy or me, it was party time. Still, if you can catch, there will always be a need for your services, even though the coaches have to balance out playing time with team success. Torlando and Twuan and Art will always be better than the rest of us, but football will always be a game of situation and of motivation and it was here that I bled impatience for most of the season.

Mike and I would talk often after practice about my ability and what I needed to do to improve. To Mike, Dudley had messed most of us up all season long. Mike would mimic Dud, "Don't worry," he would say "we are going to play you today, don't worry" and then it became a joke. And then he says, "Oh, I am sorry I didn't get you in." Mike also didn't like what Joe and Carmen did to a substitute defensive back. Carmen told him point blank to his face, you are not going to play. Man, you just don't get into his face and tell him he is not going to play. Ash (a defensive back) used to want to go out for punt return and then Joe told him, "I don't care if you are here for three years, you are never going to return a punt."

"Okay," Mike says, "maybe Ash knows he's not, but you don't say that to a kid. You just shot me down to nothing. I am not worth anything. What is the point of playing? Let him go do what he is doing, maybe he will make a play, and maybe he will get in at the end of the game. Let him find out for himself." Mike remembers seeing Ash in on kickoff one game and he was getting rocked every time, leveled. He would get up and then get leveled again. But at least now he knows what kind of game it is. At least now he knows how much he needs to grow and how much he needs to improve to play. If he had sat there the whole time, he would think that he could play. Why am I not playing? That is how he was until they put him in on kick off and now I think he will start getting better.

Mike would hear me say, "I can do this, just get me in." He would tell me point blank, "You will never be great, maybe not even good, but you don't have to be a great receiver to be able to contribute. You may have speed," he would say, "you run hard, but you came in too late. You don't have a lot of football sense." Mike would then invariably say, when you get in, take advantage of the situation. Do what you are capable of and work on it. Mike would pontificate more, and I would never tire of listening. "It's like myself, man. I am short, but then I hear the coach last year say I only play the guys who are tall." Mike heard that and couldn't believe it. The coaches were playing them because they are tall. He would then look at me and burn his frustration deep inside of me. He marched up to Carmen and told him to put him in there so he could see for himself. If he got burned and they kept picking on him and the coaches take him out, then he wouldn't care. Just let him see for himself. But he knew he could play and tackle. "Best thing for you," he would end up saying, "is to get in a game and learn for yourself what you can do. Maybe there are only certain patterns that you can run, but you should work on it in practice." Mike liked that Benjy Tremblay wasn't fast or shifty, but he tried hard and was good in the clutch and he blocked like gangbusters. "If he hadn't played from the beginning, then Chuck would never had known what he was capable of," he said. "When situations would pop up and the coaches would know to run the ball or go for a short gain, they would put Benjy in."

For Kratz, the season ending would signal his last association with organized ball, and although he railed against his lack of "playing time," "it's the German in me, Doc, I can't help it," he still soaked it all up. He came early to practice to run routes and just throw the ball around and bullshit. Stuart and Troy were planning on playing next season and, for them, this whole season was a learning experience. If anything, this year motivated them to work harder in the off-season and come in next year competing for playin' time.

For me, as the season wound down, I became philosophical about most everything, knowing I would miss the experience once it was put on the shelf. With only the Glendale and Bakersfield games left on the schedule, Chuck took me to the weekly Monday afternoon Santa Barbara Athletic Round Table luncheon, put on by the local newspaper and television channel. The lunch enabled area high school and college coaches of the sports in season to give some publicity to themselves and their team.

When it came time for Chuck to talk, after walking to the podium and summarizing our win over Los Angeles Pierce, he introduced me. He began and, although his words and their meaning were public, he looked straight at me as if to personalize their impact. "I brought Robert Sands with me today. He is a wide receiver and he doesn't like to me to mention that he is 38 years old. He works hard, very hard and gives his leadership and maturity. He is frustrated now because he thinks he should be playing more and I haven't been getting him in that much. He is a prime example of, in some cases, how a player's contribution to the success of the team takes the form of more intangible things other than performance."

There we were, the same age, the same profession, college educators, but also player/coach and he was acknowledging that which had been eating away inside of me for two seasons. In that brief two minutes, while Chuck spoke about me, the time, effort and energy I deposited came to the surface of my mind and battled with Chuck's words. I sat there and listened and wondered if this was his way of telling me that he understood how I was feeling, as if the public forum increased the weight of his meaning. Two games remained in my college career. Was this the way I was going out, I wondered?

After the lunch, that same afternoon and before practice, Dudley emerged from the coaches' office while some of the receivers and I were scanning the bulletin board and looked right at me.

"Doc," he said, "you are starting on Saturday."

"Don't fuck with me, Dud," I told him.

"You are starting on Saturday," he repeated, clapped me on the back and walked away.

As if in unison, the boys turned to me and said, "What did Dud say?"

"He told me I was starting Saturday," I said to their collective faces, and they laughed.

"Dud can be such an asshole," I muttered.

I started that next game. The opening play of the game, I dropped the only pass thrown to me. I played for a quarter's worth of plays and, as we walked off the field in victory, I felt that I had made a real contribution.

The day before that game, while Garret threw routes to the receivers, he told me that I was starting because the coaches felt I should be rewarded for my hard work. "Doc, you busted your balls all year," he said, as he pulled me aside. "They want to see you play and catch some balls. Also, I think they want to send a message to the rest of the team for next year that working hard will pay off." I dropped the next pass, and Garrett told me to frame my hands in the shape of pussy.

# Chapter 21

---

## Comeback?

Time seems to accelerate when there is not much of it; seconds race by and soon minutes trail close behind. We were getting the ball back with about 13 minutes to play and time was not going to stand still. We needed to strike soon, and often, to pull ourselves back into the game and Bakersfield knew that. After the ensuing kickoff was tipped by one of our up men, Neil Dreste covered it at the Bakersfield 49-yard line. Things were going our way. J.T. fired off a quick five-yard completion to Torlando. With Bakersfield playing a prevent defense, J.T. was getting more time to throw.

Everybody knew that we were going deep every chance we got. Not wasting time, on second and four, from the Bakersfield 43, J.T. lofted a bomb to Arthur in the far corner of the end zone. Art had slipped behind the defense and was waiting for the ball when it fell to the earth. But Art's legs got tangled in the pylon and the ball fell harmlessly to the turf. After finding Eric on a series-saving 3rd down conversion, we wasted two passes and a short gain by J.T. on a quarterback draw and faced a 4th down and the game at the Bakersfield 36. All year long we had gone no-huddle, but now,

Chuck was giving J.T. the next play even before the last one had finished and receivers were sprinting to get set up for the next pass. It was chaotic. I didn't need to look around me to know that players' faces wore the excitement of the moment.

On the field, Art, Torlando, Ryan and Eric lined up, the cream always rises to the top and this was our best unit. For once, Dudley had lined up the players that fit the play. On both sidelines, players bunched up and pushed forward to see the play. The past, present and future of this season had finally collided in these last minutes of the game and I swear that, for this play, time stood still. Nobody knew where each of us were going to be in a year; different schools, maybe not playing at all, suspended from a team or in jail. All that mattered was the next 10 seconds. This was do or die.

J.T. took the snap from the 'gun and looked for Torlando as we looked for the human highlight film. "It's going to Torlando," Kratz said, as J.T. cocked his arm.

**KIST**

*A fourth down and five, down 24 points. Stone fires to Bolden over the middle, he has the first down at the 15!! Torlando slips a tackle at the 10, a spin move, stays on his feet again, and out of bounds at the 8-yard line! What a run by Torlando Bolden. This crowd appreciates the effort. Torlando refuses to go down. First and goal Vaqueros. You watch him all season long and he still amazes you. Torlando Bolden has so many moves and they are all patented to him. A unique talent.*

We went wild on the sidelines as Torlando shook tackles, left defenders grasping for a dream and stopped the clock by going out of bounds. I had come to know Torlando for over a season and, along with everybody else, felt that I didn't know Torlando at all. Even with a game remaining in the season, he was still an enigma, distant as a galaxy, the sheen of his sweat the only real layer I, or anybody else, knew, and even that was suspect, given his practice effort. Halfway through the season, we talked for 15 minutes about his legal problems and it was all matter of fact. He had his homeys that encircled him like tightly-knit wagons. Torlando was perceptive and extremely proud of his skills on the field. That pride created a giant chip that sat on his shoulder like an anvil weighing

263

him down and blocking any help that he desperately needed off the field. The receivers, to a man, agreed that he should be destined for stardom and to a man we agreed he wasn't going to get there. We relied on him, we marveled at him, we spent too much time talking about him and, in the end, none of us were any closer to knowing him. Tony, the defensive back who went to Santa Barbara High School with him, probably came the closest to unlocking the secret of Torlando, yet he could only manage the vague stock reply, "Torlando is just Torlando."

One day, not too long before the end of the season, Torlando commandeered the video projector, still left up from afternoon film, and stuck in his 30-minute highlight video, his signature of greatness. Only a few of us were there as the lights came down and the screen came up. The tape's quality was poor, but Torlando slashed his way into our mind through amazing runs, catches and touchdowns. He was a man playing with boys. As the tape unwound in slow motion, oohs and ahhs uttered were quickly replaced by a growing cacophony of "shit," "motherfucker," "god damns" as Torlando would evade another tackler or simply explode past the defenders on his way to another long touchdown run. Torlando sat behind the projector, holding court, his voice cutting through the wall of sound, pointing out an upcoming move, a feint, giving us a running commentary on the poor defender's lack of expertise or a narration on the game. By the time the film ended, the entire team was jammed into the locker room, many trying to dress at the same time, not wanting to miss out on a move or a catch. As the lights were switched on and players went back to getting dressed, I am sure each of us were wishing that we had just a little of what Torlando was blessed with and all us knowing that even a little would make us ten times better on the field. Nobody else could have held 50 players spellbound and left us wanting more. Anybody else would have been laughed out of the room.

I guess, in a way, that was Torlando; not just a facet of his personality but, in some sad way, his athletic ability and perceptions of those around him formed the biggest part of his mystique. He had cultivated that visage so long that even he had bought into the importance of the omnipotent Torlando. Almost too late, I had discovered that I had known the real Torlando all season long. There was nothing else that mattered or existed to him. I was looking too hard for something that was at the end of my nose.

"He's fucking unbelievable," Kratz, his biggest detractor during the season, said, admiration radiating from his eyes like a son who sees his father as god. Four plays later, we again faced fourth down, two yards away from respectability and Bakersfield's end zone.

### KIST

*Stone out of the shotgun and looks to the right and fires complete in the end zone! Touchdown! What a catch! David Weismeiller. Touchdown Santa Barbara! What an outstanding grab by Weismeiller, looked like it was overthrown at the outset and David stayed with it in the back corner and comes down with the touchdown of the season and Santa Barbara closes it to 45-27.*

David came sprinting off the field, ball triumphantly held high in his hands. He was met by a swarm of Vaqueros who quickly engulfed him to where all that was left was David's hand sticking out of the pile, ball waving in the air. We were still grabbing at straws, but there was now some glimmer of hope that penetrated the fog of depression that had hung over our bench. Chuck screamed, "Don't give up! We got a shot. Come on, defense, you have to hold them!" He stormed up and down the sideline, pumping the kick-off team up, slamming pads and screaming encouragement.

"Goddamn it!" he bellowed. "We got to have it. Defense get out there and shut these fuckers down. We can do it! There is plenty of time left." Not even missing the two point conversion as Art dropped the ball dimmed our emotion. After the kickoff, the defense was exhausted even with the extra shot of adrenaline. They started onto the field, almost as if they dreaded what was coming. And what was coming was punishing Mike Gray and his alter ego, Shawn Lane.

For a brief period of time, hope surged against the currents of reality and the players were pumped up, yelling "Deefense! Deefense!" and slamming hands down on thigh pads in a rhythmic chant, as if the number of voices blended together and the rhythm of the chant would generate raw energy in the worn Vaquero players. Bakersfield started at the 20-yard line after a touchback and spent the next six minutes, eight plays and 80 yards shredding our defense, ripping gigantic holes and left it looking like Swiss cheese. Gray and Lane took turns as the Renegades kept it on the ground and moved seemingly at will. In the process, Gray went over 300 yards, Lane 140 yards and Bakersfield over 50 points as they scored on an eight-yard run by Lane.

Each play was excruciating to watch. On the touchdown, you could actually feel the air go out of our sails on the sideline. Chuck's face showed little emotion, but he turned away from the end zone and walked resignedly back down the sidelines pulling his cord from his headset with him. For a moment, he felt the pain and couldn't hide it. It was only for a brief moment and then he was clapping his hands in a sign of motivation.

"Come on, let's get one back, show them we aren't dead! Let's get them, offense! Let's not roll over and die, goddammit. Let's score on these guys!"

In any other contest, by this time, with this score, the players would be thinking about the trek across the field and obligatory handshake. But this was Bakersfield, the biggest crowd of the season, the last game of the season; for the sophomores and freshmen not coming back, the last game as a Vaquero.

Funny thing, pride. We could dance around what it meant to us, played it down, like "who the fuck cares about this stupid game," once we got buried like an avalanche. Stick any one of us on the field, anytime during the game, there was a switch turned on that ignited some kind of wicked adrenaline and, for that time we were on the field, nitroglycerine flowed like water through our veins.

Five minutes remained of football. Chance for another score. In our offense, a lifetime.

"Doc, Troy," Dud called. "You guys get ready to go in when we get the kickoff."

# Chapter 22

## Walter Mitty, George Plimpton, Hunter Thompson and Doc Ride Again

W e had the ball for one more drive and now it was a matter of respect and pride. J.T. was working his magic, a draw here, a completion there, and we were moving down the field. Torlando and Art had taken their respective seats on the sidelines and were watching the last five minutes. Chuck was into this drive, the last of the year, and he wanted to go out at least some kind of winner. Bakersfield hadn't given an inch. Fresh players were in, but they were just as good as the ones they replaced; an endless well of talent.

After being taken out for Troy on one play, I stood next to Chuck, his hand on my shoulder as we watched the next play unfold, waiting to see what happened before I went in with another play. I was out of breath, not due to fatigue, but due to the adrenaline overload. This was the one experience that I had missed all these months, the clicking of the offense in a game situation. I had been in for a number of plays in two seasons, but this was the time that electricity shot through me and wired my legs, my hands and I felt that I could single-handedly bring us that final measure of triumph. Chuck turned to me and barked the play into the earhole of my helmet and pushed me, as if he needed to, on the field.

The last week passed quickly. Twuan missed practices and I missed a practice while in San Francisco interviewing for a teaching position. Torlando was spotted on the sidelines, Art's shoulder kept him an observer, and the rest of us nursed our injuries and licked our wounds. Chuck and the rest of the coaches talked about nothing else except Bakersfield and a bowl bid.

Chuck's words, "play for pride, play for yourselves, play this as if this is the last game of your life," spewed forth like jets in a fountain, drenching those closest to the reality of what the coaches were saying and misting those coming back for another. As each practice ended, I contemplated the passing of one more day, leaving fewer practices, until it was Friday. We were through the hour of reviewing formations and in Chuck's speech and Dud's monologue and it was finally the last time we made our way across the field, the sun sinking in the west, throwing huge shadows before us, larger than life. In many ways, we were leaving the field, bigger people than when we started four months ago in August–than I started 16 months ago.

"Doc, get in there!" Dudley yelled. "Get in for Lee at Z."

He didn't need to yell. I was standing in between Chuck and him, as I had been for most of the entire game, save for the last three minutes that I had been shuttling in with Troy. We were driving and Benjy had just grabbed a fourth and 10 low liner from J.T. to give us another series in the waning moments of the game. My red helmet was already on and I fumbled with the chinstrap as I ran onto the field. The clock at the far end of the stadium said two something. Two minutes plus left in the fourth quarter.

I passed J.T. as he came over to get the play from Chuck near the sideline. Chuck, Dudley and Garret were huddled together. Ryan, Benjy and Dave milled around the line of scrimmage with the offensive line waiting for J.T. to bring the play back. I turned back to the bench to pick up the play as Chuck screamed to J.T., "Hit Doc! Hit Doc!"

Okay, the simple six-yard hitch. Off the line, sink and breakdown at six or seven yards and pivot back to the ball. J.T. came back to the offensive milling of humanity and called the play and then we split out for our positions in the formation. I jogged out to the near sideline, right in front of our bench, and set up on the line of scrimmage. Benjy slid into the slot between the guard and me. Ryan and Dave were mimicking us on the other side of the ball.

I toed the 30-yard line of Bakersfield and looked over to the linesman to make sure I wasn't off sides. He nodded I was fine. On the near sideline, the coaches and the rest of the team were 10 yards away and some of their yelling permeated the silence that suddenly blanketed my mind.

"Come on, Doc," I heard Garret yell, "get off hard!"

Dudley's voice piggybacked Garret's instructions, "Come on Doc, gotta have it. Get off hard!" Chuck just clapped his hands.

The other receivers standing around the coaches were yelling and, every now and then, I picked up "Doc" but that was about it. I glanced up the field at the white uniform and helmet of the Bakersfield defensive back. Automatically, I noticed he was playing off and setting up for man to man coverage. The inside coverage guy was between Benjy and me.

Just drive him hard and plant and the ball should be there well ahead of his late shot, I thought. I glanced down at the line and my toes. This is it. A season made in one or two plays. Catch the fucking ball! I clenched and unclenched my fingers, keeping them loose. It seemed that all my frustration and loss of sleep over not playing much this season, when I thought that I should be contributing on the field during games, rode my back like jockey on a horse. Better late than never!

I turned my head inside to see J.T. step back and settle into the shotgun position, six yards behind the center. Twuan, the lone running back, was set off to my side and almost as deep as J.T. I listened for J.T.'s somewhat soft cadence and reminded myself, even play number, off on the second count. The second "hut" came and I drove from the line. The only thought in my mind was grab the ball. I jammed my outside foot at seven yards and turned back to J.T., trying to sink my body at the same time.

I picked up the ball right after J.T. released it and tracked it, the usual frozen rope fired from the gun that was his right arm. It was high and to the outside, so I tried to stop my momentum drifting inside. I went up for the pass and grabbed it over my right shoulder, felt the ball settle into my hands, and waited for the shot in my back from the defensive back. The thought passed through my mind for an instant, "now we will see if I can hold on to the ball."

## KIST

*Now Stone fires and there is the man all season long, Robert Sands, the 38-year-old anthropology teacher who is in the process of writing a book about his experience in junior college football, and there it is and the crowd loves it. Robert Sands came out for the team last year and listen to the crowd here at LaPlaya Stadium and they love it. So Robert Sands will go into the record books, he will go into the all-time record book with 1 catch for 8 yards, at least to this point. Robert Sands etching his name into the history books here at Santa Barbara City College.*

*Nice article this week in the News-Press by John Zant on Robert Sands and he is talking about all the difficulties of being 38 and playing in a world filled with 20-year-old kids, the bumps and bruises that take a little bit longer to heal. But he is certainly a credit to this program. Chuck Melendez has named him a co-captain three times earlier this year. Sands hasn't seen a lot of action in his two years here, the sophomore from Springfield, Illinois. But a delightful ending to his City College career this afternoon, he had to wait two years, but he got that catch. And it gives J.T. Stone a season high passing for one game, a fitting way to do it, an 8-yard pickup, gives J.T. 398 yards on the game. And Robert Sands has the catch.*

All I remembered about the catch was reaching up for it, grabbing it and turning up field only to be met by two Bakersfield defenders. Watching the tape of the game, I was stood up by the two and a third one came in and all four of us fell to the turf. I got up and started walking toward the sideline. One of the Bakersfield defensive backs reached out to shake my hand, but I didn't see it. I heard the loudspeaker and the metallic voice that announced to the crowd my catch and what it meant but, already, Dud was waving me back onto the field and I started back toward the huddle.

It was second down, still two minutes to play and I didn't feel the hit. Of course, I wouldn't have felt my leg being amputated at that moment, either. I looked toward the sideline and Garret and Casey and others were shaking their fists toward me. Three plays later, we had a penalty and two incomplete passes.

## KIST

*Fourth down and 10 from the 25-yard line and Stone and company wants to take a time out to think things over. One minute forty-six seconds remaining.*

We walked over and met Chuck coming out on the field. Dudley and Garret stepped out and the trainers brought water. "Let's try a 99," Chuck said. "Come on guys, let's punch it in!" Chuck's headset was off and the flush of excitement still with him. He was coaching to the bitter end.

Dudley opened his mouth and, before words came out, I knew what he was going to say. "Come on guys," he started, "Gotta have it." We finished up the water and headed back to the line of scrimmage. "Gotta have it," echoed Garret, his face washed in sweat, his eyes hidden by shades, but a smile that was live with excitement. Gotta have it to keep playing. We lined up and the thought fleetingly banged around in my head that this could be my last college play.

## KIST

*Santa Barbara, after talking it over with Chuck Melendez, fourth and 10 will go for it, from the 25. Stone from the shotgun, blitz coming, J.T. steps up under the pressure, fires completed to Sands at the 15-yard line! Robert Sands makes the big catch, is dropped at the 14 and a gain of 11 for a first down, Santa Barbara. And this crowd eating it up. That puts Stone over 400 yards on the afternoon, 404 yards to be exact and Robert Sands' second catch.*

I ran a 10-yard down and in and as J.T. stepped in the pocket, I broke open and he delivered it to me in stride as I was running parallel to the 15-yard line. Gathering it in, I set sail, trying to ditch the defender hot on my trail. Unfortunately, he grabbed from behind and pulled me to the turf.

Gotta have it to keep playing.

## KIST

*Santa Barbara needed 10, they picked up 11. 1:17 remaining and now the clock starts and quickly stops as the back judge fires a penalty marker, offsides Bakersfield and they will march it 5 more yards. Will go inside the 10-yard line, down to the 9, where it will be first down and about 5. 1:14, Santa Barbara trying to get into the end zone one last time. Stone back to pass, fires quickly, pass completed at the 3-yard line and driven out of bounds, Troy Tremblay. He made the catch and was stuck by Kevin Burton. Cedric Ashly making the final hit at the 3-yard line. Another 5-yard pickup for Stone and will bring up a first down and goal from the 4-yard line.*

*Stone has Stewart Boyer to the near side, but he is rolling to the far side, now throws back across the middle of the end zone, incomplete. Was looking for Robert Sands and momentarily open, but pass knocked away by Cedric Ashly. Nice play.*

I was open early on the crossing route in the back of the end zone, but J.T. waited too long and the Bakersfield back got his hand in there to deflect it at the last second. A second back was coming in at my face and I would have been leveled if I made the catch. Funny thing, out of habit, after the ball rolled free beyond the end zone, I automatically walked after it and picked it up to give to the referee. In my head was Dudley screaming at the receivers all year long in practice, "If you drop it, receivers, you chase it down."

## KIST

*Second down and goal, and we can anticipate, perhaps, Robert Sands getting another crack at a touchdown here with 46 seconds left. That seems to be the big thing now, will Robert Sands get into the end zone and put a final chapter to his book. Stone looking for the corner of the end zone, Sands there once again, no flag on the play. He was in single coverage, tight coverage. Ty Thatch, hands on hips saying, "Are you kidding me, there is no penalty."*

There was no penalty. I came up to J.T. and told him to throw me the fade, the out pattern at the corner of the end zone and it was beyond my reach. A misfire to Kratz, who had entered the lineup in the last series, and a dump pass to Twuan that went nowhere ended the drive, stalled on the three-yard line.

We walked off the field after Twuan got nailed behind the line and as I slapped hands with Casey, Garrett and others, Bakersfield ran out the clock, the final score 52-27. I sought out Chuck in the milieu of players and we hugged. "Good job, Doc. You finally got your pass," he said. I found Troy Tremblay and congratulated him on his catch and Benjy came up to me and told me he was responsible for me getting a chance to be a statistic by catching that fourth down grab the series before my first catch. Some things never change.

I joined the rest of the team as they lined up to meet Bakersfield players and coaches in the middle of the field. Players slid by, faces blurred as hands were slapped. Some congratulated me for my catches and a couple of their coaches stopped to tell me they were impressed. A *News-Press* sportswriter collared me and asked how I felt. I told him something I couldn't remember until I saw it the next day in the paper.

Parents, girlfriends and friends of both teams streamed onto the turf and created a sea of humanity. I wandered around, found a friend and went over to him. He had followed my efforts over the two years; occasionally taking time to meet and throw passes to me. We chatted for a couple of minutes and then on a cloud of post game high, I slowly made my way off the field and into the locker room for the last time as a Vaquero.

## KIST

*This is the post-game show. Bakersfield comes in and wins the Northern Division, a showdown with the Vaqueros, Bakersfield winning it, 52-27. A most entertaining ball game. Bakersfield improving to 9-1 and Santa Barbara finishing out the season at 5-4-1. We won't rule out a bowl bid just yet.*

*Nathan Sparks, 3-9 for 34 yards, three sacks on the afternoon. The big star of the show, Mike Gray, 316 yards on 31 carries and 3 TDs. Shawn Lane, 16 carries, 148 yards and 2 TDs, Sparks had three carries for 16 and Patrick Duffy carried three yards on the final drive. Receiving Josh Acosta, the only man to catch a pass and that is all they needed, three catches for 34 yards and a TD.*

273

*For Santa Barbara City College, a big day for J.T. Stone. He is going to have the Ben Gay on tonight, 64 attempts, 38 completions, both season highs and J.T. a season high 404 yards, 2 interceptions. And a couple of TDs. Hit David Weismeiller in the fourth quarter, earlier hit Twuan Hill on a 44 yard TD. So J.T., who needed 304 yards to reach 3000, finished with 404 and put him unofficially at 3104 yards and a most impressive freshman season. And J.T., who has gotten better and better, and those who have been following the Vaqueros all season long, remember the 4-17, 17-yard first half performance against LA Harbor and J.T. has come a long way since then. We expect an outstanding sophomore campaign.*

*On the ground, Stone not as successful today, only 24 yards on 10 carries, Twuan Hill even less so, 0 yards on 3 carries, had the TD from 2 yards out, but that was his only bright spot on the ground. Vaquero receivers had another fine day. Hill led them with 7 catches for 70 yards, Ryan Capretta had 6-54, Eric Mahanke 6 for 53, Torlando Bolden, 5-50, David Weismeiller, 3-21, Benjy Trembly, 2-25. Robert Sands, the 38-year-old anthropology teacher, what a great story. The man who had never played football at any level, Pop Warner all the way up, decided to make it a cultural experience and try it out for size, writing a book that should be out sometime in the future, next year, called GutCheck, the story of an anthropology teacher at a junior college. Just a great story. Robert waited two years to catch a pass and today, J.T. found him twice, in fact, for 19 yards, one of them giving J.T. his 400 yards plus and breaking the season record for Stone. Robert Sands, 2-19 and nearly had a TD on the final drive. Finally, Troy Tremblay had a catch for 5 yards, Lee Green had 1 for 15 yards.*

*Santa Barbara scratching to a 5-4-1 record, 4-1 at LaPlaya Stadium.*

# Chapter 23

## Post Partum Blues

I left the locker room slowly, wanting to savor the last moments of familiarity, the last good-byes to players who I would no doubt see around campus, but would no longer be my teammates. The gang went over to Woody's and scarfed fries and downed beer and cokes as we talked about the coaches and the game. David, Eric, Ryan, Casey, Jake, the Hawaiians, Evan, Tony and two of his girls, Kratz and I filled up a huge table in front of the big-screen television that was blaring, what else, a college football game. I felt lightheaded after two beers and, with the onset of pain hitting everybody, we called it quits and trickled out of the bar.

As night fell quickly, I stopped at the field on my way home. The sun was dropping like a stone, flaming out on the horizon and the few clouds that dotted the sky wore the sunset with a coat of deep scarlets and reds. The field was empty save for the small pieces of tape that littered the sidelines and only a few joggers and stadium climbers intruded. I grabbed my camera from the car and laid down on the wet carpet, the sheen of evening dew had already laminated the grass, and snapped a couple of pictures of the crossbar and the palms. The sweet smell of the grass and the earthy mustiness of the turf were overpowering as they nudged memories of the last two years into my brain. It was finally over.

No practice tomorrow or the next day or the next season. Although I wanted it to end three weeks ago, now my catches had fueled a desire to keep playing and, as I lay there, I wished I had two more years of eligibility like Jarrett or Twuan. But I didn't. I finally dragged myself to my feet, my shoulder and knees letting me know that it was good that I didn't have any more eligibility left. The walk across the field was a swan song. The shrieks and screams of the fans and players and the thuds and explosions of contact were muted and the emptiness and silence of the stadium was deafening.

As I folded myself into the car, a car full of teenage guys screeched up besides me and emptied out. "Come on, we can get a quick game in before it gets dark," one with a football yelled when they were all out. They ran through the gate and, as I shut my car door, I heard one voice cut through the dusk. "Okay, tackle, not pussy-ass two-handed touch. We got to get ready for next year!" I drove off into the sunset with a final yank on my infant nostalgia. There was no next year.

Three weeks later, Joe and I were relaxing and drinking our usual morning coffee. No films to break down, no practices to plan, no classes to take. We talked about the chances of sophomores playing next year. "Mike Hayes is maybe a D-1AA player," Joe said. "He is small, his size hurts him, but he is a quality player. Christ look what he did for us all year long? Coffey is the same way, but he has a little more athletic ability."

"What about Twuan," I asked.

"I don't know. The Northern Arizona coach asked us about his attitude and we told him. 'Is he coachable?' he asked. We said not really. He missed practice, got kicked off the team, had a negative attitude. And he said, 'Okay, we don't want him.' I mean we aren't going to lie about him. He wasn't that good of an addition to our team. Torlando has the possibility of being a PAC 10 player, but his

276

grades are going to be the problem. He wasn't a Twuan-type player. He is lazy, but he never was a problem due to his attitude. He just wasn't a practice player or even a leader. Of all, Chris Hill is the most marketable. He has got the size, the speed, he likes to lift. These are the things colleges look for; Cal-Poly, Northern Arizona, University of Pacific, Fresno, they all have been asking about him. Hives maybe is a D-2 player. He has a lot to make up."

"Is Jarrett in the same boat as Chris?" I asked.

"He had a decent year, but nothing spectacular. I don't really think he can play at the Big Sky level, which is where he wants to play. Maybe at Northridge, maybe only a D-2 player, like Humboldt State. Johnny has a better chance, but his grades are the biggest problem. He needs to get a degree. For a lot of these players, it is the grades. They need their A.A. degrees to go on to D-1. I mean if we had the program like Moorpark, we could gray-shirt the freshmen with problems. Moorpark does that and it works like a feeder system. Chuck and I came up with a list of sophomores and what level we thought they could play at and we even put down you could play D-3."

We had the season-ending tri-tip barbecue and Chuck and Joe handed out awards. J.T. and Jarrett were named most valuable offense and defense players of the year. Dudley said a couple of words about players like me working hard and then everybody scattered, after only about an hour, to hopefully study for finals.

The season was finally over. I had my own finals to grade and purposefully shied away from writing. Everything was way too fresh in my mind and my body was in a slow healing mode. My fingers refused to return to their normal size and my shoulder was still giving me problems when I lifted. Underneath, I didn't want to sit down and start writing. Three notebooks full of notes and a huge stack of loose-leafed paper with daily scribblings sat next to my computer and 10 micro-cassette tapes filled with interviews lay in the top drawer of my desk. Every day I would leave to go to school and avoid looking at them and every evening I would come back and quickly turn on the television or read an action novel.

Christmas was coming and so was the four-week break. I knew I couldn't get past that without writing something. I missed football more than I thought I would. I would run on the track and find myself constantly looking at the field and remember a play, a catch, a drop, even remember a hit that I took. I missed the camaraderie of the players, the joking around, the laughter. I missed the one-on-one drills, the scrimmages, even the bus rides. Retirement from sports is easily the hardest type of retirement to experience. To one day just leave the arena and never be able to compete at that level again or hearing the screams of excitement and adoration is like cutting off a finger when you are a world-class pianist. All you have are the memories, and they fade in time.

Christmas came and I forced myself to get started, leafing through the notes and listening to the tapes and trying to lose the feelings I felt about not playing again. I told myself over and over again in my mind that month, "You are a college professor, you are not a college football player. Leave it and get on with your life!" I started writing, sketching out the personalities and coming up with a time line. But it seemed too dry, too objective, too removed. I was losing what I felt by trying to be more of an observer. After several attempts at getting started, I left it for a week and spent the afternoons on the beach. I started thinking that maybe I wasn't meant to write about my experiences. They were way too personal.

One evening, at the end of that week, I laid down in my bed and picked up *Fear and Loathing in Las Vegas,* by Hunter Thompson, to skim before falling asleep. I had read it many times, but I started to reread it and couldn't put it down till I was finished, laughing out loud at many of his descriptions. I lay awake for an hour thinking that was what I wanted my book to be like; a story dragged up from the ravaged mind and experiences of the author that captured the nuts and bolts of what college football was like, pulled no punches, made no apologies for it's characters; and left the reader knowing more than they knew before reading. The next day, I started writing about pain as my first account. I didn't stop writing for several years.

As I wrote, I relived those two years over and over again. I sometimes would walk by spring ball, seeing Eric, David, Ryan and Art and the new crop of receivers catching the perfectly-thrown spirals from J.T.'s gun. Every now and then, I would run into the players or stick my head inside Joe and Pat's office and ask what was going on. I was on the outside now, looking in, and it was different. Yet, the experience stayed with me. My notes would come alive when I sat down to decipher my scrawl and emotions would flood as I worked through the seasons. I would chuckle remembering Dudley's cliches or Chuck's speeches, laugh out loud at Joe's observations and then jump the fence and recall conversations from Benjy or Ryan. The more I wrote, the more I wished I had just one more year to play.

Two years later my fingers are blown up like blimps and I haven't run a route or caught more than an errant pass in the days since I walked off the field the last time as a Vaquero. Now I spend my days on the track, coaching and sprinting around the field, instead of through the secondary. I have even watched a few Saturday games from the old wooden benches and enjoyed the spectator's view. Across the field were my old teammates, my old coaches and the yearning was just as strong. But, like experience, time marches on.

"Did you play college ball?" the man drinking a beer beside me asked as we watched *Monday Night Football* at a bar just down the street from my apartment. Smoke hung low over the bar and voices hummed around us. "Yeah, I played," I said. "I was a wide receiver at Santa Barbara City College. Had a couple of grabs my last year against Bakersfield. Where did you play..."

"Let me buy you a beer."

.... *And now, glad I didn't know, the way it all would end, the way it all would go. Our lives are better left to chance, I could have missed the pain, but I'd had to miss the dance.*

*...For a moment, wasn't I the king. If I'd only known that the king would fall and whose to say I might have changed it all.*

*And now, I'm glad I didn't know, the way it all would end, the way it all would go* (*The Dance*, Tony Arata)

# *Epilogue*

---

## A Year or Two Later

**A** year and two weeks, exactly, after my last football game, Chuck Melendez, J.T. Stone, Ryan Capretta, Eric Mahanke, Dave Weismiller and the rest of the Vaqueros found themselves playing Butte College in the 1996 Holiday Inn Bowl in Oroville, California. Riding the crest of a successful 7-3 season and a national ranking, City College once again returned to football prominence and the possible beginning of another string of championship teams like the Bob Dinaberg, Carmen DiPaolo juggernaut.

The heavens opened up that early December afternoon and deluged the Northern California Butte College field, rendering J.T. Stone and the high powered Vaquero offense useless and ineffective. Stone passed for only 98 yards and, in the end, as the rain continued to pour, his motion was more like a shot putter, than one from a prospective Division 1 quarterback. The game film showed Chuck and the rest of the coaches draped in over-sized garbage bags with heads cut out, an ironic image that summed up the paradox that was the 1996 season.

"Compared to last year (1995), we took a total 180-degree turn in events," said Ryan Capretta. "From the first day of summer practice, the team was a much closer family. This year, everyone played as a team and to win, rather than for themselves."

Eric, Art, David and Ryan rode the golden arm of J.T. Stone, and City College once again led the conference and state in offense. Highlights for the year included an early season home victory over eventual conference champion LA Valley on a last-second Hail Mary pass to Ryan Capretta, a 62-14 stomping of Ventura College, thrilling victories on the road at LA Pierce and Glendale, and as in the two previous years, a chance to tie for the division title at Bakersfield, the last game of the season. The last four games of the season, the defense played like City College used to play during the years of Joe, Hopwood, and Colin.

Valleys in the season were convincing losses to Moorpark, Hancock and the season finale at Bakersfield that was much closer than the 17-0 final would indicate. In the end, the Bakersfield game, before over 5000 tailgating Renegade fans, which would have been Chuck's finest hour, turned out to be another typical City College loss. The defense held the mighty Renegade offense to few yards, but J.T., bothered by a nagging shoulder injury and ankle sprain suffered in the Ventura game and perhaps feeling a loss of confidence from his teammates sporadic play, was not up to the task and the high-powered offense was shut down.

## The Lineup

**Torlando Bolden**—Touchdown Torlando Bolden, who flashed like a comet across LaPlaya Stadium for one blazing year, left in the deafening silence of a midnight's broken dreams and promises. He failed classes, dropped out of school in the spring and resisted efforts of coaches and recruiters to get him back in school in the summer and the fall of 1996. He received jail time in the summer of 1996 after violating his probation for a second time in an Isla Vista run-in with the police in February. His jail time was waived on conditions he either go to school or get a job, of which he has done neither. Rumors swirled around school and friends that USC was extremely interested in him and would give him a full-ride if he could get his academics in order. They still are just that–rumors. He met, in the early fall of 1996, with Vaquero basketball coach

281

Morris Hodges about playing. Torlando was a standout player for four years with Santa Barbara High School, but after Hodges described what the conditions were and what he would need to do, Torlando was only a memory. Occasionally I would run into close friends and relatives of Torlando on campus and inquire about his whereabouts and the only thing that came out was Torlando was "hanging around, drinking 40s and doing nothing much else, except playing three or four games of hoop everyday."

Books could be written about Torlando, one of the many gifted black athletes who fall or, in Torlando's case, plunge through the cracks in society. He had a chip on his shoulder the size of a winter's surf and an overdeveloped sense of pride that wouldn't allow him to face up to the fact of a learning disability and the necessary grunt work he had to do to become competitive in the classroom like he was on the field. So that is where it stands now, Life, 21, Torlando 7.

**J.T. Stone**—For most any other quarterback, J.T.'s sophomore year would have been phenomenal. Ranking in the top quarterbacks in the nation, throwing for over 2600 yards in nine games and leading his team to a 7-3 record, J.T. was also selected first team WSC all-conference. Yet there was a pearl in Stone's oyster, creating friction among the team. As the season wore on, J.T. often prematurely vacated the pocket and scrambled with the ball. On one of these scrambles in the second half of the Ventura game, J.T. sprained his ankle and chose to sit the rest of the game. Many felt that he lacked moral turpitude and a backbone when he watched the rest of the game from Susan's training table. "If it had been DeGeorgia," Pat Aguilera said, "he would have been out there the next series."

J.T. missed the Glendale game due to a shoulder injury and his backup, despite throwing four interceptions, kept the boys in the game and, in the end, the defense was the big winner. Chuck was frustrated throughout the season with J.T.'s progress. After his 1995 performance, Chuck was counting on J.T. to mature on and off the field and improve and become the leader that DeGeorgia had been. It didn't happen. His second year was a carbon copy of his first year, with many of the same mistakes. J.T. continued to have problems with his decisions on the field, not staying in the pocket long enough, scrambling too soon. He rarely watched film before a game and provided little leadership on or off the field. San Diego State, Brigham Young, Cal were just some of the D-1 schools interested in J.T. In February, J.T. told me that he wanted to concentrate on his classes and try to finish up at the end of the summer of 1997.

"The D-1 schools, like San Diego, Utah, BYU, they want me to come now and be ready for the Fall and I am not ready," he said. "I want to red-shirt the first year, get caught up on my classes, work on my feet, my footwork needs a lot of improvement. I am just going to wait. If they want me, they will let me do this. Simon Banks signed late in the Spring, almost summer, and I can do the same thing. If not, if I have to, I will go D-2."

**Ryan Capretta**—Ryan's year was better th-n his first. "I just got better, Doc. I worked and worked, took hits and kept coming," he said. And he did just that. If anybody was automatic and sure-handed, it was Ryan. He personally took charge the day the Vaqueros upset mighty, highly nationally-ranked LA Valley, the third game of the season. Threading the Valley secondary, he accounted for 2 TDs and set a new school record in receiving yardage in a game. His exclamation point was the last-second Hail Mary grab over the massed secondary in the right rear corner of the end zone. One second J.T.'s desperation toss was suspended like an evening over reaching hands, the next second Ryan's hands exploded up and out of the ragged milieu of humanity and plucked the sphere from obscurity. The next moment, Ryan is sprinting down the sideline toward the Vaquero bench, the center of a celebration that rivaled Mardi Gras.

The Moorpark game, Ryan took a shot in the ribs that knocked him out the rest of that game and the Compton game. The shot, heard all the way back to Santa Barbara, ended up fracturing the transverse processes of four vertebrate. Ryan was back in the lineup in two weeks, heavily taped and wearing a flak jacket and continued his assault on defensive backs.

All through the year, Ryan remained the same quiet and reflective person that I had the fortune to play with the year before. Teaming up with the veterans Mahanke, Weismiller and Arthur Williams, Ryan stood heads above not only in his ability, but his quiet leadership. Ryan was named to the Western States Conference second team at the end of the year, an honor well deserved. In April, after receiving tepid offers from schools like Northern Arizona and Eastern Washington, Ryan was offered a full scholarship at Indiana State University. He was caught between wanting to go to USC and walk-on or traveling 3000 miles to play ball. He chose Indiana State and traveled 3000 miles to Terre Haute, Indiana in July.

**Eric Mahanke**—After grabbing 50 catches, highest on the team in 1995 and making second team All Western States Conference, Eric was primed to have an even better sophomore campaign. "I have to admit," he told me, "I thought I was going to do better than I did. In the off-season, I worked very hard and I thought my season was going to be much more productive." It wasn't. Irony of ironies, the team improved; but Eric's personal statistics didn't. Eric was selected to the 1996 Western States Conference Honorable Mention team.

The last year I played, most of the games were close or we were on the losing side right up to the very end. So Eric, being a starter, rarely came out and, when he did, he was put right back in. This year, however, as the team won, often scoring a ton of points, Eric's role was reduced and affected the amount of his playing time. "Don't get me wrong, I loved the fact that we went 7-3 in the regular season," he said. "Winning is a lot more fun than losing. But it will affect me in recruiting, I feel, because junior college stats is a big part of your recruiting process. Although this year I felt I blocked better, ran better routes and ran more with the ball after catching. I had better film." In the beginning of the season, Eric picked up where he left off last year, Mr. Clutch, grabbing everything in sight. When the scores started climbing, J.T. started spreading the "wealth" around and Eric's performance suffered.

Give him credit though, he grumbled only occasionally when I saw him around campus or after home games that I attended. Like everybody else, he was caught up in the winning fever. With no D-1 schools knocking at his door, Eric's spring was spent spreading the word and film about himself. Possibilities were similar to Ryan's, Northern Arizona, Easter Washington, San Jose State; all wanted him to walk on his first year. "I'll go somewhere and play. Don't you worry Doc," he said. Finally, in early May, the Fresno State coach called him and beckoned with possibilities of a scholarship after a year. Eric took it.

**David Weismeiller**—David made good on his word and came

back his second year. Juggling two schools again and a job bouncing at an Isla Vista bar, David contributed more than his statistics indicated. He had flashes of brilliance, a reception here, a run there, but mostly David ran the right routes and blocked the right people. In a lineup that featured Ryan, Eric and Art, all human flypapers, David's role was to add stability and a touch of leadership. He looked to graduate from UCSB the following year, but his dream of playing some more lingered on. He had talks with Eric about going to a four-year program together where Dave could finish his degree and start on a graduate program. All I could remember was Dave looking me in the eye, before the Bakersfield game of 1995 and saying, "I just want to play my four years, even though I did get started kind of late."

**Arthur Williams**—Arthur Williams in 1996 was flashy, electric, sensational, all the things 1995 promised would happen. Arthur was also moody, self-centered, and petulant, also all the things 1995 promised would happen. He caught long balls in the same breath he dropped sure catches. Good or bad, attention was never far from Arthur. Arthur again led the team in gathering unsportsmanlike conduct penalties, gathering as many as touchdowns. Arthur, at his worst, was the pivotal Bakersfield game in which he was flagged for two unsportsmanlike penalties, the second one occurring at the start of the second half. Chuck benched him and Arthur responded by slamming his helmet to the turf and then pouting the rest of the game. Arthur, at his best, was against Ventura where he broke open the game on two long touchdown bombs and 170 total yards on three completions in the first quarter alone. Of all the 1996 Vaqueros, Arthur was the most gifted. Early in the spring of 1997, after taking a visit to Portland State, he fell in love with the Northwest and signed a letter of intent with the D-1AA school, joining the two Russians, Oleg and Ruzik, as Santa Barbara transplants.

Twuan and Chris Hill and Mike Hives left Santa Barbara early in the spring semester of 1996, changed by the word of God. Twuan ended up at Georgia State College, where he played quite a bit. Chris Hill fit in nicely as a backer at North Carolina Central and Mike Hives ended up staying in Florida with his mother, planning on attending University of Findly in the Fall of 1997.

Benjy Trembly dropped out of school in the spring of 1996 as he underwent a life crisis when his girlfriend broke up with him. He lost weight, considered moving down to San Diego, and went through months of depression. He had no plans to return to SBCC and started working for a plumber and still lives in Carpinteria. Lee Green had thoughts of returning for his last year, but he never materialized in the fall. He still attends UCSB. Drone and Kon Hatcher remained on campus and were working towards finishing their course requirements. Drone talked about coming out and playing on the defense, but it was just talk.

That next fall, Stephen Kratzer moved back to Germany with his American girlfriend and went back to school. They married and, a year later, had a son. I received a letter from him not too long after that, with a photo of his son.

Both Jarrett Thiessen and John Sonoma ended up at Cal State Sacramento where they shared an apartment. After forsaking a partial ride to Cal State Northridge, Jarrett ended up transferring up to Sacramento State in the fall of 1996. Leaving Northridge after spring semester, he lost a year of eligibility. John, in the last days of August, decided on Sac State over University of San Diego due to financial reasons, and played on special teams and had limited playing time. Both are expected to contribute considerably in 1997. John still sleeps on the couch even though he has his own bedroom and Jarrett's relationship with his sometimes girlfriend went the way of most college romances, down the "shitter," as Casey said.

Mike Hayes and Tony Coffey were perhaps the two that stood out the most from that 1995 team in their 1996 endeavors, both on and off the field. Mike and Troy ended up at Shippensburg State, a D-2 school in Pennsylvania. Mike started at corner, was selected all-conference, led the team and league in interceptions, and actually ran a punt back to win a game. For Mike, the important thing was that he stayed in school, kept on track and also suffered through the loneliness of a long-distance relationship with his girl friend and daughter who remained behind in Santa Barbara. Troy roomed with Mike and actually was in a three-man rotation at wide receiver. The cold weather was not kind to their thin-skinned Southern California hides. Tony Coffey was accepted and enrolled at University of California, Berkeley, not an easy institution to get into. He came back occasionally at breaks and was making progress in his course work. He said he was walking on at Cal in the fall of 1997. For all the players, I felt that Tony's acceptance to Cal was a neon light of success for the Vaquero program.

Jerome White as of March 1997 is still serving time in the Santa Barbara County Jail as he awaits trial on the burglary and probation violation he received in the summer of 1996.

Jarrod DeGeorgia spent two years as the starting quarterback for Wayne State College in Nebraska. His second year was a personal success, although the team fared much worse. In the spring of 1997, he was signed on as quarterback for the Iowa Barnstormers in the Arena Football League.

Casey Ray finally, after one year at Ventura and three years at SBCC, exhausted all his course possibilities at SBCC and moved up to Chico to attend the Cal State school there. Unfortunately, he still needed to make up a math class, so he attended Butte Junior College in the spring of 1997 in hopes of passing the class so that he could get into Chico State. Chico dropped their D-2 football program for the fall of 1997 and Casey's dream of landing a job as an assistant equipment manager for the team to help him pay for school vanished. He did catch on with the Chico Heat, a minor league baseball team, as an assistant clubhouse guy, and spent the summer washing uniforms and running for beer and chew for the players.

Chuck Melendez prepared for his fourth season at the helm of the 1997 Vaquero squad, but that season was without one of the DiPaolos, as Joe took the head-coaching job at Bishop Diego High School in Santa Barbara. Carmen, due to a contract obligation remained at SBCC. Steve Dudley went through a blood pressure scare and found his niche as a telemarketer when he wasn't on the field. He told me, in early Fall 1997, he finally found a girl friend, didn't drink much anymore, stayed away from O'Malleys, and was enjoying life. You can't stay mad at Dud. T.K. Walter never went hunting again in November and still brings his Patton-like demeanor to the practice field and game sidelines. I occasionally surf with his 12-year-old son.

I spent the spring of 1996 entertaining the idea of playing football professionally in Australia, even going as far as contacting an agent who handled overseas player placement. The level of play would have been similar to what I was used to and the chance to play one more year was almost too good to pass up. But I did. At thirty-nine, I figured it was time to hang up my cleats. Not a day goes by that I don't think about playing one more year. I will take that addiction with me to my grave.

# *Postscript 1999*

AS I took Highway 126 through Filmore on my way to Las Vegas last month, I couldn't help but flash back to October four years ago and the specter of death that suffocated the Vaquero football coaches and players. I gunned my little Miata, leaving the last 45-mph speed limit sign, and was going 60 as I entered what we use to call the highway of death. It wasn't too far from here that Cindy Johnson lost her life to an errant rock and the meaning of mortality descended on 90 players and coaches, especially her husband, Mark. This road used to be a narrow two-lane path that ran from the other side of Filmore to Santa Clarita and Interstate 5. Complete with several one-mile long passing zones that just invited car wrecks, the highway cut through an agricultural valley with much slower-moving farm traffic. There now exists a smooth and spacious double lane asphalt corridor that gracefully winds through the orange groves. After four years, the hope for an improved and less dangerous highway has been realized.

After four years, this book has taken me on a similar path of change; the words and sentences dying many times along the way, but having just as many resurrections. It has been reorganized twice, edited many times, and finally was completed, appropriately enough on January 2, the year of the new millennium. The four years since I left my teammates have been a brief interlude for some of those players and a lifetime for others. Santa Barbara City College became a proving ground for players but, more importantly, for each individual, a rite of passage into the larger game of life. After almost half a decade, the successes outweigh the failures. For Pat Aguilera, the equipment manager at City College, each year brings in new faces and releases familiar faces to their destinies. Pat has a filing cabinet full of information concerning past players written on cards. Opening a drawer of that cabinet releases the players' spirit and breathes life into their arrogant and mean countenances frozen in the many team photos that adorn the locker room.

Jerome White is in the middle of a three-year prison sentence. Torlando Bolden, who had the eyes of so many college scouts and cops alike, finished a six-month sentence for probation violation in February of 1999. Upon tasting freedom once again, his plan included enrolling in Cal State Northridge for his last year of eligibility. That, too, never saw the light of day and, with one last chance, Torlando was on track to finish up his college eligibility playing for Chuck Melendez and City College in 1999; four years, several court appearances, some jail time. Without eligibility remaining, if Torlando is going to play again, the next step will be a leap, from junior college to the pros. J.T. Stone, who launched 60-yard rockets, could not last a summer at West Texas A&M before he returned to Santa Barbara. Never removing a slew of "Ds" from his City College transcripts, J.T. was unable to go to Cal State Northridge or San Diego State when the opportunity arose and simply sat back and watched his eligibility expire. Twuan Hill made it through a year at West Georgia College, but was expelled from school his senior year for violating team and school rules. You wonder if at some point along the way, second chances become last chances.

As for the successes, City College weaned plenty. Eric Mahanke and Arthur Williams each finished stellar careers at Fresno State and Portland State, respectively, and will be busy this spring showcasing their talents. In the summer of 1999, Eric was invited to regional NFL combines and camps on the West Coast. He is still in contact with CFL teams and Arena Football teams telling him to stay in shape, just in case. Eric is two classes shy of graduating and will work on completing those in the fall of 1999. Arthur became a legend at PSU and retained an agent and went through professional tryouts with NFL and Canadian Football League teams. He is now, like Eric, waiting for the bell to toll. Chris Hill finished his college career at North Carolina A&T and was also invited to tryouts. Ryan Capretta survived shoulder surgery and played two years and graduated from Indiana State University. Jarret Thiessen and Johnny Sonoma played out their tenure at Sacramento State. Johnny was the defensive star his last season. Even though their playing careers ended at City College, David Weismiller and Lee Green succeeded in graduating from UCSB. Mike Hayes and Troy Tremblay spent a year as teammates at Shippennburg State where Mike was the defensive star. Both came back for summer break and never returned for their senior year. Mike married his girl friend and now coaches at Bishop Diego High School.

As I sit and peck away at my computer, giving this project final touches, there is one player that has combined his talent and dreams. Tony Coffey was accepted by the University of California, Berkeley and, after red shirting a year and walking on as a non-scholarship player, will be a member of Golden Bears secondary for the 1999 season.

Four years has produced changes in my life. I remarried, took a teaching position at Community College of Southern Nevada in Las Vegas and now, as my wife lives in Carpinteria, I commute home from Sin City on the weekends and spend my summers one block from the beach. I have taken up surfing and that has become my next book project. I have written two books on sport and culture in the interim that featured my fieldwork on football. Four years is a lifetime for some, a drop in a bucket for others. For my body, the memories have never left and live from day to day. Gnarled, misshapen fingers and a creaky shoulder remind me of violent collisions encountered on the playing field. Much has passed under the bridge, but it takes only a second when I step on a field to run or flip on ESPN's game of the week for those two years of memories, rich in nostalgia, to flood my mind. Chuck Melendez, Steve Dudley, Carmen DiPaulo and T.K. Walter still coach at SBCC and Joe DiPaulo will be entering his third year as the head coach at Bishop Diego. I know that these same memories of past seasons haunt them. I have become just like them, a ghost of LaPlaya.

*Shadows lengthen on my season, as evening falls on my career.*
*So hard to let go.*

This book is in memory of Viki Paulsen, Cindy and Spencer Johnson, Dr. Charles "Bogey" McBride and # 38, Mark "Sammy" Samuels.

*"Sammy"*